JAN 2 5 2017

DATA FOR THE PEOPLE

ALSO BY ANDREAS WEIGEND

Time Series Prediction
Computational Finance
Decision Technologies for Financial Engineering
Neural Networks in Financial Engineering

DATA

FOR THE PEOPLE

How to Make Our
Post-Privacy Economy
Work for You

ANDREAS WEIGEND

BASIC BOOKS
New York

Library of Congress Cataloging-in-Publication Data

Names: Weigend, Andreas S., author.
Title: Data for the people : how to make our post-privacy economy work for you / Andreas Weigend.
Description: New York, NY : Basic Books, [2017] | Includes bibliographical references and index.
Identifiers: LCCN 2016052312 (print) | LCCN 2016056857 (ebook) | ISBN 9780465044696 (hardcover) | ISBN 9780465096534 (e-book)
Subjects: LCSH: Information society. | Information technology—Social aspects. | Online social networks. | Privacy, Right of.
Classification: LCC HM851 .W42957 2017 (print) | LCC HM851 (ebook) | DDC 303.48/33—dc23
LC record available at https://lccn.loc.gov/2016052312

10 9 8 7 6 5 4 3 2 1

To p., f., and s.

CONTENTS

PROLOGUE

When Everything Is Recorded

As information itself becomes the largest business in the world, data banks know more about individual people than the people do themselves. The more the data banks record about each one of us, the less we exist.[1]

MARSHALL McLUHAN

IN 1949, MY FATHER, then a young man of twenty-three, took a job as a teacher in East Germany. When he arrived in his new town, he needed to find someone to share a room with. At the train station, he met a man who was also looking for a place to live. My dad thought it was his lucky day. But a few days after they moved into their home, his roommate went missing. My dad was baffled. As the days stretched on, he grew worried.

Not long afterward, as my dad was making breakfast one morning, there came a knock at the door. Perhaps his roommate had returned! However, when he answered, he was greeted by several unfamiliar men, who informed him that he had won an award for teaching. It was quite a special award, and had to be presented to him in person, and they were there to escort him to the hall where he would be honored. He met this invitation with skepticism: in the circumstances, it seemed odd that the men were so dour, and that they were all wearing identical trench coats. But he had no choice; he was immediately ushered into a waiting car. To his utter alarm, he discovered that the car doors could not be opened from the inside. He had been arrested by the Soviet occupying forces.

Based on the evidence that he spoke English, my father was charged with being an American spy. None of his family or friends knew where he was. He had disappeared from the face of the earth. He was thrown into solitary confinement in a prison run by the Soviet authorities, where he languished for six years. He never learned what got him arrested, nor what got him released.

There are real, life-threatening risks to sharing personal information, because data can be used against us. Indeed, contemplating that risk is quite sobering and scary to me, specifically because I have seen how data were collected and used against my father.

A decade after the collapse of East Germany, I requested to see what information the Ministry for State Security, also known as the Stasi, had collected about my father during and after his imprisonment. I wasn't the only one curious to know what the Stasi had on my family: nearly 3 million people have asked to see their own files, or those of relatives, since the fall of the Berlin Wall.[2] Unfortunately, when the letter came from the commission in charge of sharing the Stasi's files, it seemed that everything about my dad had been destroyed.

However, tucked into the envelope with the letter I discovered a photocopy of another Stasi file: my own. I was amazed. There was a Stasi file on me? I was just a kid, studying physics. Still, the security agents had started gathering information about me as early as 1979, when I was a teenager, and had last updated the file in 1987, the year after I had moved to the United States. All that was left of my record was the cover sheet; I'd never know what information the Stasi had collected, why they had collected it, or what, if anything, it had been used for.

Back in the days of the Stasi, it was tough to get information about "citizens of interest." First, the data had to be gathered by following people, taking photographs of them, intercepting their mail, interviewing their friends, installing microphones in their homes. Then the information had to be analyzed, all by hand. There was so much to scrutinize that, at the time of the collapse of East Germany, 1 percent of the nation's working population worked full-time for the secret police. But the Stasi needed even more resources than that to collect information.[3] According to the Bundesregierung, East Germany eventually had about 200,000 citizens gathering information for it.[4]

Data collectors today have it easy in comparison. Think about a few high-profile cases. Following many months of protest and court battles, privacy activists won a small but limited victory against the NSA's dragnet surveillance of phone records.[5] Yet, few people dropped their mobile

The cover of my Stasi file

phone service during the fight or afterward, when it became clear that the metadata of their calls might be scrutinized—by the NSA or others. Indeed, a California saleswoman claimed she was fired for uninstalling an app that tracked and shared her geolocation with her manager, both during work hours and outside of them.[6] When news broke that Facebook was studying how moods spread from person to person, it caused an uproar about whether the company was "manipulating" users' feelings.[7] However, the actual use of Facebook barely changed, and Facebook continued to allow experiments to be run without prior consent of users, for the simple reason that experimentation is an essential component of online platform design. And in 2015, e-commerce giant Alibaba's affiliate Ant Financial rolled out a pilot service in China, called Sesame Credit, which analyzes individual transactions to summarize a person's creditworthiness—somewhat like having your Amazon purchase history reviewed to determine whether you qualify for credit.[8] The score quickly got adopted in other areas, including as an optional but popular profile field on a dating site in China.[9] There's no groundswell for getting rid of mobile phones, email addresses, navigation apps, social media accounts, online retail, and other digital services. Life is just more convenient with these technologies.

The shock of discovering my Stasi file could have converted me into a zealot for privacy. Far from it. In fact, the Stasi's files are nothing compared to what I voluntarily share about myself each and every day.

Since 2006, I have published on my website every lecture and speech I will give and every flight I will take, down to my specific seat assignment.[10] I do this because I believe the real, tangible value we get from sharing data about ourselves outweighs the risks of doing so. The data create opportunities for discovery and optimization. What matters is that we find ways to ensure that the interests of those who use the data are aligned with our own.

How can we achieve this? By understanding what data are being shared—and will likely be shared in the near future—and how data companies analyze and use our data. With all due respect to Marshall McLuhan, the more the data companies record about each one of us, the *more* we exist, the more we can know about *ourselves*. The real issues are how to ensure that the data companies are as transparent to us as we are to them, and that we have some say in how our data are used. *Data for the People* explains how we can achieve both of these ends.

INTRODUCTION

The Social Data Revolution
How Can We Ensure That Data Are for the People?

Every revolution was first a thought in one man's mind; and when the same thought occurs to another man, it is the key to that era.[1]

RALPH WALDO EMERSON

AT 6:45 A.M., the alarm on my mobile phone wakes me up. Eager to start the day, I carry my phone to the kitchen while I scan through my email and Facebook notifications. My phone's GPS receiver and wifi register the changes in location, logging my shift a few meters north and east. As I pour myself a cup of coffee and really start to get going, the phone's accelerometer tracks how quickly I walk and the barometer registers when I'm going up the stairs. Because I have Google apps installed on my phone, Google has a record of all these data.

After breakfast, I'm ready to make my way to Stanford University. The electricity company has put in a "smart" meter, which registers the decrease in electricity use as I turn off my lights and unplug my mobile devices. When I open the garage door, the meter detects the usage signature specific to it. Thus, as I pull my car out onto the street, my electricity provider has enough data to know I'm no longer at home. When my phone's signal gets picked up by different cellular signal towers, so does my mobile phone carrier.

On the road, a camera installed on a street corner takes a photo of my license plate in case I speed through a red light. Thankfully, I'm on my best behavior today so I won't be greeted with a ticket in the mail. But as I go on my way, my license plate is photographed again and again. Some of those cameras belong to the local government, while some belong to private companies that are analyzing the data to identify patterns of mobility—which they sell to police departments, land developers, and other interested parties.

When I get to Stanford, I use the EasyPark app on my phone to pay the parking fee. The money is automatically debited from my bank account, and the university parking team is notified that I'm paid up, so both the school and my bank can see that I'm on campus starting at 9:03 a.m. When my phone stops moving at a car's pace, Google infers this is where I have parked and logs the location, so that I can look it up in case I forget later. It's also time to check my Metromile insurance app, which has been recording data about my drive from the car's on-board diagnostic system. I can see in an instant that my fuel efficiency was lower today—nineteen miles per gallon—and that I spent $2.05 on gas for my commute.

After my day at Stanford, I'm planning to meet up with a new friend back in San Francisco. We "virtually" met each other when we both commented on a post by a mutual friend on Facebook, and liked each other's take on the topic. It turned out we had more than thirty Facebook friends in common, more than enough reason to meet up.

Google Maps predicts that I'll get to my new friend's place at 7:12 p.m., and as usual the prediction is correct within a few minutes. As it happens, my friend lives above a store that sells tobacco products as well as various paraphernalia used for smoking marijuana. The GPS receiver on my smartphone doesn't differentiate between the apartment and the store, however. As far as my carrier and Google are concerned, I've ended my day with a visit to the head shop—a fact revealed to me by the ads Google shows when I check the weather forecast before going to bed.

Welcome to the social data revolution.

Give to Get

Every day, more than a billion people create and share social data like these. *Social data* is information about you, such as your movements, behavior, and interests, as well as information about your relationships with other people, places, products, even ideologies.[2] Some of these data are shared knowingly and willingly, as when you are signed in to Google

Maps and type in your destination; others less so, often without much thought, part and parcel of the convenience of using the internet and mobile devices. In some cases, it is clear that sharing data is a necessary condition for receiving services: Google can't show you the best route to take if you don't tell it where you are and where you want to go. In other cases, you might happily contribute information, as when you "like" a friend's Facebook post or endorse a colleague's work on LinkedIn simply because you want to reach out and support her in some way.

Social data can be highly accurate, pinpointing your location to within less than a meter, but social data are often sketchy, in the sense of being incomplete. For example, unless I sign in to an app that displays my smart meter's readings (for instance, to be sure that I really did turn off all the lights in my house as I make my way to the airport), the electricity company knows when I am not at home, but nothing more than that. It's a rough data point that may or may not be of much use to me. Similarly, as I was visiting my new friend in San Francisco, while my latitude and longitude were conveyed with precision, the inferences made about my activities that evening were utterly wrong. That's even sketchier, in the sense that the data appeared quite exact but were very much an interpretation. Sketchy data have a tendency to be incomplete, error-prone, and—occasionally—polluted by fraud.[3]

Altogether—passive and active, necessary and voluntary, precise and sketchy—the amount of social data is growing exponentially. Today, the time it takes for social data to double in quantity is eighteen months. In five years, the amount of social data will have increased by about a factor of 10, or an order of magnitude, and after ten years, it will increase by about a factor of 100. In other words, the amount of data we created over the course of the entire year 2000 is now created over the course of a day. At our current growth rate, in 2020 we'll create that amount of data in less than an hour.

It's essential to understand that "social data" isn't merely some trendy buzzword for social media. Many social media platforms have been designed for broadcasting. In the case of Twitter, communication is almost always moving in one direction, from a celebrity, authority, or marketer to the masses. Social data is far more democratic. You may share information about yourself, your company, your accomplishments, and your opinions through Twitter or Facebook, but your digital traces are much deeper and broader than that. Your searches on Google, your purchases on Amazon, your calls on Skype, the minute-by-minute location of your mobile phone—all these and many more sources come together to produce a unique portrait of you as an individual.

Further, social data doesn't end with you. You create and share data about the strength of your relationships with family, friends, and colleagues through your communication patterns; you create data alongside friends and strangers alike—for instance, when reviewing a product or tagging a photo on Instagram. You verify your identity when you set up an account on Airbnb, the platform for renting a room or house, using your Facebook profile in addition to a government-issued ID. Social data are becoming embedded in homes with smart thermostats, in cars with navigational systems, and in workplaces with team-based software. Such data are beginning to feature in our classrooms and doctors' offices. As mobile phones get loaded up with more sensors and apps, and new devices start tracking your behavior at home, in the mall, and on the job, you'll have less and less ability to control the data that describe your daily routine—as well as your deepest wishes. Data scientists become detectives and artists, painting iteratively clearer sketches of human behavior from our digital traces.

These digital traces are examined and distilled to uncover our preferences, reveal trends, and make predictions, including about what you might buy. During my tenure as chief scientist of Amazon, I worked with Jeff Bezos to develop the company's data strategy and customer-centric culture. We ran a series of experiments to see if customers were happier with their purchases when they were shown editor-written versus consumer-written product reviews, and whether recommendations based on traditional demographic profiling or individual clicks were more successful. We saw the power of genuine communication over manufacturer-sponsored promotions. The personalization tools we created for Amazon fundamentally changed how people decide what to purchase and became the standard in e-commerce.

Since leaving Amazon, I have taught courses on "The Social Data Revolution" to thousands of students, from undergraduates and graduate students at Stanford and the University of California–Berkeley to Chinese business students at Fudan University and China Europe International Business School in Shanghai and Tsinghua University in Beijing.

I also continue to run the Social Data Lab, a group of data scientists and thought leaders that I founded in 2011. Over the past decade, in my work with corporations ranging from Alibaba and AT&T to Walmart and UnitedHealthcare, and at major airlines, financial services firms, and dating sites, I have been an advocate for sharing the decision-making power of data with customers and users—regular people like you and me.

No single person can wade through all of the data available today in an effort to make what we used to call an "informed" decision about some aspect of life. But who will have access to the tools that are necessary for leveraging data in service to our problems and needs? Will the preferences, trends, and predictions extracted from data be available to only a few powerful organizations, or will they be available for anyone to use? What price will we have to pay to secure the dividends of our social data?

As we discover the value of social data, I believe we must focus not just on access but also on actions. We face some decisions many times each day, others just once in a lifetime. Indeed, the social data we create today have a long shelf life. The way we behave today may influence the choices we face in the decades to come. Few people have the ability to observe everything they do, or to analyze how their behavior might affect them, in the short or long term. Social data analysis will allow us to better identify the possibilities and probabilities, but the final choice must be deliberate.

One thing these technologies cannot do is decide what sort of future we want—as individuals or a society. The laws in place that protect individuals in many countries from discrimination in the workplace or health care may not exist tomorrow—and in some countries, they do not exist even today. Imagine that you opt to share that you're worried about having high cholesterol with a health app or site in order to get advice about diet and exercise regimens. Could your worries be used against you in some way? What if the law made it permissible to charge you a higher rate for medical care if you refused to stop eating deep-fried food and slouching on the couch after you've been presented with a menu of your health risks and recommendations for healthier choices? What if a manager used a service to crawl the web for information about you, and then, based on what he learned, decided that your lifestyle isn't a good match for a job at his company and he won't consider your application? These are real risks.

If the sole person creating and sharing data about you was yourself, you might be able to withhold information that you thought might be risky. It would cost you a lot of convenience, but it could be possible. However, we do not live in such a world. You have no control over much of the data about you. This fact will become more palpable as social data are utilized by businesses and governments to improve effectiveness and efficiency.

Because social data are so democratic, the questions about how best to handle it touch each and every one of us. Technology is moving fast, and the companies that collect and analyze our data are primarily in the business of creating and coding information, not creating and codifying principles. Many of those questions are being considered on an ad hoc basis, if they're being considered at all. We should not leave decisions about principles that will deeply influence our future in the hands of the data companies.

We can agree to have all of these data collected, combined, aggregated, and analyzed so that we are in a better position to understand the trade-offs in decision-making. Human judgment is crucial to evaluating the trade-offs intrinsic to any important decision. Our lives should not be *driven* by data. They should be *empowered* by data.

Principles for the Post-Privacy Age

As we've come to appreciate the increasing role of data in life, there have been several efforts to safeguard citizens' interests. In the 1970s, the United States and Europe adopted broadly similar principles for the fair use of information. Individuals were told they had a right to know who collected what data about them, and how these data were being used. They could also correct data about themselves that were inaccurate.[4] These protections are perversely both too strong and too weak for the world of new data sources and analytics that is being built today.

They're too strong because they assume it's possible to keep tabs on all the data collected about you. Amazon might be able to explain in accessible terms exactly how the data the company collects about you are used. It might even be able to do so in a way that helps you make better decisions. But reviewing all this information would require investing a lot of time. How many of us would take the time to trawl through all the relevant data? Would it be useful to you to see how Amazon weighs each data point, or would you prefer to get a summary?[5]

At the same time, these protections are too weak, because even if you could check every bit of data you have created and shared about yourself, you will not get a full picture of the data about you, which includes data created and shared by others, such as your family, friends, colleagues, and employers. The businesses you visit online, as well as most of those you visit in the physical world, also create (and sometimes share) data. That goes for strangers on the street and a number of other organizations, public and private, with which you interact. Who decides whether these data are accurate or inaccurate? Because data today come from so many perspectives, having the right to correct data about yourself doesn't reach nearly far enough. Finally, even accurate data can be used against you.

With the massive quantitative and qualitative shifts in data creation, communication, and processing, the right to know and the right to correct are clearly insufficient. Thus far, the attempts to update these guidelines have focused almost entirely on maintaining individual control and privacy.[6] Unfortunately, this approach is borne out of ideals and experiences that are technologically a century out of date. Standards of control and privacy also force individuals to enter an unfair contract with data companies. If you want your decision-making to be improved by data, you usually have to agree to having your data collected on the data collector's terms. Once you've done that, the data company has satisfied the legal requirement to give you individual "control," regardless of how much choice you really had or the effects on your privacy. If you want to maintain personal privacy, you can instead withhold your consent to data collection and forfeit your access to relevant data products and services, reducing the value you get from your data. Enjoy your individual control then.

Today, what we need are standards that allow us to assess the risks and rewards of sharing and combining data, and provide a means for holding companies accountable. After two decades working with data companies, I believe the principles of transparency and agency hold the most promise for protecting us from the misuse of social data while increasing the value that we are able to reap from them.

Transparency encompasses the right of individuals to know about their data: what it is, where it goes, and how it contributes to the result the user gets. Is the company observing you from the "dark" side of a one-way mirror, or does it also give you a window with a view to what it does with your data, so that you can judge whether (and when) the company's interests are aligned with your own?[7] How much data about yourself do you have to share to receive a data product or service that you want? Historically, there has been a strong information asymmetry between institutions and individuals, with institutions having the advantage. Not only do institutions have more capacity to collect data about you, they can interpret your data in comparison to others' data. The balance between what you give and what you get needs to be clear to you.

Consider how transparency is designed into the shopping experience at Amazon compared to the traditional relationship between customers and retailers. When you are about to buy an item, should a retailer remind you that you already bought it, potentially losing a sale in the process? At Amazon, if you try to buy a book you've already bought from the site, you're greeted with the query "Are you sure? You bought this item already, on December 17, 2013." If you buy a track from an album of music and then decide to buy the rest of it, Amazon will "complete the purchase," automatically deducting the amount you have already spent on the track from the current price for the album. Amazon surfaces and uses data about your purchasing history in these ways because the company wants to minimize customer regret. Likewise, many airline frequent flyer programs now send you a reminder that your miles are about to expire rather than letting them quietly disappear from the company's books.

Unfortunately, transparency is far from the norm. Consider the far-too-typical experience of calling your favorite customer service center. At the start of the call, you'll inevitably receive the warning: "This call may be recorded for quality assurance purposes." You've got no choice: you must accept the company's conditions if you want to talk to a representative. Okay, but *why* is that recording accessible only to the business? What, really, does "quality assurance purposes" mean when only one side of the conversation is assured access to the record of what was agreed? The principle of data symmetry would also give you, the paying customer, access to the recording.

Whenever I hear that my call might be recorded, I announce to the customer service rep that I might also record the call for quality assurance purposes. Most of the time, the rep plays along. Occasionally, however, the rep hangs up. Of course, I could record the call without asking for the rep's permission—which, I should note, is against the law in some places. Then, if I don't get the service I was promised, I could appeal to a manager with my evidence in hand. If that still didn't work, I could upload the audio file in the hopes that it might go viral and the company feels pressured to fix things quickly—as Comcast did when a customer tried to cancel services but was rebuffed again and again, finally succeeding after his recording started trending on Twitter.[8]

You shouldn't have to break the law to level the playing field in this way. To make transparency the new default, you need more information to be public, not less.

But transparency isn't enough; you also need agency.[9] *Agency* encompasses the right of individuals to act upon their data. How easy is it for you to identify the data company's "default" settings, and are you allowed to alter them for whatever reason you like? Are you able to act upon the data company's outputs in any way you choose, or are you gently nudged (or forcefully pushed!) toward only some options—mostly the options that are best for the company? Can you play with the parameters and explore different scenarios to show a smaller or bigger range of possibilities? Agency is an individual's power to make free choices based on the preferences and patterns detected by data companies. This includes the ability to ask data companies to provide information to you *on your own terms.*

On a fundamental level, agency involves giving people the ability to create data that are useful to them. Amazon wholeheartedly embraced uncensored customer reviews. It didn't matter to the company if the reviews were good or bad, five stars or one, written out of a desire to gain approval from others or to achieve a lifelong dream of becoming a book critic. What mattered was their relevance to other customers who were trying to figure out what to purchase. Reviews revealed whether a customer regretted a purchase even though she did not return the item for a refund. These data helped customers decide if a recommended product was the best choice for them. Amazon gave customers more agency.

Many marketers talk about targeting, segmentation, and conversion. I don't know about you, but I don't want to be targeted, segmented,

sliced and diced. These aren't expressions of agency. We
hat the leaders of every company will, on their own, em-
_iples of transparency and agency. We must also go beyond
these principles: we need delineated rights that help to spell out how to
translate transparency and agency into tangible, hands-on tools.

If we can get data companies to agree to a set of meaningful rights and
tools, it will lead to what I call "sign flips"—reversals in the traditional
relationships between individuals and institutions. Amazon's decision to
let customers write most of the content about products is a sign flip, and
the social data revolution will provide many more similar opportunities.
As individuals gain more tools to help them make better decisions for
themselves, old-fashioned marketing and manipulation are becoming
less effective. Gone is the day when a company could tell a powerless customer what to buy. Soon, you will get to tell the company what to make
for you. In some places, you already can.

Sign flips are an important element in how physicists see the world.
They are often associated with phase transitions, where a change in an
external condition results in an abrupt alteration in the properties of
matter—water changing from a liquid into a gas when it is heated to
the boiling point. The effect on society of the increasing amount of data
can be compared to the increasing amount of heat on a physical system.
Under certain conditions—when data companies provide transparency
and agency for users—a sign flip will take place that favors the individual
over the institution; that is, it will benefit you, not the company, or the
company's chief marketing officer.

We the people all have a stake in the social data revolution. And if you
want to benefit from social data, you must share information about yourself. Period. The value you reap from socializing data often comes in the
form of better decision-making ability, when negotiating deals, buying
products and services, getting a loan, finding a job, obtaining education
and health care, and improving your community. The price you pay and
the risks you take in sharing data must at least be offset by the benefits
you receive. Transparency about what data companies are learning and
doing is essential. So, too, is your ability to have some control over data
products and services. Otherwise, how could you possibly judge what
you give against what you get?

Balancing the Power

Information is at the center of power. Those who have more information than others almost always stand to benefit, like the proverbial used-car salesman who pushes a lemon on an unwitting customer. As communication and processing have become cheap and ubiquitous, there's a lot more data—and a lot more risk of substantial information imbalances, since no individual can get a handle on all the data out there.

Much of the data being created and shared is about our personal lives: where we live, where we work, where we go; who we love, who we don't, and who we spend our time with; what we ate for lunch, how much we exercise, and which medicines we take; what appliances we use in our homes and which issues animate our emotions. Our lives are transparent to the data companies, which collect and analyze our data, sometimes engaging in data trafficking and too often holding data hostage for use solely on their terms. We need to have some say in how our data are changed, bartered, and sold, and set more of the terms on the use of our data. Both sides—data creator and data company—must have transparency and agency.

This will require a fundamental shift in how we think about our data and ourselves. In the first chapter, I explain several of the ways data companies analyze data, adopting the metaphor of the refining process, whereby the companies transform raw data into products and services. Then, in Chapter 2, I turn to individuals and their attributes, and how the cumulative digital traces of our lives—our searches, clicks, views, taps, and swipes—are destroying any illusion of privacy, creating new concepts of identity, and indicating honest signals of interest, whether we want them to or not. Next, in Chapter 3, I shift the focus from the individual to the connections between individuals, and how social networks reveal and reshape trust in the digital age. I then in Chapter 4 look at how our context is being recorded at finer and finer resolution, as sensors of all types—not just cameras—are networked, and the data they collect are analyzed to infer our location, emotional state, and level of attention.

With this foundation, I lay out the six rights that I feel are essential to ensuring that future data of the people and by the people will be data for the people. Two of these rights—the right to access data and the right to inspect the data companies—are committed to the cause of increasing transparency. The remaining four rights are focused on giving us more agency, through the right to amend data, the right to blur data, the right to experiment with data, and the right to port data to other companies. Applying these rights to our data and their use will have consequences for how we buy, how we pay and invest, how we work, how we live, how we learn, and how we manage public resources, as we will see in the closing chapter on turning these six rights into realities.

We are poised at a hinge moment, when the relationship between the people who create data and the organizations that create products and services from that data is being redefined. We are not playing the old game better, faster, and cheaper; we are playing a qualitatively new game, with new rules, which will require us to also redefine the relationship between customers and retailers, investors and banks, employees and employers, patients and doctors, students and teachers, and citizens and governments. It's time to take a stand and truly understand the use of data, so that we can realize the benefits and monitor the consequences. Then we can assess whether our interests are aligned with the data companies. As with most new technologies, it's not the machine that changes everything. The revolution will arrive as people use the machine, adjust their expectations, and change their social norms in response.

Data of the people and by the people can be for the people—if we rise to the challenge. I invite you to join the revolution.

1

BECOMING DATA LITERATE

Essential Tools for the Digital Citizen
How Do Data Refineries Work—And What Is Your Data Worth to Them?

> In the 18th century a person able to read aloud familiar passages from the Bible or a catechism would be counted as literate; today someone who could read no more than that would be classified as functionally illiterate—unable to read materials considered essential for economic survival.[1]
>
> **GEORGE MILLER**

"DATA FOR THE PEOPLE" is not some empty slogan. Every day we are presented with data products and services in the form of rankings and recommendations based on social data. The traditional "Mad Men" of marketing have been replaced by data scientists running algorithms on the multitudinous digital traces that a billion people leave behind every day. Even more important than the exponential growth in our data set is the change in our mindset. To be full participants in the social data revolution, we must shed the old mindset of passive "consumers," who take in whatever is placed before us, and embrace a new mindset, that of active co-creators of social data. The balance of power is shifting between sellers and buyers, bankers and borrowers, employers and employees, doctors and patients, and teachers and students. This is how data of the people and by the people can and will become data for the people.

In fact, the demand to ensure data for the people couldn't be more important. The most important raw material of the twenty-first century is data. Data are the new oil.[2] This analogy is illuminating in several ways. For more than a century, our economy and society have been largely shaped by the discovery of oil and the development of techniques for extracting, transporting, storing, and refining it to create products used by everybody on the planet. Today, the capacity to transform raw data into products and services is transforming our lives in ways that will rival the industrial revolution.

Crude oil cannot be used in its raw form. It has to be refined into gasoline, plastics, and many other chemical products. Refined oil, in turn, has fueled the machines of the industrial age and played a role in the manufacture of most of the modern economy's physical products. Similarly, raw data are pretty useless on their own. The value of data is created by refineries that aggregate, analyze, compare, filter, and distribute new data products and services. Instead of powering the apparatus of the industrial revolution, refined data powers the apparatus of the social data revolution.

Happily, data are very different from oil in fundamental ways. The amount of oil in the world is finite, and the less of this resource that remains, the more the cost of exploiting it goes up. In contrast, the amount of data created is increasing, while the cost of the technology required for communication and processing is decreasing. By the end of 2015, more than 50 percent of adults owned a smartphone.[3] The average American spends about two hours each day on a mobile phone.[4] It's estimated that we touch our phones between two hundred and three hundred times a day—for most of us, that's more often than we touch our partners in a month.[5] And each time we use our phones, we create data. In contrast to oil, we will never run out of data.

Our use of oil is constrained by the fact that it is scarce and physical; our use of data has to take into account that data are now abundant and digital. Only one entity at a time can have the right to use a particular stock of crude oil or a product refined from it, while many can simultaneously access the same pool of data and create many different products from it. Our laws and social norms are based on the idea that goods are in short supply. For instance, in the absence of abundant data, we created insurance—a way to protect ourselves against the costs and consequences of terrible events occurring in our lives. Because it was impossible to know a specific person's chances of being burgled or contracting diabetes, insurers grouped people together, pooling the risk and charging everyone in the pool an average rate for coverage. As more and more data are produced, we will be able to make predictions about risk on an individual level—and get charged individually, too. We can close our eyes and pretend the data do not exist, or we can acknowledge that they do and think about how this should change the way we go about our lives. What sort of world do we want to create with this new resource?

New technologies can be empowering when we have the tools to utilize them. Before the printing press was invented by Gutenberg, books were in short supply and sharing news with far-flung audiences was expensive. The majority of the population gained no benefit from spending long hours learning how to read. Before the web was invented, George Miller, then a professor of psychology at Princeton, wrote about modern standards of literacy. He was worried that too many students were leaving school without the level of advanced reading, mathematical, and scientific literacy necessary to get a job in an economy dominated by the "knowledge industry."[6] Now I believe there is another, just as pressing, need for a new kind of literacy: data literacy—skills like understanding how data refineries work, learning what parameters can and cannot be changed, interpreting errors and understanding uncertainty, and recognizing the possible consequences of sharing our social data. Such literacy is necessary for a world in which most of our decisions will be guided by the recommendations and analyses of data refineries.

The Data-Refining Process

It is not surprising that one of the first significant data refineries, Amazon, is in the retail sector. To succeed as a retailer, you have to know which products to stock for your likely customers, which entails keeping track of data about inventory, prices, advertising, and customers' buying habits.

Two hundred years ago, the bulk of the data a shopkeeper had was the inventory on the shelf and the money in the till, recorded at the end of each day in a paper ledger with a fountain pen. For similar products available at similar prices, the customer had to decide what to buy based on information about the credibility of the product's promises, the attractiveness of the product's packaging, and the say-so of his neighbors, family, and friends. About 150 years ago, a few companies—most notably,

Montgomery Ward and the Sears & Roebuck Company—delighted customers in small towns across America by publishing mail-order catalogs with more than ten thousand products listed in them. These innovative companies knew which items a particular customer ordered and where he wanted them shipped, and they could see which products sold in which region. One hundred years ago, the catalog companies opened physical showrooms and stores, relying on an army of analysts to rake through past sales data and predict future consumer demand, in order to stock products cost-effectively.[7] Fifty years ago, the retail landscape changed again. The mail-order companies and their storefront businesses could more easily characterize American customers by using the newly introduced ZIP-code system for addresses.[8] Over the next couple decades, companies gleaned detailed demographic information about people living in these geographic units. The adoption of credit cards in the United States starting in the mid-1960s simultaneously provided a method for efficiently collecting transaction data for individual customers. That was as personalized as data got, pre-web: where you lived and how much you spent where.

Data broker Acxiom, which was founded in 1969, and others sliced and diced household data, lumping individuals into consumer segments such as "Apple Pie Families," "Blue Blood Estates," "Shotguns and Pickups," and "Suburban Soccer Moms," among several dozen other labels.[9] These labels—some of them even worse in their stereotyping—were developed when data brokers only had information from public records and mailing-list purchases.[10] Brokers could look up the property assessments for homes in a ZIP code and learn which had a swimming pool. "Segmentation marketing" was a godsend in the days when data about consumers were scarce. By the turn of the millennium, Acxiom's annual revenues had grown to about $1 billion.[11]

It was natural for data brokers to explore opportunities for extending their segmentation analysis to online retail. A year before I joined Amazon, I was invited to work with a team at Acxiom on how they might add a digital component to their ZIP-code and household-based data. The big issue for Acxiom's managers was figuring out how to attach the right email addresses to an existing household record. While Acxiom was contemplating one small step—adding one new data field to its database—Amazon and others were about to make one giant leap—into the abundance of social data. I vividly remember trying to explain to Acxiom's managers that online data—this was six years before the first iPhone—meant that companies would soon be in a position to know far more than the demographic profile of a household. Retailers would gain the capacity to track every search query, click, and purchase, to capture every abandoned "shopping cart." With these data at their disposal, companies could really start to market their products and services to individual customers—that is, to a segment size of one.[12]

Amazon is sometimes called the "Everything Store," for its mission to stock everything, but it could also, more profoundly, be described as the first "Save Everything Store," in light of its dedication to storing every bit of data about its customers and products.[13] Given that Amazon offers hundreds of millions of products, it can't show you every product it carries. The scale of digital inventory makes it impossible to browse page by page through the entire company catalog. And if you don't tell Amazon what you're looking for, there's no way the company can tell you about the products it can deliver that might be a match for you. You have to give data to get a ranked list of search results. You no longer have the option of keeping your interests to yourself until the moment you reach the checkout.

When I arrived at Amazon in 2002, one of our goals was to move beyond analyses at the level of ZIP code and make full use of every interaction our customers had with the site. My team and I identified five hundred personal attributes for each user, starting from a number of questions. For instance, did the distance between the shipping address and the nearest bookstore or mall make a difference to how often the customer shopped at Amazon or how much he spent? Did a customer's choice of credit card predict anything about her future buying patterns? Was a customer who shopped in two or more categories worth more in sales each year to Amazon than someone who only ever bought books? Does a customer order different things during the day versus in the evening? Our analyses informed many of the company's decisions, such as whether to spend a dollar on marketing or a dollar on price reductions.

Our analyses also helped determine what to show customers as they decided what to buy. We discovered that a customer's purchase history often was less predictive of a product's likelihood of getting bought than the product's relationship to other products. There are different relationships between items, and the relationships can be computed in various ways. Similar products could be inferred by comparing product specifications or analyzing the overlap in the words that appear in product descriptions, but the most important data for recommendations were how often two products were purchased or viewed together. If there was a pattern of customers buying two items together, those products were mapped as complements. If there was a pattern of customers clicking on two similar items in the same shopping session, the products were mapped as possible substitutes. When customers looked at an item, the queries, clicks, and purchases of previous customers were combined and analyzed to suggest substitutes ("What other items do customers buy after viewing this item?") and complements ("Customers who bought this item also bought"). Just as helpful, however, was the distillation of these user data into a summary of the decision-making process, by sharing the *percentage* of people who clicked on a product and eventually purchased it (or a substitute).

Thus Amazon developed its recommendation system on aggregated clicks and purchasing data. It also built a platform through which third parties could sell products on the site, offering space in its warehouse for these companies' products, which expanded the universe of data available for analysis. Rather than creating tens of customer segments—the typical "Suburban Soccer Moms" and "Shotguns and Pickups" of mail-order catalogs—Amazon could cater to a segment size of "one-tenth," reflecting the changing needs and interests of each person.[14]

Saving data was not revolutionary, in and of itself. What set Amazon apart was its commitment to refining data in ways that help customers decide what to buy based on their own interests, preferences, and current situation. But too much personalization can scare off customers. *New York Times* reporter Charles Duhigg gave the wonderful example of a young woman whose purchases triggered Target's algorithms to start sending her promotions for maternity products. Her father was outraged. However, a few days later his daughter told him that she was pregnant. Target's algorithms had been correct.[15]

Amazon changed marketing by using all the data its customers created in their interactions with the site. It also gave customers the ability to create data in the form of product reviews. This experiment turned traditional marketing, with its emphasis on controlling brand and product communication, on its head. Customers were eager to share their experiences with other customers, and often trusted the reviews of other customers more than the descriptions provided by product manufacturers, marketers, and sellers. If many people gave an item a low rating, it didn't matter if an expert or staff member loved it. Allowing customers to publish reviews also provided far more coverage of everything for sale in the Everything Store, and it gave customers a chance to scan a range of opinions, not simply one person's. Eventually, Amazon got rid of its editorial staff and allocated its resources to developing algorithms for displaying the most useful customer reviews at the top of a product's page. A dollar spent on technology and data improved the shopping experience for customers more than a dollar spent on curation.

Amazon's data refinery has changed how a billion people shop. In 2015, nearly half of online retail purchases in the United States started with a search at Amazon.[16]

Just as we don't need to understand every intricacy of an internal combustion engine to drive a car, we don't need to understand every intricacy of Amazon's algorithms to find a product that matches our interests and needs. It's more important that we understand the basic mechanisms for how the machine works and establish rules for safely operating it. As we create and share data from more sources and sensors, either we can stand by and let others decide the terms of use—scrolling through twenty-plus pages after which we blithely click the accept button—or we can choose to help establish new norms of interaction. We can treat social data refineries as mysterious "black boxes," or we can become data literate and demand meaningful ways to influence the refineries so that the value we get from them is worth what we give to them.

What's Your Data Worth?

We already rely on social data in making many everyday decisions, as when we decide which product to buy on Amazon or where to go for dinner and how to get there. As social data are created in more areas of our lives, we will increasingly depend on data refineries to help us make some of the biggest decisions in life, including who we pick as a romantic partner, where and how we work, what medications we take, and how and what we study.

In many cases, the true meaning of the data we create emerges only when we're comparing our data to the data created by others. With the amount of social data available to the refineries increasing exponentially, we can now hope to get answers to many questions that we'd never before expected could be answered. We may even be inspired to ask fruitful new questions we've never before thought to ask.

Algorithms find patterns that humans cannot see without computers. Such patterns can help guide our decisions. The value of sharing data with a refinery is defined by how useful its outputs are for our decision-making, whether we're negotiating deals, buying products and services, applying for a loan, looking for a job, obtaining health care and education for ourselves and our families, and improving our community's safety and public services.

Thinking about how the outputs of a data company benefit us is a significant shift from the customary debate over how, when, and why companies and governments collect our "digital exhaust"—that is, the data we create day in and day out. Some argue that too much data is being collected, and that the best option for individuals is to share less about themselves—or to demand payment for the data they create and share. Our focus on the inputs misses the potential benefits. I think we should demand something far more valuable than a little financial handout in return for our raw data: we should be asking for a seat at the controls of the refineries—for the chance to influence the outputs on terms that are fair and understandable to us.

First, let's consider the difference in value between raw and refined data. If I enter "Andreas Weigend" into the Google search box, Google reports that there are "about 122,000" pages with the words "Andreas" and "Weigend" on them. There is no way for anyone to sift through all those pages manually: at the rate of one page every five seconds, a phenomenally fast click-and-review rate, it would take a full week for somebody to get through them, which is completely infeasible. So that leaves us reliant on the order in which Google ranks the pages for us. Google could list the most recent mention first. That might be ideal if I'm interested in the most recent news about myself, but not if I'm looking for the video of a class I taught a few years ago. Another option would be to count the number of times my name appears on a page and list the pages in that order, with the most mentions being the most relevant.

That might be somewhat helpful if I'm sorting articles and want to find the one in which I'm quoted the most. But think about how this type of ranking would help if, instead of looking up my name, I were searching for a "cheap iPad"—about 350,000 results. The click-bait specialists would load up pages with popular search terms (as many of them still do) and I'd be stuck wading through result after result trying to find a link to a page that was actually useful.

To improve its search result rankings, Google looks at more than the words on a page, assessing a page's usefulness from multiple data sources. Google's engineers started by ranking the relevance of pages based on the number of other pages that pointed to them. These incoming links provided a measure of people's attention. As people discovered the importance of incoming links in determining a page's rank in search results, the field of "search engine optimization"—including disreputable link farms—was born. Google's algorithms had to adapt, learning how to detect which incoming links were created by honestly interested individuals and which were created on behalf of a page's owner. Now, in addition to the link structure of the web, Google has nearly two decades of data on which pages people visit in response to a search query, as well as dwell times (how long they stay on the page before navigating back to the list of search results and clicking on another link). A page is moved down in Google's relevance rankings when many visitors click on it but, after a cursory glance—what is called a "short click"—they swiftly defect in search of something better. However, high Google page rank doesn't guarantee that the information on a page is correct; it simply indicates the amount of attention people have given it.

How many searches are conducted on Google each day? How many photos are posted on Facebook? One of the basic skills of being data literate is learning what data are plausible, implausible, or impossible. Exact numbers are not important; being data literate means being able to see whether something makes general sense—or could be an order-of-magnitude mistake. Physicists often argue in terms of orders of magnitude, or factors of 10, when making these kinds of assessments. They would say the order of magnitude of people using Google and Facebook is 1 billion, since it is certainly more than 100 million and less than 10 billion.[17] They would then assume that the average number of searches for a typical user is on the order of 10 per day, since it is certainly more than 1 and less than 100, and the number of Facebook photo posts is 1 per day, since it is certainly more than 1 a month and less than 10 a day. This gives us an order-of-magnitude estimate of 10 billion Google searches and 1 billion Facebook photo posts every day, for just two common social data activities.[18]

When you acknowledge that there are billions and billions *more* points of social data being created every day, you can begin to see why your stream of raw data isn't particularly valuable, in a monetary sense. This is very different from the sentimental value your personal data might hold for you. That adorable photo of your dog that you posted on Facebook is probably of interest to no more than one hundred people, or 0.00001 percent of the site's users. It is only through the aggregation and analysis of data from millions of people that correlations and patterns that are useful can be found. Subtract one person's data and the refineries can still arrive at the same conclusions from everything that's left. The individual misses out completely, while the refineries miss out on essentially nothing—the input of one person among a billion.

What's more, data inputs aren't always as discrete as a Facebook photo post. A single data point may be like a pebble, or even a grain of sand, dropped into the ocean—hard to find but distinct. Or it may be like a drop of ink, which gets diffused throughout the water on a microscopic level until its molecules are so homogeneously distributed that the ink is no longer separable. Data literacy also involves knowing when your data can be deleted point by point and when they have dissolved into the aggregate data of all users. As I mentioned earlier, at Amazon a click on a product was associated with a click on another product or with a product purchase. If a customer did not want the purchase to show up in his purchase history, he could delete the entry. But it is impossible to remove the click from Amazon's product recommendation system since it wasn't associated with the customer. Again, this demonstrates the similarity between refining oil and refining data. After a certain point, the oil from an individual well can no longer be removed from the process.

This understanding of the quantity and quality of data is partly— though not entirely—why I think that it's wrongheaded to ask to be paid for your data. Microsoft Research philosopher Jaron Lanier has become a cheerleader for data compensation in the form of "micro-payments," a stance he has presented with great passion since the publication of his book *Who Owns the Future?* in 2013.[19] One of his pet examples is the language translation service available from Google. Why should Google get all the advertising revenue, he asks, when all the people who helped to improve the company's algorithms by suggesting and correcting translations receive nothing? With each suggestion and correction, Google's model for translating text does improve, even when a new contribution duplicates the work of earlier contributors. The model learns from these duplicates to put more weight on that suggestion.

Lanier's contributors do receive something for their efforts. There's a high probability that they, too, benefit by using Google's service tool for translating texts. They are paid not in money but in refined data products and services.

Now think about some of the data created on Facebook every day. If you post a photo of your dog, you clearly created that data. But what if you post a photo of a group of friends at a birthday party. You took the photo and posted it, but the commercial value of the post for Facebook is based on the traffic that it inspires and the refined data about relationships and interests that are embedded in people's interactions with it. Should you get 100 percent of the payments attributed to the sharing of those data? Or should you split it with everyone tagged in the photo? How about with everyone who adds a comment, like, or tag on it, which means the photo becomes part of their activity for friends to see? These reactions are far more numerous—and far more helpful to improving Facebook's services. Lanier doesn't discuss these data—he might not think of them as "creative" content worth being paid for. But these digital traces are the bulk of the raw material for the data refineries whose outputs we depend on, day in and day out.

If refineries were forced to make a reckoning of the value of all your clicks and searches, all your likes and tags, relative to everyone else who touches these data and adds them, you can bet they'd start asking users to pay for access to search results, recommendations, and rankings. Developing algorithms costs money, and doing this analysis would require developing an algorithm specifically for the purpose of assigning attribution and value to every bit of data—including how the value of data changes over time.

It's not merely the cost and difficulty of solving this problem of attribution that makes Lanier's proposal for micropayments a nonstarter. First, let's consider a simple order-of-magnitude argument. If Facebook shared every cent of its profits—about $3.5 billion in 2015[20]—with its users (with no dividends paid out to its shareholders), each user would have received about $3.50 for the year. Is having unlimited access to a communication platform for a year worth more to you than a cappuccino? If so, you're already getting "paid" for your data. Second, in many cases you have to give data to get a refinery's service, as when you share your location with the Uber ride-sharing app. You can decide you no longer want to provide data to the data refineries, but then you'll have to forego the products and services they provide. Third, many of the outputs of refineries—from product recommendations to predictions of when drivers will be in high demand—are created only by refining individuals' raw data. While your specific data might not change the results you see, it is appropriate for refineries to ask every person who uses their products and services to contribute data.

For these reasons, I believe that instead of demanding payment for your raw data, you need to be demanding more powerful ways to gain control over how, when, and why you share, what your data can be used for, and what you get as a result. The data refineries that are most successful make it clear how the data you contribute improve the refined data products offered to you. We spend a lot of time as a society debating whether restrictions should be put on how organizations can use raw data and not nearly enough time on what tools they should offer in order to foster transparency and agency.

Refineries do not reduce you to a bunch of numbers to be bought and sold—at least, not necessarily. If there's one lesson I want you to take away from this book, it's that social data can help *you* make better decisions—not just help some megacorporation develop a better targeted advertising campaign. I believe that, as much as you are the data you create, you are the decisions you make. This is the value of your data for you.

Exploration Versus Exploitation

The data-refining process also involves trade-offs between exploration and exploitation. Hearing those words, you might be imagining a dark and seedy street corner, but instead I want to transport you to the blaring neon lights of the Vegas Strip and a bank of slot machines. In the field of artificial intelligence—where computer software learns from incoming data—the "multi-armed bandit problem" is a sort of king, an exemplar of the dilemma of whether you're better off exploring new options or sticking with the best option you have seen so far.[21] Say you just walked into a casino and heard someone seemingly make a fortune at a particular slot machine. What would you do? Would you spend the rest of your evening at that machine, exploiting your observation that it has paid out more than other machines since you arrived, or would you explore other machines, looking for data that might identify a potentially better chance of a jackpot? Of course, collecting data about the performance of the machines takes time; because casinos are in the business of making money, the game is set up so that gamblers lose on average. Ideally, the computer theorists say, you'd spend some time observing the slot machines and try to detect a pattern. While a statistician could suggest how much or little time to spend on each of the casino's noisy slot machines, you would still have to decide whether to explore a new option or exploit what has worked thus far. The multi-armed bandit problem may seem to have little to do with the output of data refineries, but the balance between exploration and exploitation is a key issue in how recommendations are ranked for users and how users pick which recommendation is best for them. Here it's helpful to reconsider the analogy between oil and data. When petroleum geologists and engineers are working a reservoir, they have to weigh a trade-off: whether to put significant resources into extracting every drop from an active well, spending the money to dig deeper even though the field may be drying up, or to shift resources toward looking for a new field that might yield oil more efficiently. Data refineries also have to make decisions about how best to allocate resources to maximize inputs, outputs, and efficiency. When it comes to data, the most important resources to manage are the time and effort of users.

When search engines like Google present a list of websites in response to a query, they don't show you dozens and dozens of very similar results that all match the same aspect of what you are looking for; they include options that allow you to discover pages with a range of relevance to your search term. Occasionally, it's very clear that you're searching for information about a particular thing—for instance, if you type "*Panthera onca*" into the query box. But if your search term is "jaguar," the search engine should show you not only webpages about the cat (or, for that matter, about the car or the old Mac operating system).[22] The search engine's algorithms create clusters of "jaguar" meanings based on the words on the page, the links between pages, and people's navigation among the pages and shows a selection from each cluster to explore—and hopefully ensure that you find what you're looking for.

An offshoot of the one-armed bandit is called the "optimal stopping" theory or "fussy suitor" problem, which was first described by Martin Gardner in his "Mathematical Games" column for *Scientific American*. Gardner's version involved slips of paper with numbers written on them, anything from "small fractions of 1 to a number the size of a 'googol' (1 followed by a hundred 0s)."[23] You mix up the slips of paper and turn them over, one by one, until you come to a slip that you think might be the largest number in the stack. Over time, the slips in the thought experiment were transformed into suitors going out on dates. You go on a date with a person and have to decide: Do you keep dating around, or do you stop because *she's the one* (of those you've met so far)? You're facing a real-world, high-stakes choice between exploration and exploitation.

For obvious reasons, users of dating apps or sites are constantly negotiating the fussy suitor problem. Early dating sites were designed to let users specify their preferences for people based on weight or height or geographical distance ranges, and they ranked their dating prospects accordingly. A user decided to click on a photo of a possible dating prospect, who we'll call Sam. The site didn't know what it was that inspired him to click on Sam's picture. Was it the fact that Sam was the first person on his list? Was it because Sam has dark hair or wears glasses? Was it because there's an ocean view in the background, and he's interested in someone who lives by the beach, or in someone who likes to take beach vacations? Any number of things might have interested the user, but he still had to decide whether to send a message to Sam or to keep looking. And while a traditional matchmaker would strive to find the perfect mate for every one of her clients, a dating site lets the user decide whether he wants to see more suggestions, as well as whether he wants to see more of the same or something completely different.

For the most part, data refineries have been making decisions about how to set the balance between exploration and exploitation by observing how deeply users explore the recommendations, and whether and when they return. However, the optimal setting often depends on the user's immediate context. The fussy suitor may be looking for Mr. Right or Mr. Right Now—and it is hard for the refinery to correctly guess which it happens to be in this particular moment. Transparency demands that users get to see the refinery's settings; agency demands that users have some ability to affect them.

At MoodLogic, a music recommendation start-up I co-founded,[24] we gave each user at any given time control over the balance between exploration and exploitation—in this case, between supplying music similar to what she usually listened to and exposing her to unfamiliar music. We analyzed the user's existing digital music library and created a model to find songs, artists, composers, instrumental lineups, tempos, and genres that matched the songs on the person's hard drive. Our model predicted both how much she would like a new song and how confident (or not) we were in making that recommendation. Then we let the user choose between two settings. The "safe" setting played music we predicted she would love, with little variation from song to song. In the "explore" setting, she got unfamiliar pieces of music that we thought there was a chance she'd love, but also a chance she'd hate. The choice was hers—and created data that we could also use to improve MoodLogic's algorithms.

Though data may seem infinite, time is not. Decisions have to be made. The wonder of social data is that the outputs of the refining process can themselves become inputs.

Learning from Errors

People like to feel confident about the decisions they make. It's reassuring to be able to list the pros and cons of a choice (*Do I accept this job offer in a new city or accept the matching offer from my current employer?*), weigh the options against each other, and pick the one that better matches our current situation, goals, and comfort with risk. In the past, people would gather data by talking with family, friends, colleagues, and mentors. They had to make decisions in a "small data" world.

It's now possible to look up job satisfaction ratings on Glassdoor, a platform for anonymously reviewing work environment and compensation.[25] More than 400,000 companies have been reviewed on Glassdoor, and the site receives 500,000 new reviews by employees each year. Amazon, for example, has 8,000 reviews of jobs, 8,000 reviews of job interviews, and 14,000 reports of salary covering 1,400 job titles. A person considering a position has more data available than ever before—but not the time to read and analyze 8,000 reviews and compare them to her current workplace. Which reviews are accurate, and which are most relevant to the job being considered? Could some of the reviewers have misread a question and clicked a lower rating by accident?

All data are prone to error. In the days of small data, the people who collected data made it their job to get to know each and every data point, weeding out and correcting most errors by hand. And it's a good thing they were able to check everything, because often decisions for a whole community or state were based on data from these very small samples of people. An error in the total unemployment claims made in a state in a week—for example, typing 254 instead of 2541—could accumulate, impacting annual unemployment figures and, in turn, affecting government economic policy. The US Bureau of Labor Statistics' longitudinal surveys of workers had a sample size of around 10,000 people—the same order of magnitude as the number of Glassdoor reviews from Amazon employees.[26]

It is reasonable to assume that the rate of errors in data does not depend on the amount of data collected. If we now have access to a hundred times more data, we can expect roughly a hundred times more incorrect data points. But we no longer have the ability to hunt down and remove individual errors and mistakes from the data.

However, the exponential growth in data itself offers the solution to the problem of the exponential growth in the number of errors. Because people are constantly creating new data in response to the refineries' outputs, algorithms can learn to identify what might have been an input error. Google asks if you meant to search for "Andreas Weigend" when you type "Andreas Weigand" because a percentage of previous users changed their queries after seeing the initial results.

When refineries combine data from multiple sources, they can detect such input errors for us. One day in July 2012, a service called Google Now appeared on my phone. It scanned Gmail for information in my e-tickets and updated me on the status of my flights, often before the airline did. Simple enough. But the sophisticated data analysis of Google Now still managed to surprise me. One morning, as I was getting ready to pack up my bags in Freiburg, the app informed me that I needed to leave for the airport immediately. According to my schedule, my flight wasn't supposed to depart for hours. Airlines don't typically shift a scheduled flight's departure time forward by more than a few minutes. It didn't make sense. Still, trusting Google Now more than my calendar, I decided to make a move; maybe Google had identified a huge traffic jam en route to the airport. When I arrived, I realized that the flight time had been entered incorrectly in my calendar. Google had ignored that manually entered data and sent me a reminder based on the e-ticket in my Gmail. (Three years later, Google would automatically add the flight to my Google calendar after the e-ticket landed in my inbox.)

We've become accustomed to letting refineries point out and correct mistakes like this; it's a useful service. The question is whether we will accept similar corrections in other parts of our lives as we create and share more data.

Refineries also have to interpret what is signal and what is noise. "Signal" and "noise" are statistics jargon for data that are relevant—signal—and data that are random and thus irrelevant—noise. Social data are complicated because what is signal and what is noise may vary from user to user and from context to context. When a friend on Facebook tags you in a photo in which you don't appear, is that signal or noise? It depends. If he has tagged you in the photo accidentally, mis-clicking on your name instead of Andrew's, who appears right below you in his friend list, that's noise—the social data equivalent of static interfering with your radio's reception. If he has tagged you in the photo because he wants you and your friends to find out about the events captured in the snapshot, it might be annoying, but it is still a signal; it is not noise, statistically speaking.

Learning from user feedback is crucial for improving a refinery's algorithms. By this, I don't mean that you're asked to sit down and fill out a customer survey or attend a focus group. Fostering an ongoing "conversation" with users enables a refinery to improve and personalize its products and services. Each choice you make helps the refinery adjust the ranking of the options. But you, as a user of the refinery, also learn to change what words you search for to get results closer to the ones you were looking for—not just to avoid typos but to emphasize your interest in different categories or aspects of a topic.

However, your interactions with a site or app are also constrained by the options the refinery presents to you. I think query refinement could be made much more dynamic, by allowing users to play with the refinery's confidence intervals, as my colleagues and I did with the music recommendations at MoodLogic. As Glassdoor accumulates many more employee reviews, it will have to find ways to refine that data further for it to be even more useful to users. A model might estimate which reviewers' assessments are most relevant to a user—not simply by job title or office location but by other data shared with the site, such as career goal or preferred work environment. But no matter how much data comes in, there will be uncertainty in the estimates.

Being data literate means realizing that a recommendation is a percentage chance, and that any decision requires a trade-off between risk and return—even when they're based on so much data that the uncertainty seems very small. A refinery should not be making the decision for you. It should be empowering you to take advantage of far more data by removing some of the risk of errors for you.

With the help of refineries, we can access and analyze a rich data history, discovering patterns and predicting trends, not all of which will always be correct. This approach to thinking about our data and ourselves is very different from what most of us are used to.

Turning Data into Decisions

"Data! Data! Data!" [Holmes] cried impatiently. "I can't make bricks without clay."[27]

ARTHUR CONAN DOYLE

When I was working as a post-doctoral fellow at Xerox PARC (Palo Alto Research Center) in the early 1990s, we used a supercomputer to analyze road traffic patterns. One of our goals was to predict travel times. Being physicists, we studied traffic like a fluid, trying to identify the conditions that caused a "laminar-turbulent" transition—the shift from a smooth flow to stop-and-go. By today's standards, we didn't have much data, so we had to make a lot of assumptions to create our traffic simulation models.

The problem of knowing when you will arrive at your destination has now become trivial since pretty much every car has someone traveling in it with a mobile phone that indicates the car's location in real time.

One company in the field, a Microsoft spin-off called Inrix, analyzes the geolocation data of more than 100 million individuals' phones each day to identify where cars are going—and, just as important, where they're not—to infer trends in the movements of people and products.[28] For its analyses, Inrix gets data from mobile carriers on which cellular base station those 100 million phones are connecting to. Inrix sells this refined data to Garmin, MapQuest, BMW, Ford, and other companies that want to provide mapping and route-planning services to drivers. Inrix also advises governments on urban planning issues, including where to build new bridges, install new traffic lights, and situate new public hospitals and other social services.

Inrix's traffic updates demonstrate how data from many devices, aggregated and "joined" by a refinery, can be far more empowering for decision-making than any one individual's raw data all alone.[29] Anticipatory systems based on social data will advise us—and potentially nudge us—on a trajectory of decisions about our relationships, finances, jobs, health care, and many other things. It also highlights the crucial role of interpretation in the data-refining process. Refineries model data in three "flavors": description, prediction, and prescription. Description characterizes the past. Prediction extrapolates from the past and present to the future, with the assumption that there is no interaction with or manipulation of the system that would change the outcome. Prescription shows us what to do, based on analysis of the past, in order to achieve a desired outcome.

Descriptive statistics summarizes data—for example, by grouping similar data points into clusters. Such descriptions of data can provide a context for decision-making by setting a benchmark against which you can measure your particular circumstances. If you want to know the current location of traffic jams in Manhattan, you can look at how quickly cars are moving on the streets by tracking the geolocation of mobile phones and identify bottlenecks. But even this relatively simple exercise involves some interpretation. You might see huge amounts of data indicating stationary cars near the MetLife Building. But is that because MetLife is near Grand Central Terminal and several busy taxi stands, where you've got a number of taxi drivers waiting for passengers, plus a number of passengers joining them, so quite a few mobile phones are over-reporting "stalled" traffic there? If you want to know if your store is doing well this holiday season, you can tally up your sales, but you need to compare them against something else. If you compare them against your sales at the same time last year, this would not take into account changes in the local economy. Instead you can compare your sales to those of similar stores in the area.

When I was at Amazon, we looked at the time lag between when a person viewed an item and when she bought it. Some of the data points were obviously erroneous because the time difference was negative, and it simply wasn't possible for someone to buy a product before she'd viewed it. We didn't know why these data points were wrong, but we threw them out. We were left with a bunch of data that indicated that quite a few customers waited eight hours before buying an item. How strange. It was only when we noticed that some of the computers at Amazon were set on US Pacific time and others were set on Greenwich Mean Time that we realized the eight-hour lag was an artifact of different international time zones being applied to different clicks. As is often the case, what initially seemed to be an exciting new insight turned out to simply be a mistake.

Interpreting data is an iterative process. Here is a case in point. An airline wanted to target mobile phone advertising to potential business class passengers and asked a team of data scientists to find smartphone owners who were passing in and out of New York's JFK airport on a regular basis. The problem was that the people who most frequently go to any one airport aren't business travelers: they're airport and airline employees. The data scientists discovered this in the data by observing the phones' patterns of movement. One set of frequent visitors—airport workers such as counter clerks, mechanics, and baggage handlers—came and left each day on a clear shift schedule. Cabin crew based in New York City were harder to delineate, but they seemed to be identifiable by the sites and apps they accessed through the airport wifi: few were searching for hotels or logging in to Uber to get a ride, and more were likely to sign in to a dating app on their way out of the airport.[30]

The second way to think about data refining is predictive analytics, which involves taking data and generalizing to future cases, including likely behavior and events. For instance, city planners have used Inrix archives of traffic data collected at one-minute intervals to assess the impact of an event—whether it's a highway accident, a construction project, or a big concert—so that better contingency plans can be formulated for the future. Hedge funds have used Inrix data on the amount of traffic to shopping malls and big-box stores to decide whether to buy and sell shares in retailers long before the release of quarterly sales figures. Analysis of geolocation data collected on Black Friday 2012 correctly forecast a major bump in sales for the entire holiday season.

Similarly, Amazon relies on predictive models in its business decisions, including how many extra warehouse staff and how many extra delivery vendors it needs to hire to fulfill orders during the busy holiday season. This is a typical decision-science problem: how do you weigh the cost of late delivery to customers against the cost of excess delivery capacity? Amazon analyzes shipping capacity at a highly granular level, day by day and city by city. In 2013, the company's predictions were wrong—as they were for several major retailers and shipping vendors that year. Many packages arrived after Christmas, infuriating customers.[31] After doing a root-cause analysis, Amazon revised its model to make more accurate predictions and allocate resources accordingly. As a result, the company was able to offer free shipping with a guaranteed delivery by December 24, 2014, for purchases made two days later than it had in the previous year.[32]

Because many data refineries are in the business of recommending purchases, you have to be on the look-out for the possibility that the rankings have been created in ways that aren't aligned with your interests. One of the earliest big data initiatives was the Sabre Global Distribution System for flight reservations. Sabre was originally launched in 1960 as a project of American Airlines, which invested a huge amount of resources into developing it. In 1976, Sabre was installed in travel agent offices and other airlines' flights were added into the mix.[33] By looking at flight-booking patterns, American realized that travel agents were most likely to choose the flight listed first on the screen, and that few if any flights appearing after the first page of results got selected.[34] American tinkered with the algorithm that ranked the options to give preference to its own flights. The customers didn't know about this bias in the top options presented to them. And given that the travel agents were getting a commission, they had little incentive to find a cheaper flight for the customer. However, two rival airlines, New York Air and Continental, discovered that their flights were getting buried in the results, even when they added new routes and discounted fares—two of the variables that should have helped to raise their flights in the system's rankings.[35] A congressional investigation ensued.[36] The bias finally stopped when the government prohibited it in 1984.[37]

Such manipulation is much harder to pull off when the users of a data refinery aren't middlemen but the end customers, who are more likely to pay attention to whether the suggestions match their preferences. I worked with Agoda, a Bangkok-based hotel reservation site, on developing a recommendation system. At first, it might seem that the best option for the company's bottom line would be to sort the hotels by the amount of profit that Agoda would make. If a hotel is willing to give a bigger commission to Agoda, why not put that hotel at the top of the list? Some customers who were shown results ranked by Agoda's profit went ahead and booked the room, but might later regret their decision. Other customers looked at the top options and assumed Agoda didn't have inventory of the sort of hotel they liked and decided to book a room through a competitor. What if the ranking was based instead on the preferences of each individual traveler? In the long run, it was better for Agoda to align its interests with those of customers.[38]

The final level of working with data is prescriptive analytics, taking the data you have and determining how to change conditions to reach a desired outcome. A classic example is the data analysis involved in NASA's moon landing.[39] To get Neil Armstrong and the American flag on the moon, the engineers at NASA had to analyze a continuous stream of data about the landing module's position in space. The space engineers needed to do more than summarize that data (description), and they needed to do more than forecast when and where the module would hit the lunar surface (prediction); they needed to identify which action to take next in response to the data about the module's changing situation in order to improve their chances of actually getting a man on the moon. After each firing of one of the module's jet thrusters, they would learn the exact effect the force had on the trajectory of the module. They'd then predict how and when and for how long the thruster needed to be fired again to reach their goal.

Being data literate involves understanding that assumptions are built into description, that uncertainty is inherent in prediction, and that feedback is fundamental in prescription. Is it reasonable for a data refinery to place you in a marketing cluster based on your Google search history? Is it possible for a refinery to judge a job candidate's suitability for a position based solely on LinkedIn connections? Is it plausible for a refinery to suggest a change in a person's exercise regimen based solely on her Facebook check-ins at restaurants?

Experiment, Experiment, Experiment

Refineries don't merely describe, predict, and prescribe; they experiment. Indeed, every time you shop online, whether you're looking for modern masterpieces at Amazon, moccasins at Zappos, or mates at Match.com, chances are that you're the subject of some experiment. Data refineries depend on experimentation in order to improve the products and services offered to users through a process known as A/B testing.

In science, causality is established in an experiment by changing one variable, the independent variable, and comparing the response in a "treatment" group against a "control" group for whom the variable has not been changed. A/B experiments typically begin with a question— for example, "Should I stock more red umbrellas or blue umbrellas if I want to maximize the number of umbrellas I sell?" This question appears pretty simple, but it throws up many of the complications of devising a good A/B experiment. An umbrella seller might try to detect the right choice by setting up his stand on a particular corner and offering only red umbrellas on the first day of his trial and only blue umbrellas on the second. He might even choose to run the experiment on two consecutive Mondays, when the workers in the area might be more rushed as they head out the door and thus more likely to forget their umbrella. But while he has controlled for location and day of the week, he didn't take into account one of the most important variables in determining whether someone wants to buy an umbrella, red or blue: namely, whether it is raining.

Data refineries have far more variables to take into account than our umbrella seller. Amazon runs A/B experiments to decide everything about how pages appear, from the size of the search box on the home page to whether the checkout dialog appears on the left or right side of the screen to how much descriptive text about the product should be visible without a second click. Google famously ran an A/B experiment to determine the shade of blue used for advertising links. According to

Google insiders, the final selection from among the fifty choices boosted advertising revenue by $200 million annually.[40]

Descriptive analytics provide opportunities for recognizing "natural experiments," situations in which a condition has changed by chance or by mistake (that is, not as part of the design of the experiment) and its effects can be observed—for example, when there is a bug in the rollout of software. The developers for Amazon's website in France—Amazon.fr— initially forgot to add the cost of shipping at the time of checkout. This mistake, and the immediate surge in orders that followed it, gave Amazon an idea for how much free shipping would increase orders.

Prediction is at the heart of the scientific method: a scientist creates a model that makes a prediction, carries out an experiment, and measures whether the outcome corresponds to the prediction. If it doesn't, the scientist changes the model and repeats the process.

What most interests me in the realm of social data are experiments that involve prescription, allowing a user to change a parameter and see how that might change the output or outcome. A refinery using data to identify a traffic jam happening right now can alert drivers, providing a longer predicted travel time for the slow route and suggesting alternates that appear to be moving faster. If most drivers select the same alternate route, a new traffic jam might build up there. A refinery could suggest a variety of options and inform drivers what percentage of other drivers in the area have already selected a particular route, so that they can decide if they might want to take a different option. Or a refinery could use those data to try to optimize traffic flow by anticipating where a traffic jam is likely to occur in the next few minutes and changing the timing of traffic lights to prevent it from happening.

One of the best minds in the field of A/B experimentation is my former colleague Ron Kohavi, who left Amazon in 2005 to build the Analysis and Experimentation team at Microsoft. Ronny and his team ran hundreds of experiments on about twenty websites (including MSN.com and Bing), trying to formulate the basic practices behind good online experimentation. Based on this experience, Ronny says: "getting numbers is easy; getting numbers you can trust is hard."[41] I wholeheartedly agree. Further, the same can be said for one of the most fundamental aspects of data refining: making recommendations is easy; evaluating recommendations is hard.

Lots of things can go wrong when running A/B tests on websites. To begin with, web crawlers account for 15 to 30 percent of the pages viewed on some sites—and unless a refinery wants to be optimized for machines, these visits by robots have to be identified and separated out from visits by humans.

It can also be tempting to assign users to treatment or control groups in ways that appear to be more efficient than doing so at random. However, as smart as this may initially seem, many nonrandom ways of sampling influence an experiment's results and pollute the analysis. For instance, if a user deletes cookies on a frequent basis, she might be assigned to one group on her first visit during the experimental period and to a different group on the next. In some experiments, the assignment to a group might be correlated with the site a user was on when she clicked a link taking her to either a treatment or control version of a page. Are people more likely to click on the ad for an umbrella because they were just at the Weather Channel, which is running nonstop stories about a possible hurricane? Because the assignments weren't random, the results would be biased.

In addition, scientists try to consider variables that may affect user behavior but which they haven't built into their experiment. An experiment's results can be biased by a bug that crops up in the version of software presented to one group but not to others. How software runs on different platforms can also be an issue. Users who access the web on an iPhone versus an Android phone aren't independently and identically distributed across the entire population. An experiment might seem to show that iPhone users visit a site more often than Android users but, in actual fact, the software—not the user base—was the difference: the default page refresh rate might simply have been set higher on iPhones. Coming up with such possibilities and investigating them is a daily delight for data detectives.

Companies have been running tests on customers for decades, conducting trials of products and packaging long before the web. What's new is being able to run experiments in real time, rapidly receiving feedback that can be incorporated into the development of products and services, including those of the data refineries. In the past, the "round-trip" time between idea and result was measured in months. Now, in our connected world, the time frame has collapsed to minutes. This is fundamentally different from the timescales of medical trials, where the effects of a change in a drug's formulation may take weeks, months, years, or decades to show up.

As social data become ever more integrated into our problem-solving and decision-making, refineries will develop products and services in contexts with great significance in our lives, including health care and education. We as a society will have to consider which social data experiments we want to have run, and which results we can trust. When is it enough to collect data for an hour or a day, and when would it be better to conduct an experiment over a longer timescale? In the setting of education, for instance, there are no obvious correct answers. To evaluate what an A/B experiment tells us about improving the way we teach students, we must first choose the goal against which the data are being tested. As I said above, making recommendations is easy; evaluating them is hard.

And this process should not be scary to us. We've all benefited from social data experiments, gaining access to services and products that were unimaginable two decades ago but are now considered as essential to modern life as the delivery of water or electricity.[42] There will be far more innovation in the use of social data; only the bounds of budgets, social norms, and creativity will hold things back. To benefit from the work being done at the big data refineries, we must embrace the fact that we are all experimental subjects—and inspire data scientists to run experiments that enlighten our decisions. We shouldn't be left in the dark.

That's why, before we turn to the new data rights that I argue need to govern the data refineries, we need to become better acquainted with the three categories of social data—our clicks, our connections, and our context. As we'll see, these data sources challenge many of society's existing norms, including strongly held, often emotional ones. How do we establish a personal identity? To what extent is privacy an illusion? What does it mean to be a friend? How do we decide who to trust, when, and for what? How much are we influenced by our environment, and how much do we influence our environment? It may surprise you to learn that your searches on Google, your interactions on Facebook, and the sensors on your mobile phone hold the answer to these questions.

CHARACTER AND CHARACTERISTICS

The Stand-off Between Digital Privacy and Digital Honesty
Are You the Data You Create?

One does what one is; one becomes what one does.[1]
ROBERT MUSIL

I'm a physicist by training, as are many of the people experimenting with social data today. That's not really surprising when you think about it: the digital traces we leave behind as we browse the web and use our mobile phones are very much like the trails and counts captured by a particle detector. In fact, working in experimental particle physics was the perfect training ground for conducting experiments in e-commerce.

In high-energy physics, you can't really observe the particle in and of itself. All you can do is observe the interactions of the particle with the detector you built. Physicists infer the properties of the particle by analyzing those interactions. As an undergraduate, I worked at the CERN particle physics lab near Geneva on data from a bubble chamber experiment, which involved measuring the trajectory and radius of the microscopic bubbles formed as a particle entered the chamber and interacted with a near-boiling liquid. The path and size of those bubbles were used to calculate the particle's electrical charge and mass. This principle of indirect observation applies to every experiment in particle physics: no one will ever see a Higgs boson, but most physicists are sure the particle exists given the indirect traces that have been observed.

People, like particles, have properties that can be ascertained only by watching how they interact and value other people and things—a bit like

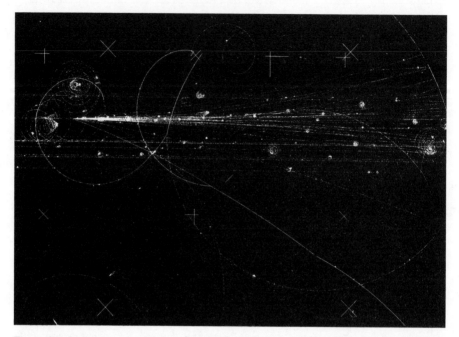

The trails of a proton creating twenty-six charged particles in a bubble chamber experiment at Fermilab. Reprinted by permission of the Fermi National Accelerator Laboratory.

the mathematician hero of Robert Musil's *The Man Without Qualities,* who depends on the world around him to define his very character.[2] The traces we leave reveal a great deal about us, challenging our ability to live life in private. Our traces also allow the data refineries to observe and interpret our behavior, then to predict our actions and interests—whether we know them or not.

The new social data platforms, where we actively create and share data about ourselves, give us an opportunity to express ourselves as never before. We are able to "curate" the self, not merely by changing the style of our hair or the cut of our clothes—what was called conspicuous consumption. Now, in what I call conspicuous communication, we can easily change the characteristics of our digital identity, from profile photos to the pseudonyms we select on various platforms. In the early days of the internet, we thought anonymity would grant amazing new freedoms, but adopting and discarding identities have real costs and consequences for people. It is natural to want to establish rules for safeguarding our character, given the risk of having these data used against us, but being anonymous also decreases our opportunities to benefit from these data.

For many people, the knee-jerk response to the possibility of data being used against them is to ask for stronger privacy protections, since privacy is sacrosanct. Yet many privacy protections actually make it more difficult to hold people to account. The deficit of accountability runs counter to the very principles of transparency and agency that can help us gain personal value from our data. In the world of social data, the old rules are no longer adequate; the economics of ubiquitous data creation and dissemination require us to develop new frameworks and new ideals.

But before we look to the future, let's examine the illusion of privacy. As it happens, privacy is a concept that was only rather recently enabled by technology, and the concept may not be up to the task of protecting us in the age of social data—at least not in its current incarnation. We shouldn't be fighting for privacy simply because it was a pretty good response to people's problems a hundred years ago.

A Brief History of the Brief History of Privacy

For most of history, we humans have lived our lives in public. We shared our living spaces not just with close intimates but with extended family, who gathered with us around an open hearth and knew our comings and goings. "Neighborly" behavior was maintained through close observation. Those who broke society's rules were subjected to merciless gossip; when people *really* broke the rules, they were ostracized, or worse.

Chimneys might very well be the first privacy-enabling technology.[3] In the seventeenth century, the chimney became a common feature in European houses, allowing more families to divide their homes into private rooms with walls and doors that shielded individuals from the prying eyes of their relatives. Around the same time, a cluster of agricultural innovations changed how people could earn a living.[4] By the middle of the eighteenth century, food production was growing faster than the population—and the population was growing fast. Many people moved to the cities, where the first factories of the Industrial Revolution were going up.

City living was anonymous living, and urban dwellers locked their doors to prevent strangers from entering their abodes. There was a cost to this newfound privacy: the design of fireplaces, which were usually quite deep to permit pots to be placed over the fire, was incredibly inefficient. Smoke built up in small rooms—this was the price of a private space. Conditions finally improved in the 1740s, when, who else, Benjamin Franklin suggested a design, the "Pennsylvanian Fire Place," that did a better job of heating a room while also forcing the fire's smoke up the chimney.[5] Finally, ordinary people could shut their doors without fear of asphyxiation. The home became the *sanctum sanctorum,* a place where people could expect some semblance of privacy and safety. With the Fourth Amendment to the US Constitution, Franklin and his fellow Founding Fathers went further, enshrining a right to security against illegal search and seizure of the person in the protection of his dwelling space.

While home life was becoming more insulated and private, political life was not. In our earliest experiments in democracy, voting was a decidedly social activity. The point, after all, was to encourage freedom of expression among regular citizens. As recounted by Harvard history professor Jill Lepore, for the first century of the United States, men voted in public, raising their hands or lining up on one side of a room (just as they still do in the Iowa presidential caucuses). "Casting a 'secret ballot,'" Lepore says, was deemed "cowardly, underhanded, and despicable," an undermining of the openness and direct communication many thinkers believed was an essential ingredient in democratic governance.[6] For example, beginning in the 1850s, the English philosopher John Stuart Mill argued that a secret vote was vulnerable to "selfish" interests,[7] and that "not secrecy, but publicity, should be the rule."[8] A gentleman should vote with public rather than private interests in mind, and what better way to ensure this than to have his vote out in the open and accountable—in other words, transparent.[9]

In those days, when white property owners alone were enfranchised, the best technology available—paper ballots—was deemed to be elitist. Paper required voters to be literate, and not all men with property were. Eventually, however, paper won out as a more stable medium for recording votes than flailing hands or moving bodies. At first, voters were required to bring their own ballot papers to the polls. To make voting easier, they could mark the ballot in advance, or have somebody else do so for them. Those who could afford to print up ballots for others were practically invited to manipulate the choices available. Sometimes this led to flagrantly self-serving campaign tactics, as when a political party listed only its own candidates on a ballot paper supplied to loyal party members as well as random passersby. The paper ballot was adopted not for its privacy-enabling attributes but for its permanence. A permanent record could be re-counted.[10]

The first secret, government-printed ballot was used in an election in the Australian town of Victoria in 1856. It took a generation for the system to be adopted in Britain; cities and states in America began the switch in the late 1880s. The new approach was a limited success. The proportion of the American electorate who turn up at the polls has never again reached the 80 percent level common in the middle to late nineteenth century,[11] perhaps because there is little social cost to not voting.

Around the time the secret ballot was gaining popularity, a couple of lawyers in Boston were making the case for a new "right to privacy." In what is considered to be the first use of the phrase in 1890, former law firm partners Samuel Warren and Louis Brandeis railed in the *Harvard Law Review* against the increasing intrusions into people's private lives. The offenders? "Recent inventions and business methods"—including photographs and circulation-hungry newspapers trading in gossip.[12] As with many inventions, this "right to privacy" was devised to solve a personal problem: Warren and his family had recently been the victim of unflattering and unwanted sketches in the society columns.[13] They clearly didn't live at a time when a billion photos a day were being posted on Facebook.

Alas, the good lawyers, so eager to save their wives and daughters from social embarrassment, conflated the desire to control depictions of yourself with the right to manage what other people say about experiences they've shared with you. In a robust democracy, no one, not even someone suspected of illicit behavior, is compelled to express their thoughts and feelings to others. If you share your secret with someone, there is always a possibility that your confidant will share it with his confidants. Laws can't stop indiscretions, but social norms might—in those cases when the "public" gains more benefit by keeping things quiet. In engineering, it's often said that the purpose of communication is to transmit information. But as Facebook's founder, Mark Zuckerberg, intuited, the purpose of information is to give people an excuse to communicate.

A century ago, when Brandeis was confirmed to a seat on the US Supreme Court, the right to privacy was among his most passionate causes. Brandeis began to tie the right to privacy to Americans' strong beliefs in personal liberty. Take *Meyer v. Nebraska*, a case fought over whether the state of Nebraska could make it illegal for teachers to give instruction in the German language. This was just after World War I, and anti-German sentiment was running high. The Supreme Court's majority asserted that a person had the right "to contract, to engage in any of the common occupations of life, to acquire useful knowledge, to marry, establish a home and bring up children, to worship God according to the dictates of his own conscience, and generally to enjoy those privileges long recognized in common law as essential to the orderly pursuit of happiness by free men," no matter where he made his home.[14] An attack on the right to privacy was an attack on freedom, according to Brandeis.

Our personal choices seemed secure, locked away from peeping eyes and judgmental tongues—or so we fooled ourselves into believing. Aberrations like the McCarthy hearings were "outliers," a snooping into personal politics that was permitted because Communism was a great menace to free society. But our default assumption of privacy would dramatically flip with the development of tools for discovering information and communicating on the internet.

From Walls to Windows

In 1996, when Larry Page and Sergey Brin attacked the problem of web search by looking at the link structure between webpages, they had to rely on public data. Every webpage crawled by Google was public. Someone had written the page and put it up on the internet so other folks could read it, and someone had linked to it.

Developing Google's algorithms and building its network of servers required a lot of money, and Larry and Sergey figured out that the best way to pay for that was by selling space for ads based on a user's search. Advertisers "purchased" keywords, phrases, and categories they believed matched the interests of their likely customers. The payoff was immediate. Advertisers who used Google's personalized ad option had four times as many people clicking through to their sites compared to the average, including ads placed on pages with content related to the product.[15]

People's search data were a valuable commodity because they provided an observable trace of the things that attracted attention.

In April 2004, Google obtained another source of data about user attention when it launched Gmail, which analyzes the content of an email to determine the ads that appear on the service's web interface. Until this moment, most people thought of an email as equivalent to a letter—something sealed in an envelope, intended for the eyes of the addressed recipient only. Privacy advocates argued that Gmail users would be "giving away" their most personal communications to Google if they signed up. Today it is the most widely used email service in the world, with more than 1 billion active users every month.[16] Most of them are aware that their correspondence will be "read" by Google's computers in exchange for free email. This deal—which includes being shown personalized ads—is accepted knowingly and willingly.

Google's aspirations as a company go well beyond search and advertising. The prototype for Google Glass, released in March 2013, incorporated sensors capable of observing and recording the wearer's surrounding environment from her point of view. Critics raised concerns that Glass would be used to publicly share conversations without a person's consent. But it's not as though Glass is the sole piece of technology that can be used for such a purpose. A handy audio-recorder or mini–video camera can easily do the same job. Or you could pull out your mobile phone, which has those sensors and several more. Instead of having to pull out a device to record a moment, wearables like Glass make it even easier to start a recording of events happening around you.

A few months before Gmail's launch, a website called Facemash went live at Harvard. In what is now a legendary story, then Harvard undergrad Mark Zuckerberg wrote software to "scrape" headshots from the online directories of nine residential houses so students could vote on which of two random photos was "hotter."[17] The site was wildly popular with Mark's classmates—and wildly controversial. Mark was in a lot of hot water with the university, which said he had violated copyright and individual privacy rights when he published the photos without permission. Once again, photos were being used by a new communication format as a way to satisfy the very human desire to gossip. Judge Brandeis would have been horrified, but within a decade Facebook would be the default communication system for a large portion of the world's population.[18] As of 2016, about one in four people around the world was on Facebook, with more than 1 billion people accessing it each month via their mobile phone.[19] Mark was pushing the boundaries of social norms, and a lot of people were eager to enter the uncharted territory of digital identity with him.

Of course, as Facebook grew, the company realized that it, like Google, could make money by getting into the online advertising business. The content of people's posts created even greater potential for targeting ads than an email message. People were identifying their relationship status, education level, political persuasion, and religious beliefs; creating lists of their favorite movies, TV shows, books, and music; reporting their travels; and sharing opinions about a host of brands and ad campaigns. They were uploading photos of themselves, their kids, their beloved dogs and cats. All of this was intended for a "public" of family and friends. I was at Facebook's headquarters on the day in the summer of 2008 when the site began personalizing ads.[20] The new ads had a feedback button. When a user clicked that she did not like an ad she was shown, she was asked to give some reason. Reading through these responses as they were coming in was eye-opening. For the most part, people weren't complaining that the ads were using too much of the personal information they had shared on Facebook; they were complaining that the ads were using *too little* of it. A typical example: "My profile says I'm a man and I'm interested in men. Why am I getting ads to 'meet single women'?" Users were asking to see ads that actually matched their interests.

The year 2016 marked the thirteenth birthday of Facebook. Very soon we're going to witness a generation of people who have had their entire childhood shared on Facebook by their parents and grandparents long before the kids could officially open their own accounts. In the past, a person graduated from high school with a handful of identity documents: a birth certificate, an immunization record, a transcript of grades, and a diploma. Most would also have a driver's license.[21] Some might have a reference from an employer or religious authority, maybe a passport. In contrast, every preteen now comes preloaded with social data, created by parents, grandparents, aunts, uncles, older siblings, and family friends. You can find sonograms from before a child's birth, commentary on difficulties maintaining a toddler's discipline, prayers about ill health, and details of physical appearance, skills, and hobbies. Why does Facebook still require its users to be at least thirteen years old in order to sign up for the service? Doesn't it make a lot more sense to set up a Facebook account for every baby at birth?[22] This would help to ensure everyone has a unique, authoritative identifier available to them, which they can choose to use or not. In addition, social data could be tagged with an account's ID, and this would give people the ability to curate the data attached to it when they're older—that is, when the rules say they're old enough to decide for themselves.

We've evolved from the open hearth and its assumption of a public existence, with little experience or expectation of privacy, to enshrining a "right" to personal and political privacy behind the walls of our bedrooms and voting booths. As the internet became entwined in the fabric of social existence, we were more than happy to "go public" with our lives in exchange for free and immediate contact with family, close friends, and distant strangers. Building up the idea of privacy and dismantling it all happened in the span of just a couple centuries—a blip in human history.

village gossip
no privacy

chimneys and urban migration (1600s)
social anonymity and the invention of privacy

US Fourth Amendment (1792) and the adoption of
the secret ballot (1856–1896)
privacy gets political

"The Right to Privacy" (1890)
privacy enshrined in law

Google, Facebook, and beyond
privacy is an illusion

For the past hundred years we've cherished privacy, but the time has come to recognize that privacy is now only an illusion. We *want* tools for managing attention, belonging, and communication. Judge Brandeis came up with a great idea, but it was an idea of his time, when data were scarce, communities were localized, and communicating was costly. It was easy back then to stop someone from publishing a photo of you that you didn't like. Not so today. Further, anonymity is not the default setting of democracy. It's better to write rules for the realities of the present and the possibilities of the future than to romanticize privacy and hope the rules of the past will protect us in the future. To put data to work for the people, we need transparency and agency.

Rather than expending energy on delineating what's public and what's private, and then building walls to keep the data in (or out), let's focus on the ability to truly be ourselves. Doing so will allow us to take full advantage of the data refineries and to balance the potential upside of sharing with the potential downside.

On the Internet, Everybody Knows You're a Dog

When it comes to social data, it's no longer about whether you have privacy or not. Not anymore. There's a classic *New Yorker* cartoon by Peter Steiner with the punch line "On the Internet, nobody knows you're a dog."[23] Things have changed a lot since 1993, when the cartoon made its debut. Today, a better adage would be "On the Internet, everybody knows you're a dog. Sporting a blue collar. Interested in cats. Owners on vacation." That's because you've shared this information with social data refineries in order to communicate with your friends and get personalized recommendations. The price involved seeing an ad for Puppy Chow. People assumed they could be anonymous on the internet.

But long before Facebook, data exposed personal identity. In the mid-1990s, computer scientist Latanya Sweeney decided to find out exactly how anonymous an "anonymous" database of health data was.[24] The Commonwealth of Massachusetts decided it was in the public interest to share information about state employee hospital visits with the research community. The government officials weren't dumb; they knew it was inappropriate to share these data with people's names attached, so they removed identifiers, such as each person's name, address, and Social Security number. In order for the data to be useful for improving health policy, they kept a few bits of relevant data: sex, birth date, and ZIP code. By comparing those three bits of data to a second database—the voter registration rolls for the city of Cambridge, which was publicly available for a twenty-dollar fee—Sweeney was able to pinpoint the record of the state's governor, and "in a theatrical flourish, Dr. Sweeney sent the Governor's health records (which included diagnoses and prescriptions) to his office."[25]

Sweeney estimated that 87 percent of the American public could be identified if you knew a person's sex, birth date, and ZIP code.[26] Later research put the figure closer to 63 percent—still a staggeringly high number given that this could be done without access to more unique characteristics like the ones people share every day on Facebook and other social data sites.[27] An order-of-magnitude calculation reveals why it takes so few data points to pinpoint a person's identity. With about 40,000 active ZIP codes in the United States, and a total population of around 300 million people, on average a ZIP code has about 7,000 residents, approximately half of whom are male and half female.[28] If you assume an even distribution of births across the days of a calendar year, about 10 men or women in a ZIP code would share a birthday; factor in the birth year, and this surprisingly big number makes sense.

Next, consider the social data available to a typical refinery. The idea that a person couldn't be identified by digital traces was shattered when two big refineries shared "anonymized" social data with researchers. First, internet service provider AOL released three months' worth of anonymized search logs of 658,000 users for academic study. The data were also analyzed by two *New York Times* journalists, who managed to track down several individuals based on their search history.[29] They could do this quite easily because people like to search for themselves and their relatives, or for directions from their home address. Second, video-renting site Netflix announced a contest to increase the accuracy of predicting a person's future rating of a movie. Since the researchers participating in the competition needed data to build their models, Netflix provided "100 million movie ratings, along with the date of the rating" from 480,000 customers.[30] The customers' names weren't included, but two researchers at the University of Texas at Austin, Arvind Narayanan and Vitaly Shmatikov, managed to "de-anonymize" people in the data set by comparing the anonymized data to reviews posted on IMDb.com, the Internet Movie Database.[31] Since those reviews were already public knowledge, what difference did it make? Well, the Netflix customers didn't post reviews for every movie they rented, and some of their "private" movie picks were quite revealing—or so argued the plaintiff in *Doe v. Netflix,* who feared her identity as a lesbian had been outed to the 50,000 researchers who had access to the Netflix Prize database. (The lawyer who filed Jane Doe's suit had previously fought to close down a Facebook feature that automatically posted a user's Blockbuster video rentals for friends to see; going forward, you had to "opt in" to such sharing.)

Even if you are comfortable having your movie rental history shown to the world, chances are you would be quite uncomfortable having your entire search history revealed. If you're like the majority of people, the most frequent address you enter into Google Maps is your home address. Where you live, where you want to go, what you need to buy, who you are curious about, and what you are worried about: these are among the most intimate details of our lives.

Now imagine being able to see an individual's searches in real time. When visiting a friend from Stanford who was working at an internet search engine start-up in the 1990s, I got to watch as a string of user queries were received. One of them caught my attention: someone had just searched for "how to commit suicide."[32] What do you do? Do you track down the user through his internet service provider and IP address, then alert a suicide hotline? Would that be an invasion of privacy? Do you first try to understand the query against the user's history, hoping to interpret the person's motivation and put a more specific probability on the action "predicted" in the human response to the query? Perhaps he is a novelist researching a character, and harbors no intent to harm himself. But then you see the person's next search is for "Golden Gate Bridge"— where more than 1,600 people have committed suicide.[33] Now do you step back from the monitor, from the individual, take a deep breath, and return to the job of improving search quality, ignoring that a person's life might be at risk? There's no easy answer here.

It is possible to gain insights into humanity's preoccupations by analyzing search terms in aggregate. Google Trends identifies how interest in people, places, things, and ideas changes over time. For instance, searches for "cyberbullying" and "transgender" have been on the rise over the past few years, with those for "privacy" on the decline.[34]

Similarly, e-commerce transactions reveal attributes about you, and occasionally about the people in your life. For Amazon to deliver your order to you, it has to know which address to ship it to. It's in your interest to make sure the address is correct if you want to get your package. Your purchase history, however, may be a confused mix of things you bought for yourself and for others. Amazon allows you to mark an item as a gift and ignore it when making product recommendations for you.[35] Using these data, the personalization algorithm learns to treat an item you say you bought for someone else differently from your other purchases. If you buy a shirt for a woman as a present, you are sharing data about her physical build when you select the shirt's size. If you buy the shirt during the week or two before Mother's Day, and the recipient has the same family name as you, Amazon's algorithm can infer your relationship. Amazon might even send you an email a year later recommending great Mother's Day gifts.

The "Your Amazon" page provides some degree of transparency and agency for users. You can see some of your raw data, including your purchase history, and control which of these are refined into personalized recommendations. You can also add items that you've purchased elsewhere, whether recently or decades ago. In 2014, Facebook adopted a similar approach, giving you access to your Activity Log, a list of friend requests, likes, stories and photos in which you are tagged, event RSVPs, and more. You can delete individual data points from your history, should you wish. And because your digital identity on Facebook is used to generate personalized ads, deleting bits of your Facebook history affects which ads you see.[36]

Deleting a few likes from your history of activity is unlikely to hide your overall pattern of behavior. In fact, Facebook activity reflects the personality attributes of a user quite accurately, as David Stillwell of the Psychometrics Centre at Cambridge University has found in his research. Stillwell recruited thousands of Facebook users to take a test that assessed the strength of their "Big Five" personality traits—openness, conscientiousness, extraversion, agreeableness, and neuroticism—and then asked a separate group of subjects to review the individuals' Facebook profiles and give their own assessment of their personality. The two assessments matched surprisingly well. People tend to present an accurate portrait of themselves on Facebook—they are themselves when they are curating their social media presence.[37] If a group of human strangers can assess your personality from your Facebook Timeline, you can be sure an algorithm can as well. Revealing your secret tendency toward neuroticism is the price you pay to keep your friends up to date on the events in your life.

In 2013, Stillwell and his colleague Michal Kosinski, along with a team at Microsoft Research, launched the app YouAreWhatYouLike to find out how well personality traits such as IQ, ethnicity, political beliefs, addictive substance use, and sexual orientation could be predicted from what a person does on Facebook. In 88 percent of cases, the authors said, their "model correctly discriminates between homosexual and heterosexual men," based on likes alone, even when those likes weren't explicitly connected with political issues or rights.[38] According to the researchers, among the good predictors of male homosexuality were likes of "Mac cosmetics" and "Wicked the Musical"; good predictors of male heterosexuality were "Wu-Tang Clan" and "being confused after waking up from naps." Apparently, liking "curly fries" and "thunderstorms" accurately predicted high intelligence.[39] Employers are allowed to use IQ and personality tests to screen job applicants. Someone soon you may be asked to install an app that tries to deduce whether you're exaggerating your propensity to be highly organized or calm under pressure.[40]

Data about your attributes might also coalesce without your active involvement. The huge numbers of photos posted online are a case in point. Not every photo of you is within your control, let alone your copyright. If you attend an event and someone snaps a photo as you're passing by, it's only a matter of time before your face is recognized. Facebook's artificial intelligence research group, led by Yann LeCun, can identify whether two photos show the same face, nearly matching the performance of humans.[41] The system, called DeepFace, analyzes the faces in photos and, if a human has tagged a name to a photo with the same face, DeepFace attaches the tag to the untagged photo. Other software is being developed to analyze the background and context of a photo, distinguishing whether you're standing in a crowded bar or on an isolated mesa. If you tend to be photographed in one situation more than in another, an algorithm might classify you as a social butterfly or a lonesome adventurer.

As Microsoft Research scientist Cynthia Dwork and others have shown, the very existence of data and databases opens everybody up to information disclosures. The point of a database is to get answers to queries, and a sequence of queries can be framed in such a way that only one person in the database provides a positive answer to all of them. Cynthia often demonstrates this with the example of asking what percentage of people in a medical database of Microsoft employees carry the sickle cell trait, then asking how many employees who are not female, curly-haired distinguished scientists have it. The difference between the two answers tells you if Cynthia—the only female, curly-haired distinguished scientist at Microsoft—has the trait.[42]

People share data with a refinery to obtain personalized results that help them in their decision-making. A database like the one described by Cynthia Dwork is relatively specific and constrained about the sort of data it collects—that is, "small data." In comparison, the traces being collected by today's "big data" refineries are mind-boggling. To get useful outputs from a refinery, you have to provide accurate inputs, such as your true interests and preferences. If you are not willing to give these data, you can expect nothing better than the recommendations for the "average" person in the population—meaning, you're going to get whatever is most popular or relevant to Joe Public. If you supply incorrect data, chances are you'll get outputs that are totally useless to you. There is a trade-off: more utility, less privacy.

What's in a Pseudonym?

The decision to exchange or withhold identifying information carries consequences. Disclosing identity in one context may produce risk or harm; in another, not disclosing identity may produce it. Our distinct digital traces make anonymity practically impossible.

Still, it wasn't until Facebook that real names were a common sight on the internet. Pseudonyms were the norm. This was partly an issue of logistics. Some names are so common it was impossible to let everyone adopt a username that was the same as their real name when there was no other means for differentiating the users; some sites didn't provide usernames with enough characters to accommodate longer names. At the same time, there were also people who didn't want to reveal their real name because they feared negative consequences such as identity theft, stalking, or repercussions at work or in their community for voicing unpopular opinions. In any case, you could create a different username—or several usernames—for every newsgroup or service you used, if you wanted to do that. As a result, the first decades of the internet were marked by an unprecedented fragmentation of identity. And in the process of adopting multiple pseudonyms, we explored new ways of interacting with others.

Traditionally, a person's identity has consisted of simple data, like your name, date of birth, height, eye color, nationality, and place of residence—basic information that could be used to verify that you really are who you say. The ability to verify a person's identity is necessary in the enforcement of many rules and norms. For centuries, we have used identity passes to prove that we are allowed to enter a territory[43] or checks and check cards to prove that we have money safeguarded in a distant bank vault that can cover the cost of a purchase.[44] Your age or citizenship grants you certain privileges and responsibilities in society, such as the ability to vote or drink alcohol in public spaces, or the duty to pay taxes or serve in the military. We have learned to accept that we have to hand over a government-issued ID or number, enter a passcode, or answer a series of questions about our frequent flyer numbers or childhood pets in order to do quite a lot in life.

Many of the digital traces you leave are produced through your interactions with physical devices, and quite a few of these interactions are distinct enough to identify you, too. As people spend more time accessing the web through mobile phones and tablets, many data refineries are investing significant resources to exploring ways to stitch together a single identity across multiple devices based on behavioral regularities. In addition to requiring users to sign in, digital traces provide clues to who is using what device. For example, some people tend to make the same typographical errors again and again, catching and correcting certain ones more frequently than others. People also have idiosyncratic ways of looking for information online.

Your physical interaction with devices leaves traces, too. Uri Rivner, co-founder of the Israeli company BioCatch, believes that digital fingerprints in how users operate a computer, tablet, or mobile phone are "a way to authenticate your mind by observing what you do and how you do it."[45] BioCatch designs its data collection by forcing users to perform actions that verify their identity without their realizing that this is what they're doing. The company isn't interested in what you're searching for but in how you're searching for it. Do you thump your touchscreen vigorously or gently pat it? How much tremor is in your hand when you hold your mobile phone? Where on the screen do you indicate that you want to scroll up and down? How quickly do you drag your mouse? Do you prefer to launch new tabs from links or to navigate back and forth from an existing tab? BioCatch's clients include banks looking for additional ways to authenticate their customers.[46]

There are other areas in which real-time data analysis can help to verify identity—for example, when credentials aren't reliable or readily available. Web- and app-based games for children have to negotiate a range of issues, from user safety to appropriateness of content. On the simplest level, a site that offers games for six- to sixteen-year-olds has to find a way to ensure the right games are suggested to each user. And the games' developers aren't merely concerned about whether an eight-year-old might start playing a game that's rated as appropriate only for teenagers; a child will quickly get frustrated by games that are too difficult for her, and bored by games that are too easy. A site can't depend on the age entered into a user account profile, since siblings who share a computer might very well start playing a game while another family member is signed in. Instead, the sites analyze the player's interactions with the game to estimate her age. Often as a site safety measure, players can choose only between prescribed sentences in chat dialogues, in order to decrease the possibility of a player inadvertently sharing an address or other sensitive data with an adult pretending to be a fellow child. It turns out that older kids choose different scripted answers than do their younger cohorts. In addition, game sites' models are reportedly able to identify the age of a child within an accuracy of three to six months based on mouse movements, because the development of fine motor skills is highly correlated with age in children and young teenagers.[47]

Fooling a machine-learning system that looks at such implicit traces is a lot harder than faking explicit attributes. If you're in a hospital and a person wearing a white coat and a stethoscope around his neck asks you to undress, you're probably going to assume that the person is a legitimate doctor. Yet, people have been known to adopt a false identity, for one reason or another. In January 2015, a seventeen-year-old was taken into custody by police after spending a month at a Florida medical center posing as a doctor—a white coat and stethoscope having got him past the hospital's security guards.

Historically, pseudonyms have been used as a means for exercising freedom of expression. When "Publius" published the first of *The Federalist* papers in 1787, "he"—that is, Alexander Hamilton, James Madison, and John Jay—was batting off scathing criticisms of the newly released draft of the US Constitution. Few of the combatants in the debate revealed their identities.[48] George Eliot, born Mary Ann Evans, adopted her pen name to avoid the stereotypes commonly attached to nineteenth-century woman writers, who she said—in an anonymous essay, no less—wrote "silly novels" marked by "the frothy, the prosy, the pious, or the pedantic."[49] She wanted her characters and her words to be taken seriously, which, she believed, would be impossible if readers prejudged her writing by the name on the book's cover.

Sometimes, the motivation for adopting a pseudonym is less about freedom of expression than about making a break from past history. In 1947, a man called Hans Fallada (his "real" name was Rudolf Ditzen) penned *Every Man Dies Alone,* the fictionalized account of a German husband and wife who begin a quiet campaign of resistance against the Nazis. Fallada had been commissioned by a Soviet cultural attaché to review Gestapo files and weave a great anti-fascist tale out of them.[50] Yet, Fallada wasn't concerned about tying his well-established writing identity to the politics of this book. He'd adopted his pseudonym years earlier. It seems he wanted to divorce his writing and his literary reputation from a notorious suicide attempt.[51]

These three famous pseudonyms share a characteristic: their owners wanted them to be persistent and to gain a reputation. Publius always wrote in support of ratifying the Constitution. Eliot and Fallada used their pen names for all of their published works. These authors wanted to have their creative output tied to a single identity.

In the early days of the internet, adopting several pseudonyms seemed like a great option. Unfortunately, there was a problem: it's easy to create a new pseudonym, but how can you be sure this new username does not correspond to a person who was booted off the site a week earlier? A site might insist on having an email address registered with every pseudonym, but email accounts are easy to create, too. Some platforms responded by creating complicated registration forms, which make it slightly more costly to set up a new account, but such obstacles don't prevent a dedicated fraudster from hiring a legion of people or bots to fill them out. The "social cost of cheap pseudonyms," in the coinage of economist Eric Friedman and information scientist Paul Resnick, can't be eradicated this way.[52]

Could the cost of pseudonyms be increased enough in some way so that they are as useful as a real name? It depends on the situation. When trust needs to be established from the very first interaction, it makes sense to adopt a "real name" policy; doing so allows you to import a history of past behavior—say, with your bank or your credit-card company. In contrast, adopting a pseudonym requires you to build up a reputation over time, starting from zero.

When I was at Amazon, we looked at whether customer reviews were more valuable to other users if they were posted under a pseudonym or a real name.[53] We knew that if we required users to sign in to their Amazon account, even if they chose a pseudonym for their display name, they would be less likely to post "unuseful" reviews. We'd also seen that customers gave more weight to non-anonymous reviews. Thus, whenever an Amazon customer changes his display name, all of the bylines on his reviews, past and present, are updated to show the new name so that his reviewing history remains intact. The person's identity and reviewing history is persistent, but the pseudonym presented to the public doesn't have to be. Amazon could have insisted on a real-name policy for reviewers, since every one of Amazon's customers has a real name—as confirmed by the account's credit card. However, it turned out that the most important factor was whether Amazon indicated that the reviewer had actually bought the product. People do put more trust in opinions that are signed—but in this case, with data about a reviewer's purchase rather than a name. Reflecting this finding, Amazon changed how it computes the "average" star ratings for a product and increased the weight on verified-purchase reviews.[54] (Amazon has also sued several companies for allegedly paying customers to write "five-star" reviews.[55])

There are other trade-offs to anonymity. Consider the subtle differences between filling out a paper "comment card" at a place you frequent and answering an online survey. Although a comment card is ostensibly anonymous, many people don't fill them out, and not just because they're lazy. People know they might be identified from a number of attributes—their handwriting, their word choice, the topics that they raise, and the time at which they stuffed the card in the box. They may fear repercussions for sharing negative comments. Further, an anonymous comment is, by definition, a "one-time game." There's no dialogue between the two sides, no chance to clarify a person's meaning or intentions, and no incentive to cooperate. This allows the recipients of the feedback to dismiss it—as noise, an outlier, something specific to the moment and not indicative of the need to make a change. Anonymous feedback can be shrugged off as self-serving or malicious.

Online discussion boards like Reddit have to address the problems inherent in anonymity through machine learning. Reddit usernames can be utilized for every interaction with the community or just for a single post or vote, never to be heard from again. Every pseudonym is given free rein to express itself, and people are encouraged to try on various personas when contributing to the platform. At no time in the process are users asked to attach an email address or a real name to the account; the site's founders had no desire to hold people accountable in this way. Accountability develops in other ways. After you post something interesting, others chime in, amplifying your post or comment or arguing against it, adding their own comments or upvoting or downvoting earlier ones. If a post or comment is downvoted often enough, it is pushed to the bottom of the rankings and gets listed under the heading "comment score below threshold"—though it can still be viewed, and voted on, by anyone who makes the effort to look for it. Reddit encourages a dialogue to develop between users and ultimately lets them decide which comments are worth their time and which ones aren't.

What matters most to Reddit is that the discussions that get featured on its "hot," "rising," and "controversial" lists are genuinely interesting to lots of different people, not lots of different pseudonyms. Being ranked among the top twenty-five discussions on one of those lists often leads to widespread attention across the internet. Instead of spending lots of time and money on human moderators to enforce rules and regulations, Reddit has relied on machine learning to decrease "vote fraud," where individuals adopt different usernames not to express opinions but to upvote their postings and downvote others'. When multiple pseudonyms are active and in sync, originating from similar IP addresses or displaying similar writing styles, the pseudonyms are "ringed" together as confederates.

Votes received from confederates are given less weight, and might get entirely ignored.

Honest Signals

In 2016, more than 100 million people turned to apps and websites to meet people for casual encounters, dating, courtship, and long-term relationships. The problem is how to find a person who wants what you offer and offers what you want, and—the hardest part—returns your interest when you are looking for it.

When it comes to dating, some people are truthful, on some topics, some of the time. The distribution of truthfulness varies from one person and one situation to another. Sometimes people might just be experimenting to find out what they really want. What people say is one signal. What they *do* is another. The signals revealed through a person's actual behavior are what social scientists call "honest signals."

Designing a dating app's user interface and recommendation algorithms is particularly challenging, since users might consider certain attributes dear to their heart when their site usage tells a very different story about who they find attractive. Christian Rudder, one of the co-founders of OkCupid, has shown that users may not fully realize or want to admit the strength of their racial or ethnic preferences.[56] But a simple count of clicks and contact messages will quickly reveal these preferences.

It's a bit like the old problem of movie ratings. When Netflix asks users what they think of critically acclaimed films like *Citizen Kane* or the documentary *Blackfish,* a huge proportion of people give them five-star ratings because they believe they're *supposed* to rate them highly. Netflix can recommend films to you based on your ratings, but those ratings are only as useful as they are honest, and you have to be able to see evidence that responding truthfully is going to benefit you. Netflix found that a more honest signal of your interest in a category of movie is how long you actually watch the video. In other words, viewing data are more useful than reviewing data for making recommendations.[57] This phenomenon is related to Richard Nisbett's observation that people often don't understand the cognitive processes behind their behavior and decisions. There are limits to our capacity for self-understanding and introspection.[58]

In the real world, some preferences and attributes are uncertain. Most people don't dismiss an amazing potential date for being a few months older than their ideal. Yet, while working as a consultant with several dating sites, I discovered that far more people were reporting their age to be twenty-nine than thirty.[59] This could not reflect reality. Did the bogus twenty-nine-year-olds lie about their age when they initially made their profile, or did they change it after interacting with the app and realizing they were "too old" to show up in response to searches conducted by the users they were interested in? This got me thinking about how seeing users' edit history might change their behavior.

Some edit behavior would be considered acceptable and understandable. For example, after a few dates a person might decide to revise the interests he listed because he felt he was overselling his rock-climbing prowess or discounting how much he enjoys going to concerts. Similarly, he might revise the description of who and what he is looking for. Other changes might raise red flags for other users—such as frequently toggling between saying he is single and saying he is in a relationship.

Imagine a scenario where users have the ability to see not just the edit history but also the communication history. A common problem on straight dating apps is that women are often inundated with hundreds of messages while some men get no messages at all. To stimulate more symmetrical communication, dating apps have tried to limit the number of messages a person can send over a certain period of time. But because the inventory on dating apps changes daily, with users cycling in and out of circulation, this is a recipe for frustration. What if Miss Match activates her profile the day after you've used up your monthly quota, and by the time you can send messages again she's disappeared? You don't know if the algorithm has buried her further down the search results because you didn't get in touch earlier, or if she's started dating someone else. Rather than enforcing hard limits, a dating app or site might increase transparency and reveal the honest signals of user behavior. For example, each profile could indicate how many messages the person has sent and received in the last day, week, and month, as well as the average response rate and response time. This would put everyone in a better position to decide whom to contact.

Such dashboards are already being used on some dating apps. The gay dating app Jack'd provides data on a user's reply rate to incoming messages and descriptive statistics (the distribution of age, ethnicity, body type, etc.) about the people he's actually shown interest in (not just what he said interested him on his profile). For simplicity, Jack'd's data on a user's tastes are not based on clicks or incoming or outgoing messages, but solely on the user's "Favorites" list and the "Match Finder" tool, which allows users to express interest in someone and sends an alert only when both parties say they're interested. This transparency allows users to fully explore not just their options but their chances. If a guy you want to approach replies to only 12 percent of messages, then you might decide to spend your time contacting someone else—especially if 90 percent of the users who catch his eye describe themselves as having "big muscles" and you are anything but that.

More private than these explicit signals to other individuals are the richest data any dating site has: the trail of clicks each person leaves behind while exploring user profiles. Interpreting the motivation behind those clicks is complicated, however. When working with Match.com, I came across a user who had blocked a large number of black women. The obvious hypothesis was that he was racist, right? Wrong! When we looked at his filter settings and his clicks, it became clear that the opposite was true: he was singularly interested in black women, specifically in those who described themselves as "curvy." To avoid wasting time and effort, he was blocking those women he'd already tried to hit up but with no luck. These are the fun problems to solve as a data detective. Coming up with good stories and telling them well are essential to understanding data.

To tell a story with data, you have to find a way to take the perspective of the user. And as with any story, the context is important. What we want changes with the time of day—or the time of night. When I was advising Singapore-based dating site Fridae, we observed that the kinds of profiles users explored at 2 o'clock on a Friday afternoon were different from those they explored at 2 o'clock on a Sunday morning. Fridae's data science team then had to decide how to use that information for ranking the profiles it presented.

Dating sites are increasingly giving users the option of revealing who they "really are," by encouraging them to add links to a Facebook profile, or to an Instagram or Twitter account. But that doesn't mean bad behavior has disappeared. Sebastiaan Boer, a data scientist at the mobile dating platform Skout, wrote an algorithm to filter out inappropriate messages.[60]

It was informally called "the creepinator." What was inappropriate? Whatever was identified by the clicks and interactions of users. If someone was blocked by lots of users, he was a creep—probabilistically speaking. And if someone sent repeated, unreciprocated messages to a specific user, he may be creepy—to that person. Over time, the algorithm learned what content tended to be found in messages that got a user blocked or went unanswered. Typically, negativity creeped into the messages. Words such as "nasty" or "ugly" were one hallmark, but defining inappropriateness was more nuanced. One person's turn-off was someone else's turn-on. If a pattern of blocking emerged, the creepinator stopped messages from being delivered. In addition, excessive messaging to a specific user without ever getting a response would get throttled. The creepinator's goal was to maintain a positive environment for the majority of users.

I started this chapter by mentioning how my education and experience as a physicist have helped me design, run, and analyze experiments with social data. Many social data experiments involve watching how changes in the design of a refinery influence how people behave. If you let a dating app user see that a person he is interested in rarely responds to messages, will he spend time carefully crafting a message for the object of his attraction, or will he skip the effort and look for someone more likely to respond? What's more likely to encourage a creep to stop sending messages, an administrator telling him to stop or getting zero responses? How does experimenting with identity attributes change a user's response rates? If a person experiments with identity, when does it cross the line and turn him into a fraudster in the eyes of other users? Greater transparency about users' behavior allows people to decide for themselves whether the character presented in a profile matches up with the characteristics of their Mr. Right (or Mr. Right Now).

Calling for Accountability

When it comes to privacy and accountability, people always demand the former for themselves and the latter for everyone else.[61]

DAVID BRIN

Another pseudonym is playing a significant part in the formation of identity: your phone number. When telephones were first installed in homes, an operator would phone you, announce the other party, and ask whether you wanted to accept the call. That job of a human making the connection was soon replaced by machines. With the development of rotary pulse dialing and automatic exchanges, people called each other directly, and you had to reveal that you were available to receive the call in order to find out who was on the other end of the line. Yet, as long as the price of making a phone call remained pretty high, families got very few unwanted phone calls. When prices started falling, telemarketing became financially viable. Then, in 1990, around the same time as the web was invented, a tone-dialing system was introduced, making Caller ID possible.

Initially, there was some resistance to the idea that your phone number—and possibly your name—would be automatically transmitted to the person you were calling. But now this has flipped, and people are unlikely to accept a call when the caller's identity has not been shared with them. "Unknown" numbers are sent to voicemail. In order to get people to answer your call, you have to let them know it is you calling. You might feel more secure not sharing your own number, and you might also feel more secure if callers shared their number with you. But communication works better when it is symmetrical—that is, when both sides know each other's identity.

Alex Algard, the founder of the online phone number directory Whitepages, believes it's possible to force greater transparency on phone communications for the benefit of all users. By taking advantage of its massive database of phone numbers, Hiya (formerly called Whitepages Caller ID) provides identification for incoming calls, regardless of the caller's settings or the contact list on your mobile phone—an especially useful service in these days of increasing phone "spam." Hiya assigns a category, such as "telemarketer," to the phone number based on mining online sources and analyzing the pattern of calls from the number to Hiya subscribers. As a society, we have to decide if both sides of the conversation have a right to know the identity of the person on the other end of the line. If the answer is yes, then we have to also decide what each of us is allowed to do with that data.

This issue is somewhat tricky, however, because a persistent identity is a necessary but not sufficient condition for generating trust. Knowing who someone is merely provides a means by which you can call an individual to account if that person misbehaves. I know a couple people who have posted screenshots on Facebook of what they felt was inappropriate behavior on a dating app. In the first case, the other party wouldn't take "I'm not interested" as an answer; in the second case, the other party was insulting. Both recipients could have hit the "block" button and left it at that. But both of them decided to share the bad behavior with their friends.

What are the expectations of privacy when you communicate with someone today? The recipients of the unwanted dating messages noted above could argue that sharing these "private" messages served the best interests of their community of friends. The screenshots served as a warning to other individuals who may be on the app about those cases of misbehavior. Indeed, neither culprit's photo nor username was blurred in the screenshots, so there was nowhere to hide among the recipients' Facebook friends. Similarly, if your boss sends you an unfair email rant, you can easily forward it to your friends or post it online. The law might say you were in the wrong for doing so, because the email was a "confidential" communication, intended for distribution solely within the company. But sharing the email also has a public benefit—it lets potential employees know a bit more about the company's working conditions.

To some extent, how we react to a person sharing a private communication depends on how trustworthy we think she is. A screenshot can be faked very easily. On a discussion board like Reddit where users are essentially anonymous, you have little way of verifying the poster's identity, let alone the messages themselves. On Facebook, the poster is usually a person we know (or who knows someone we know). And since accounts are hacked only infrequently, the person's decision to post the screenshot is reined in by the downside of having friends know she might share private messages with others. Still, this doesn't mean we should assume the screenshot is real. It might have been fabricated with the intent to discredit someone.

After the screenshot, real or fake, was posted, it was just like any other piece of data: it could be shared by anyone who came across it. What if one of those Facebook friends was outraged or amused by the message and took a screenshot to share with her friends? Or if a friend of that friend decided to tweet it? Next thing you know, a facial recognition algorithm has identified and labeled the photo with the person's name. By then, it will be deprived of its original context, perhaps even the identity of the person who first shared the screenshot, but it will be discoverable by anybody searching for information about the person.

What protection might a person get for their character online in the future? One option was suggested by the European Court of Justice in May 2014, when it ruled in favor of a person's "right to be forgotten." A Spanish man was tired of prospective employers and landlords turning up an article about how he'd lost his home because of unpaid taxes, especially since he'd gone on to pay off his debts.[62] He didn't ask to purge the official records of the foreclosure. He simply wanted the page to stop showing up when people searched for his name on Google. The court decided that people should have the right to have pages removed from search results when they felt they were being harmed by them. On the first day after the European Court ruling went into effect, more than 12,000 requests were submitted to Google; the average has settled to around 700 requests per day.[63]

Google has publicized some of the requests to remove links that were submitted to the company after the Spanish man's victory. An Italian woman asked that an article about the murder of her husband more than a decade earlier be removed from search results for her name. A Latvian activist who was injured during a protest asked that an article about the protest be removed from search results for the person's name. A German teacher "convicted for a minor crime" more than a decade earlier asked to have an article about the conviction removed from search results, too. In each of these cases, Google decided that the individual's right to be forgotten outweighed the "public interest in the content."[64] These requests appear reasonable, but should it be up to Google—and, presumably, its lawyers—to decide what is in the public interest?

Back in 1890, when those two legal eagles, Samuel Warren and Louis Brandeis, made their case for a "right to privacy," they were particularly interested in an individual's fundamental ownership of a *personality*.[65] Who wants to have an embarrassing snapshot published for everyone to see, without having any say in the matter? The idea was that the law should require people to treat each other humanely. The original concept of a "right to privacy" was intended to preserve dignity.[66] It was commonly believed at the time that unchecked liberty would lead to a tyranny of the masses. Liberty was a bad thing.

An insightful paper by two law professors, Paul Schwartz at UC–Berkeley and Karl-Nikolaus Peifer at the University of Cologne, looks at how notions of privacy and personality protect us (or fail to do so) in the courts.[67] They describe two books, the first of which is a "kiss-and-tell" memoir by a best-selling American author recounting her struggle with vaginal pain and its effect on her physical and psychological health, including her relationship with her former boyfriend. The author never named the boyfriend and changed details of his life, but the man said his friends and business associates all knew about their relationship, and the depiction of their sex life had caused him to suffer "severe personal humiliation" and "considerable damage to his reputation."[68] The judge agreed that the man was identifiable, and that he had been painted in a pretty bad light, but asserted that the public benefit of the memoir was greater than the harm to him. Only a small circle of people could identify him based on publicly available attributes, and that was most important. The other book, published in Germany, was an autobiographical novel featuring thinly veiled versions of the author's ex-girlfriend and her mother. Though the novel contained "a traditional disclaimer that all characters in it were invented," the German judge found that any person who knew the ex-girlfriend or mother could see the characters were based on them.[69] In this case, the judge ruled that, since the ex-girlfriend's sex life was ostensibly private, only the ex-girlfriend's rights had been harmed, while her mother's interfering involved other people, and thus was publicly known already. The German "right to personality" protected the girlfriend from the indignity of having her sex life sold for public titillation. The novel was pulped.

These two court decisions seem almost quaint when you think about my friends posting screenshots from a dating app on Facebook. Let's assume the screenshot is real. How then should a judge take into account the right to privacy and the right to personality? Is a chat on a dating app presumed to be private? Would it matter if the screenshot obscured the name and photo of the person who'd sent the unwanted messages?

I also mention these decisions because of the critical role that weighing public benefit against private harm plays in them. The exponentially increasing amount of social data clearly presents unprecedented opportunities. In which cases does the harm to an individual outweigh the aggregate benefit to the masses? With more data refineries being designed for supporting decisions in areas ranging from finance to employment and from education to health care, we need to develop more sophisticated tools for evaluating these trade-offs.

As scientist and award-winning science fiction author David Brin notes, it seems everybody wants privacy for themselves and accountability for the people they interact with. You can't have it both ways. And because privacy is an illusion, we all need to get used to being more accountable. A good start is to be more accountable to our friends.

CONNECTIONS AND CONVERSATIONS

Identity and Reputation in the Social Graph
Who Do You Know, Who Do They Know,
And Who Do You Trust?

A man's friendships are one of the best measures of his worth.[1]

CHARLES DARWIN

A friend of a friend of mine, a young woman whom I'll call Rebecca Davis, recently got approached online by a recruiter about a possible new job. The recruiter had noticed Rebecca's profile on LinkedIn; she seemed to be a young marketing professional on the rise, someone who got kudos from her colleagues, including a few from her days as an intern at a well-respected Silicon Valley firm. It was an awkward situation, however, because Rebecca isn't a real person. She's the invention of our common friend, who decided to see how hard it would be to create and maintain a fake personality online.[2]

Rebecca exists on several social media platforms. She started her life on Facebook, where she went about the difficult task of getting people she couldn't possibly know in the real world to accept a friend request. She might have sought out D-list celebrities looking for fans, or tweens hoping to tally up more virtual pals than their peers at school, but the algorithms would have easily spotted a profile whose friends consisted only of such undiscriminating types. Instead, Rebecca sent a friend request to a select group of targets:

> Hi, my name's Rebecca. I really love my name—it's so much of who I am. I bet you feel the same way, too. So I'm trying to make friends with everybody else called Rebecca on Facebook![3]

She also reached out to all the Rebekahs, Beckys, Beccas, and Rebas on Facebook that she could find, because our friend realized that a genuine human would group those names together as essentially synonymous.

Amazingly, Rebecca quickly built up quite a social network—not just fellow Rebeccas but those Rebeccas' friends. She started to receive birthday wishes, so she did what friends on Facebook do: she reciprocated each time Facebook notified her of an event in a person's life. She also posted occasional status updates and food photos, and asked for general advice about dating and her job. Neither Facebook's algorithms nor Rebecca's friends could work out that she wasn't a real person, because the account behaved like a human would. With all these friends and messages, Rebecca's identity was established by her pattern of digital communication.

Eventually, it seemed time for Rebecca to get a profile on LinkedIn. Based on her date of birth and posts, she had graduated from college and needed a job. By now, she had an email account and a Facebook profile to prove her existence on other social networks. Her inventor bestowed Rebecca with an internship, an entry-level job, and a first promotion in one fell swoop.

But creating a believable career track on a website dedicated to professional networking is more difficult than creating a Facebook profile, especially when the site starts suggesting contacts whose tenure at a company overlaps with your purported days there. Still, more than a dozen people who worked at companies where Rebecca had supposedly worked added her as a contact. She even got a few endorsements for her work. Was it that people were confusing her with another, real Rebecca, or that people were so eager to extend their network of contacts that they accepted Rebecca's contact request without looking too closely? In any case, Rebecca's supposed experience and mutual connections were enough to attract more than one recruiter's eye.

Being able to see a handful of mutual confirmations and interactions is often sufficient evidence of a person's humanity, as Rebecca's profile can attest. What makes a fake person with a Facebook or LinkedIn profile appear more authentic than a stranger with no profile at all? Let's begin by distinguishing between five categories of data associated with a Facebook account:

1. your username and password, allowing you to sign in to Facebook as well as other sites and apps using your Facebook log-in;
2. attributes about yourself that you declare on your profile, such as your hometown, your place of residence, your phone number, the schools you went to, the places you've worked, and your gender identity and sexual orientation;
3. your list of mutually confirmed friends and groups;
4. your posts, comments, and likes—that is, the data you share with your friends; and
5. your interactions with your friends' posts, comments, and likes—that is, the data you and your friends create together when you interact on Facebook.

The first two categories are relatively static data—information that doesn't change or changes somewhat infrequently, and which isn't open to comment by others. The rest of the data—our connections and conversations—change at a time scale of weeks, days, hours, sometimes even minutes, and are, by design, set up as a dialogue.

Of course, some of our connections and conversations reveal more about us than do others. Data refineries like Facebook and LinkedIn specialize in measuring, aggregating, and analyzing our communication networks and patterns to improve the recommendations made to us—including the recommendations about the people we know or might want to get to know. People have been gathering information about whose advice to take and whose word to trust for thousands of years. Now the capacity to map human relationships at the scale of the whole world is transforming how we make decisions. And the more transparency and agency we demand from the refineries, the more value we'll get in exchange for sharing details of our personal relationships.

Darwin was especially attuned to the "duration of a man's friendships" as an indicator of the man.[4] But in the era of social data, duration is merely one of several dimensions of friendship that can be measured, aggregated, and analyzed. If you rarely if ever interact with somebody online, a data refinery knows it. What does it say about you if your relationship with another person goes no deeper than a single click? Quite a lot, as it happens.

Your Neighborhood in the Social Graph

You may have noticed that the first two categories of Facebook data that I described—name and characteristics—communicate a traditional concept of personal identity. In some contexts, these bits of data are verified by authoritative institutions, such as a government agency checking your name, date of birth, and physical appearance against its records when you apply for a driver's license. To confirm your identity, some data refineries might ask you to supply a scan of a government-issued ID. For many of our activities online, however, new forms of identity verification are emerging that are based on the structure and pattern of relationships and communications between people, or your social network.

Identity is both personal and social—think of your association with a place of worship, club, sports team, employer, or other organization. Much of the time, we construct our identity relative to others, announcing to people that we consider ourselves a member of various groups through our actions and interactions. The anthropologist Robin Dunbar proposes that human language evolved out of a need to "groom" friends and family; chatter allowed us to stroke each other more efficiently than pulling nits out of tangled hair.[5] In other words, gossip isn't always merciless; it can also be supportive, confirming mutual intimacy and feeding our social circles with news. It allows us to share useful data about how well or how badly members of our group are conforming to social norms. We kick out people who have a pattern of bad behavior and provide positive feedback to reinforce the performance of good behavior.[6] Humans are conspicuous communicators of relationships.

Dunbar believes that we evolved to perform this grooming in person, and that we are cognitively incapable of juggling more than around 150 relationships at a time.[7] Our brains, our bodies, and our tools have changed and developed since our hominid ancestors branched off from their primate cousins some 4 million years ago. We aren't chimpanzees or bonobos, despite how much DNA we share with them. We can travel halfway around the globe in less than a day, and videochat with a person thousands of miles away. New possibilities for creating and maintaining relationships are emerging, enabled by mobile and social technologies. Data refineries make it possible for us to gain access to pertinent and personal information about millions of real and potential friends.

Mark Zuckerberg popularized the use of the term "social graph" to refer to how people are connected on Facebook,[8] which uses algorithms to analyze those connections in order to recommend new contacts and content. The term comes from the field of graph theory, the mathematical study of pairwise connections. In essence, there is only one social graph, and you live in a neighborhood of it, your particular social network.[9] Today, with more than a billion people using Facebook, we're getting close to digitizing the entirety of the social graph. This was quite unexpected. Before modern communications, the largest social networks studied were on the scale of a village, a school, or a company.

Pre-internet studies of social networks give a sense of the incredible richness of data now available to Facebook and other platforms for communicating with your friends and contacts. The psychiatrist J. L. Moreno began to create "sociometric" diagrams, or graphs, of interpersonal relationships and influence in the 1930s.[10] In a notable case, he investigated the cause of "an epidemic of runaways" from a school for delinquent girls in New York State.[11] The girls who had decided to flee the school lived in various dormitories and came from various backgrounds. The superintendent was stymied and asked Moreno for help. Moreno mapped the friendships between students, noting their feelings toward one another, as well as their activities and intelligence level. Some girls were the center of attention, attracting admirers into their social orbit; some pairs described having an equal feeling of friendship, fastening to each other with a mutual bond. The runaways were all strongly connected. The runaways shared friends, but they also shared attitudes and values, Moreno argued.[12]

Moreno's analysis suggested that the social graph influenced a person's decisions. But would this be the case in other areas of life? One answer comes from research conducted by sociologist Doug McAdam into the motivations of activists who applied to take part in the famous Freedom Summer of 1964. Committing to the civil rights project proved "physically and emotionally harrowing," and three activists were kidnapped and murdered within days of arriving in Mississippi.[13] The nightly news made it all too clear that this was going to be a very risky endeavor, and

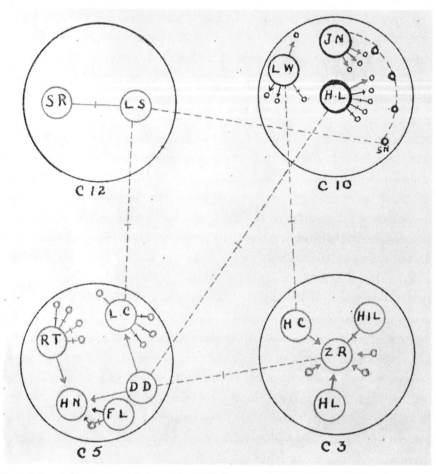

One of Jacob Moreno's early "sociometric" diagrams tracing the connections between runaways and non-runaways at a school for delinquent girls. From *Who Shall Survive? A New Approach to the Problem of Human Interrelations* by J. L. Moreno, courtesy of Jonathan D. Moreno.

not everyone who applied ended up participating: about 25 percent of accepted applicants withdrew before the summer's start.[14] By studying the project's application forms, McAdam learned that those who made it to Mississippi were more likely to have strong ties with another Freedom Summer participant or civil rights activist—and this was more important than any previous personal history of activism.[15]

More generally, mapping relationships and communication patterns provides insight into the movement of information and the concentration of expertise. Business school professors and management consultants have made a practice of comparing the difference between the formal organizational chart (who reports to whom) and the informal flow of information (who goes to whom with what kind of a problem).[16] Often, social network analysis can be used to identify bottlenecks in communication flow—and prescribe ways to improve corporate management. For example, IBM's Institute for Knowledge-Based Organizations determined that a mid-level manager at a petroleum company had such a high "reputation for expertise and responsiveness" that "the number of information requests he received and the number of projects in which he was involved grew excessively." As a result, the manager was under a lot of stress and the company's projects were getting delayed.[17]

These sorts of early social network analyses were often based on data collected through interviews, surveys, and, very occasionally, direct observation of subjects. Today, with most communication being digital, researchers have access to the digital traces of the social graph. Analyzing phone logs is one of the simplest ways to discern a social network—true even in the days before mobile phones. To connect you, the phone company needs to know what number you wish to call; to bill you, it has to know how long you stay on the phone. Phone companies are proficient in this data tracking. In 1991, MCI Communications unveiled the "Friends & Family" program in an attempt to wrest customers from AT&T, which controlled two-thirds of the long-distance market.[18] MCI asked customers to list up to twenty numbers that they could call long-distance at a discounted rate—they got 20 percent off their bill if they made more than ten dollars' worth of long-distance calls in a month. They could even name people who weren't MCI customers, and MCI would contact those individuals to sell the loyalty plan to them. Within two years, 10 million customers were enrolled in the plan.[19] The phone company had given customers a financial incentive to persuade their frequent contacts to switch to MCI.

Email messages provide another data source for social network analysis. In the late 1980s, Michael Schwartz, then a professor of computer science at the University of Colorado–Boulder, wanted to solve the problem of how to discover people on the internet who shared interests with you. (This was a few months before Tim Berners-Lee proposed the architecture for the World Wide Web and made finding things on the internet considerably easier.[20]) Mike analyzed two months of email communications at fifteen universities and research labs, including UC–Berkeley and Sun Microsystems. Using email "header" data—just the sender and the recipient—Mike constructed the social graph of 50,834 researchers, suggesting possible future collaborations.[21] One million messages then corresponded to two months of email data. Facebook Messenger and WhatsApp now handle 1 million messages every second.[22]

As these examples show, the social graph is a network of people constructed from their interactions. In the terminology of computer science, the social graph is made up of nodes—each node represents a person—connected by links, or edges. Some people tend to form connections with people who are similar to them in some way, be it their status (attributes) or values (attitudes), a phenomenon called *homophily,* from the Greek for "love of the same."[23] The interactions between people create a structure of links, and the weight of an edge connecting two people increases as they interact more. Some people have a few deep, heavy edges, interacting with a handful of other people frequently, while others spread themselves thin, making shallow connections with lots of people.

The structure of a social network reveals a great deal. A network may have a small number of nodes, most connected to each other, appearing quite dense and cohesive; it may have a large number of nodes sharing few connections, sparse and disjointed; or it may have several clusters of highly connected nodes with a few connections linking the clusters. Dense, cohesive social networks indicate high levels of trust specifically because more nodes in the network have direct, personal knowledge of the other nodes. Sparse, disjointed networks indicate lower levels of trust because there are fewer direct channels for information and more ways to reconfigure the network if problems arise. Diverse, loose networks tend to provide avenues for discovering new ideas and opportunities via peripheral knowledge and connection. Sometimes these asymmetries change over time, as in the case of your relationship with a parent, and how, at different stages in your life, you were either the one more likely to make a phone call or the one to receive it.[24]

Online, just as in real life, some relationships are more balanced than others. Sometimes this is due to the rules and conventions of the social network. On Twitter, you can follow or mention anyone of interest to you, whether or not that person is interested in you as well; a last resort for stopping unwanted interactions with users is to block them. Connections are one-directional, and often, the conversations are, too. On Facebook, connections are two-sided, mutually confirmed.

A mutually confirmed friendship does not imply that it is perfectly balanced. The number and direction of interactions between two people expose other dimensions of a relationship. As two people interact again and again, the edge connecting them increases in weight; however, the weight on the edge might be greater in one direction than it is on the other. For example, you might be quite interested in connecting more regularly with your friend Mark, because you'd like him to introduce you to a potential investor for a start-up idea you have. You've met at several events and email once in a while, but these are almost always fleeting encounters. In your eagerness to secure some of Mark's attention, you comment on some of his status updates, "like" a couple of his photos, and send him a direct message on Facebook. For every ten contacts you make, Mark reciprocates once—an order of magnitude seems to separate your levels of interest. However, when Mark does eventually get in touch, he replies to the Facebook message, not to a comment on a news story he's posted or a like on one of his vacation photos. That direct reply indicates a different type and category of interest—and possibly a higher level of interest, too. Facebook's algorithms take into account such nuances in communication to determine whose posts to bring to your attention.

Stanford sociologist Mark Granovetter has researched the strength of the ties that bind people in a relationship. In his seminal 1973 paper "The Strength of Weak Ties," he puts forward a definition of the level of relationship strength as a "combination of the amount of time, the emotional intensity, the intimacy (mutual confiding), and the reciprocal services which characterize the tie."[25] Individuals in a network exchange not just emotions and information but influence and services, too.[26]

In the past, sociologists conducted field surveys to find out who talked to whom in a village or a firm. Marketers dreamed up discount plans that would entice people to suggest their contacts. Now the traces of our interactions are used in real time by Facebook and other social data companies. These services are transforming the nature of our relationships.

The New Social Capital

As we've created online social identities, we've begun to redefine the terms of friendship. In the past, we had to spend most of our time gathering food and friends around us. While it has become a lot easier to get food and connect with friends, we aren't any wiser about how we should be spending our time.

The feeling of friendship involves the sequential revelation of information.[27] Developmental psychologists have found that children between the ages of five and nine call each other friends if they share their toys with them. Slowly, this develops so that friendship is defined by two-way cooperation, a balanced reciprocity by which the child shares a toy with a playmate if the playmate shares a toy with her.[28] As we get older, we may continue to share "toys," but more often what we share are secrets. There's a dance between two people as they get to know each other, conversation by conversation. One person shares a little bit of information that we would usually protect from disclosure, then the other reciprocates. The practice of building a relationship through "sustained, escalating, reciprocal, personalistic self-disclosure" is so common that one team of psychologists was reportedly able to induce closeness by getting two strangers to share the answers to a series of increasingly intimate questions with each other.[29]

Implicit in the concept of a "secret" is that there could be a risk to sharing the information with someone else. Georg Simmel, one of the founders of the field of sociology, noted: "Every relationship between two individuals will be characterized by the ratio of secrecy that is involved in it."[30] As we form a friendship, our trust in the other person must deepen to overcome this risk. If one person keeps a secret from the other, especially a secret that's somewhat similar in gravity to a disclosure the other person has made to her, it changes the balance of the relationship. The exchange of trust will likely break down, and the bond between the two will become weaker.

These imbalances are reflected in the edges of the social graph, but they also govern how we interact with data refineries. People are more likely to share information when they receive information in return. As we have seen, the most successful refineries encourage and reward users who contribute raw data that visibly improves the services and products offered to them. This is why symmetry works so well as a guideline for aligning the interests between data providers and data refineries: give-to-get is human nature.

When communication technologies were limited to sending smoke signals, chatting in the village square, or mailing letters, when sensing technologies were limited to a person's eyes, ears, nose, mouth, and skin, the scope of human influence was quite localized. That's changed in the past century. We're now influenced by advertising and mass marketing on a global scale, via radio, TV, and, most recently, the web. We used to get recommendations from our relatives and next-door neighbors, maybe from some actor playing the role of a "discriminating customer" sharing his "five-star experience" of a high-end hotel chain.[31] Today, we get recommendations based on the data created by a billion people. Our local neighborhood in the social graph is essential for filtering and personalizing these data for us.

For the most part, Facebook serves as a platform for communicating with your friends. Your interests are aligned with the refinery's: it wants to show you stuff you're interested in so that you'll come back. When you come back, the refinery learns more about you—what posts you spend time on, which of the friends recommended to you inspire you to click—and, of course, by learning more about you, Facebook's algorithms can also do a better job of choosing which ads are going to be of most interest to you, which allows the site to make money.

Out of your clicks and browsing behavior, Facebook identifies how you actually allocate your attention, recording who and what interests you and how your interest changes over time. Do you spend an hour poring over the vacation albums posted by a new friend you find attractive, or less than a minute clicking like buttons under your sister's latest series of baby photos? These data are a signal of the priority and strength of your relationship interests at a specific moment in time—much more accurate than trying to think later about how you spent your time, and much more useful in sorting incoming data than the rules of social obligation. It is primarily from these honest signals, the traces of your attention and interest, that Facebook constructs your News Feed.

The News Feed distributes and surfaces social content based on personal relevance. The Feed creates a positive feedback loop: content that is a good match for the users who see it tends to get more likes, which motivates the original poster, and perhaps other people who see the post, to share more content like that. In contrast, a negative response is often known only to the viewer. Facebook gives users the option of expressing in two clicks, "Show me fewer posts like this in the future," but it doesn't notify the poster that the content wasn't to a person's liking. The Feed puts us in a state of "continuous partial attention," a term coined by tech visionary Linda Stone to describe the sense that we are constantly observing, and being observed by, our friends. Linda believes that continuous partial attention "involves an artificial sense of constant crisis"—the brain is perpetually on alert, scanning whatever is on the News Feed and other ever-scrolling data sources, however small a part this is of what you potentially could be shown.[32] Imagine what life would be like if you saw absolutely everything your friends posted on Facebook.

Facebook analyzes these interactions in very granular terms. For example, different media types, such as a status update versus a photo, differ in how much they influence the weight of the edge between two people. Facebook has built an ontology of topics and classifies interactions based on it, according to Ding Zhou, a former technology lead at Facebook.[33] In the real world, I go to my doctor for medical advice but not for advice about how to fix my computer. On Facebook, we also respond to people's posts based on whether we think they are especially interesting, expert, or authoritative in an area up for discussion.

Yet, Facebook is not the only digital communication platform that can detect who you are most likely to contact, and when. Your mobile phone and Skype keep a log of your incoming and outgoing calls— who called whom, when they talked, and for how long. In fact, if you use Skype for work calls, Skype could analyze that data to identify your professional contacts, including which clients or colleagues get most of your attention.

You can safely bet such information is being used by companies to understand who you are connected with. After the success of MCI's Friends & Family program, other companies looked for opportunities to assemble social graph data that could be used to acquire and influence customers. In 2001—before Facebook—Amazon launched the "Share the Love" program. After you bought a product, Amazon would ask if you wanted anyone to be told about your purchase. If you did, and shared those individuals' email addresses with Amazon, Amazon would send your friends an email about the product offering a 10 percent discount on its purchase. This wasn't simply a chance to be altruistic while advertising your good taste or cutting-edge style, however: if any of the people who received the email bought the item within one week, you got a 10 percent rebate of the price you'd paid. This mutual discount created an incentive for you to supply real email addresses to Amazon; fake or out-of-date addresses presented absolutely no benefit to the referring customer, bypassing one of the plagues of early email marketing programs. It turned out that the conversion rate for this "social" offer was significantly more effective than standard promotional offers that came from Amazon without a referral from someone you knew. Share the Love was a tool for constructing a verified social graph of customers based on the psychological principles of reciprocation and social proof.

Similarly, when AT&T introduced a new product to the market, the company decided to conduct an A/B test to compare the success of a campaign based on traditional segmentation marketing to one based on the social graph data.[34] The marketing team at AT&T knew quite a bit about their customers—where they lived, how long they'd been with AT&T, what plans they'd chosen, whether they'd remained loyal to the company or switched back and forth between carriers. To explore the effectiveness of the social graph compared to these traditional data, the experiment was very simple: if a person you called regularly had already bought the product, the company marketed the product to you. Unlike the Share the Love program, the customers had no idea why they'd received information about the product. There was no personal referral attached. Yet, the customers with earlier adopters in their "calling graph" were nearly five times more likely to sign up.[35]

Did AT&T's customers have a higher likelihood of buying the product because of homophily, the tendency of people to have closer ties to people who are similar to themselves? Did they buy the product because the marketing materials reinforced positive mentions about the product that they might have heard from friends? Or were they more attentive to a friend's opinion if they had already heard it before in a marketing campaign? The data couldn't say. But it was striking that the social graph was so much more effective than customer profiling. Predicting your interest wasn't about finding out who you are, but about who you know.

Designed for the People (with the Data)

Who you know is particularly important in the professional world. Mark Granovetter, the Stanford sociologist of social networks, found that people were much more likely to find a new job through acquaintances rather than through closer friends, employment agencies, or want ads. Perhaps that's not very surprising, since people have a greater number of acquaintances than close friends. But they didn't merely find job leads this way—the jobs they found through their weak ties in the social graph were more satisfying and paid better.[36]

Granovetter's findings date back to the 1970s, when information distribution was slow and expensive—there were no emails, no online job listings.[37] In those days, many professionals routinely got hired "for their Rolodex," a carefully collected and cultivated list of contacts that could be tapped to broker deals and find new business leads. You may still believe your Rolodex is the most valuable professional resource you have. You may also believe that your company should be even more protective about the list of clients that its employees have built up over the years. Most managers have had it drilled into them that this information advantage is what sets a successful business apart from its competitors.

LinkedIn was set up in part to ease the process of communicating with your strong and weak business ties alike. While Granovetter was interested in finding the weak ties that helped a person get to where he was, LinkedIn was interested in helping users find the weak ties that would assist them in getting to where they wanted to be. Say your goal was landing a new client or customer or job, and you knew the name of your target, but you didn't really know her personally—or who among your existing contacts might. When you searched for your target's name, LinkedIn told you how many degrees of separation you'd have to bridge in order to get a personal introduction. If you enrolled in LinkedIn's paid service, you were shown the names of the people linking you with your target. That service was designed for the people who needed data. There was a treacherous imbalance here. The people who needed data didn't have much to offer to those who did. In fact, when LinkedIn first started offering its services, people complained about getting so many contact requests that sometimes it seemed the messages were barely a step above spam. One commentator called LinkedIn "a system for subsidizing the poor networking skills of the unconnected with the strong networking skills of the well connected."[38]

Ellen Levy, the former vice president of strategic initiatives at LinkedIn, said the real breakthrough came when the company figured out how to design the site for the people who have data, not for those who need it. Ellen has a PhD in cognitive psychology from Stanford, where she studied how to display information given the scarcity of time, which you can see in her approach to LinkedIn as well as in her own career.[39] "The worst time to build a relationship is when you need something—that would be a transaction, and that's not the same thing," she has noted. "One of the best ways to build a relationship is to help someone when there's no ulterior motive for doing so."[40] If LinkedIn was simply duplicating your Rolodex, there was no reason to use it—especially if the one, unique service you experienced while visiting the site was a bunch of strangers asking to be your contact. LinkedIn had to give data to users in order to get data from them.

The challenge for LinkedIn was to deliver services that would inspire its users to create and share more data about their professional social network. Often, it was only when people needed a favor that they got in touch with professional acquaintances—exactly the opposite of Ellen's advice. Users needed excuses to communicate more frequently. LinkedIn began sending alerts when contacts added skills and experience, changed jobs, or celebrated work anniversaries. It provided forums where users can post articles showcasing their expertise and comment on relevant news, which provide yet more excuses to communicate. If users gave LinkedIn access to their calendar, it would send relevant information about the people with whom they had scheduled meetings. The company has also begun offering professional skills development, with users receiving rewards in the form of training programs based on their profile "completeness" and quality as well as on their number of contacts, published posts, and other activities on the site.

Another option was to give users the opportunity to endorse their contacts' professional skills. Doing so indicated your willingness to help someone even though there was no obvious benefit to yourself. It might, in some cases, even trigger a desire to reciprocate in kind. And different interactions have different weights in LinkedIn's social system. Most people would agree that a carefully crafted testimonial is stronger than a click to endorse a skill. Furthermore, the popularity and reputation of the person endorsing you matters, as well as whether your tenures at the company overlapped or you worked in the same or different departments. Each of these factors can be assigned a value, and the importance of such shared events decays over time. If you last worked with someone a decade ago, the weight of that person is smaller than that of someone who you are currently working with.

This becomes important when you step back and consider how LinkedIn generates revenue. Sixty percent of LinkedIn's revenues come from recruiters using the site's data to identify and entice potential employees. LinkedIn also offers other products, including lead-management tools and analysis of economic and employment trends, to corporate customers. The raw data are supplied by individuals, not HR departments, as companies have no incentive to publicize the experience or quality of their top talent to their competitors' recruiters. In exchange for these data, LinkedIn provides free services to individuals who share data about their work and career, such as suggestions of people you might know or want to know, opportunities to access business advice in the form of columns and slide presentations, and information about who is viewing your profile.

The asymmetry of power in professional relationships plays a role in how LinkedIn reveals information about profile views. When LinkedIn alerts you that someone has viewed your profile, you may be curious to see who the person is. But if you're a manager trying to learn more about the experience and interests of people you might want to interview, or about the managers at a rival firm you'd like to poach from, you don't necessarily want them to know you've been poring over their LinkedIn profile. LinkedIn has made it easy for users to switch back and forth while viewing profiles with or without revealing your name. You can choose to browse people's profiles anonymously while revealing only your city of residence or your industry of employment. If you reveal your full name, you get to see which people are checking out your profile, by name, city, or industry, depending on how they choose to be identified. If you go anonymous, you do not get to see that data. LinkedIn records every profile you've viewed, of course, no matter what settings you choose, but it determines what data you have access to based on the granularity of the data you reveal about yourself.

In my work with the dating site Skout, I considered what levels of transparency might be most appealing to users. We didn't charge people to set up a profile, since the more users there were on the site, the more attractive it became as a destination for online dating. We wanted as much "inventory" as possible. We also realized that if we charged members to look at profiles or to contact people, they might use the site less. We did, however, have access to something valuable: their honest signals of interest in other users in the form of their clicks. Members might be willing to pay for a list of the people who had shown some inkling of interest in them but hadn't yet made that interest explicit by sending a message. In the end, we rolled out a premium feature that allowed paying members to see both who had clicked on their main photo and how deeply each user had explored their profile—for instance, how many photos were viewed and whether and when the person last returned to take another look. We also explored the option of a "VIP" membership, which would let users poke around people's profiles in stealth mode for an extra monthly fee—making members pay for the privilege of hiding their honest signals from others.

When I post a photo on Facebook, I do so expecting that my friends might see it. Today, all I can do is guess who is interested in a post based on likes and comments. Should Facebook let me decide if people can see the photo only if they are willing to let me know that they've seen it, something like having your signature automatically added to a "guestbook" beneath the photo? If I invite a friend to my house and there's a photo album on the coffee table, my friend expects I'll be aware of whether she glanced at it, flipped through the pages, looked at it with great attention, or—unbelievably!—took out her phone and snapped a photo of my pictures because she wanted to be able to have a copy for herself. Facebook doesn't let us see who is looking at our photos, even though it has that data. A Facebook friend could download every single photo I ever posted on Facebook, and I'd never know. I would like the tiers of symmetry that LinkedIn has built into its profile views to be available at more refineries and about more types of content.

How might being able to see your friends' digital "footsteps" change your relationships with them? Would you be more or less likely to look at a friend's photos if you knew he had checked out all of yours without leaving a comment or liking any of them? Would the amount of time he spent looking make a difference? Most people are more likely to moderate their behavior—reducing their number of clicks and views—if they know they are being observed. Sites and apps, including Facebook, want users to interact as much as possible: it gives them more data about users' true interests. And when clicks and views are honest signals of interest and attention, of course they help refineries do a better job of fitting content to the user, whether the content is news or advertising.

Many of a refinery's decisions about which services to offer and how to present them to users take into account that social data exist in an *ecosystem*. In ecology, an ecosystem is a community of interacting organisms in an environment. Many ecologists argue that the interconnectedness of living things cannot be managed well only by considering problems at the "local" level of the individual; instead, the health of the entire global ecosystem needs to be considered. If one tries to optimize conditions for one individual or one species group, it may throw the entire system out of whack. Think of Thomas Austin releasing two dozen English rabbits on his estate in Geelong, Australia: he wanted to improve his hunting prospects at the weekend, but the descendants of those rabbits are now a major scourge, causing massive soil erosion and the destruction of native species.[41]

The need to optimize the health of the whole ecosystem comes into play especially when social data are being used to match people with other people. Every person is unique, and nobody has more than twenty-four hours of attention to allocate over a day. Individuals you might be interested in don't always have the ability to reciprocate your interest. In contrast to Amazon, which is in the business of recommending and selling mass-produced goods, we can't simply get more copies of a person. If Facebook suggests you might want to add Amy to your list of friends, but Amy has already maxed out the number of friends she can have, you're going to be disappointed. If a dating app suggests you might be interested in John, but John already has dates lined up every night of the week with people he finds more interesting than you, you're going to be disappointed. It's better for the app to recommend a person who is able to reciprocate at least some of your interest. Anything else breeds disappointment faster than rabbits. And when people feel disappointed, they generally create and share less data: why share when you aren't getting value out of it?

I believe we can better understand how these sorts of networks evolve by considering ideas from the study of dynamical systems. During the 1960s, physicists discovered that dynamical systems can sometimes exhibit a property called "chaos," which means that, no matter how well the initial conditions of a system are known, you cannot predict the system's behavior in detail over the long term. Chaos theorists have also shown that seemingly small differences can have big effects over time, because nearby trajectories diverge exponentially. In some cases, the system amplifies random noise, what is called the "butterfly effect" after the talk "Does the Flap of a Butterfly's Wings in Brazil Set Off a Tornado in Texas?" given by the MIT mathematician Edward Lorenz.[42] Similarly, slight differences in the design and parameters of data refineries—like Facebook's choice to provide no "dislike" button, or to let users see edits made to comments and posts—might lead to very different behavior among individual users in the future and influence the structure of the social graph.[43]

Over the next several years, we will have the chance to observe a natural experiment in how small design differences have big effects on the evolution of social data ecosystems by comparing two of the world's largest messaging platforms, Facebook and WeChat. When WeChat was launched in China in 2011, it had a bit of an unfair advantage, since Facebook was blocked in the country. Within four years, WeChat had grown to over half a billion users, most in China—roughly the same number of users that Facebook boasted after four years of opening accounts to nonstudents.[44] So the two platforms have approximately the same growth rate.

Yet, the product managers at WeChat and Facebook have made very different assumptions about what people want from a communication platform. Facebook was borne out of the Harvard tradition of residential hall yearbooks, which are archived for posterity. In contrast, WeChat's parent company, Tencent, started out as an online gaming company. When a game is over, it's over; the final score, and a record of high scorers, might get saved, but not every move the player made. This attitude carried over into Tencent's messaging platforms.[45] WeChat's design has been focused on ephemeral communication: once a message is read, it is deleted from the company's servers, residing solely on the user's device. If you lose your mobile phone, you also lose your communication history.

Another significant difference in design between the two platforms involves how users connect with each other. When you receive a friend request from a person you can't quite place based on her name or profile photo, should you be able to see the list of her friends, or at least the list of friends the two of you have in common? The answer you give crucially depends on where you grew up. An American Facebook user would think, *Of course I want to see the list of her friends, because it helps me decide whether to accept her friend request.* Scanning through a list of mutual friends will usually clarify that she went to the same school or once worked at the same company or has some other tie that makes her "acceptable" as a friend.

WeChat never shows a person's friends to other users. The social graph is not visible. A Chinese WeChat user would think, *Of course I don't want her to see my list of friends, because it might reveal information about me that I don't want her to know.* Users cannot explore the friends of their friends, let alone contact them, without an introduction.

WeChat has created novel options for finding people on the app in the absence of reviewing a friend list. For instance, if you meet someone in person, you can scan a WeChat-generated quick response (QR) code on her phone and be taken to a screen where you can add her as a friend. Users can also create ad hoc chat groups, a tactic sometimes employed when a group of people, whether personal friends or professional colleagues, are arranging a place and time to meet in person. This provides a personal introduction, because you have to be invited to the group by someone who is already a member of it, as well as a shortcut to discovering new contacts. Once you've joined, you can see all the other members, and decide to send friend requests to those you want to stay in touch with.[46]

Because WeChat doesn't let users see other people's contact lists, it can employ the social graph as a tool for confirming identity. If you forget your password and get locked out of the app, WeChat shows you a security code and a set of users' names and photos. You need to contact the users in the list who are your friends in some other way and ask them to send you the code. As soon as at least two of them do so, WeChat unlocks your account.[47] This "challenge response" method, which requires confirming your identity by demonstrating knowledge of your social network, is much more secure than asking for your mother's maiden name, your first job, your pet's name, or other standard questions, some of which can be found by searching for your posts and friend connections on the internet.[48] In trying to unlock your account, you reveal information to WeChat about your relationships, because you want to choose friends who will respond quickly.

However, I suspect the choice to hide WeChat contact lists from other users had more to do with the value attached to contacts in Chinese business and society. WeChat is extensively used in China for communicating with professional contacts, and being public about your network may be a tad too revealing for some people. A competitor might look to see who you've recently added as a contact and draw conclusions from that about your business strategy—and tack accordingly. At the same time, you don't have to worry about whether you'll be judged by the "company you keep" because your contacts aren't visible to others.

As social networking platforms evolve and the amount of social data increases, we'll need more features that help us manage our relationships in the context of the overall health of the ecosystem. The connection strength across edges changes over time. You may have a pretty good sense for how often you call your mother versus your best friend, or how you've started to ignore emails from a vendor whose products no longer interest you. You may be less aware of how often you call one colleague versus another to get work advice, and may not even have noticed that you are no longer shown some of your friends' updates on Facebook.

We've seen how dashboards on dating sites can help you decide how to allocate your time and attention when exploring potential new relationships. Refined data about your social network could similarly help you maintain your existing relationships. An early cloud-based phone service, Skydeck, which provided caller identification and call-blocking services, experimented with a product that alerted users to calling patterns that they might wish to change.[49] I remember receiving a notification that I wasn't calling a friend as frequently as I used to. The notification nudged me to contact him so our relationship wouldn't deteriorate.

Refineries can do more than just alert an individual to changes in behavior; they can share insights gleaned from analyzing their users in aggregate. For instance, Facebook has observed that online interactions between two people steadily rise in the one hundred days before the couple announces they're in a relationship together, then once they publicly change their relationship status, their interactions via Facebook abruptly drop off. At the same time, the content of their communications shifts, with more positive words used in their posts and messages.[50] Researchers have also found a special "signature" that predicts two people are in a romantic relationship based on the distribution of friends they have in common across their social networks.[51] Even if they don't explicitly say they're "in a relationship" with each other, Facebook knows. Drawing on a wide range of data sources—being tagged in the same photo, checking in at the same event—a refinery can infer the strength and dynamics of our relationships.

Distinct patterns of interpersonal communication aren't limited to the realm of romance. Imagine a manager interviewing candidates for a job. One candidate who seems especially promising has emphasized her great relationship with a big firm. The manager might know the candidate's purported contact at the firm well enough to pick up the phone and ask for his opinion of her. Or the manager could instead ask the candidate to share a characterization of her professional relationships and communication patterns "certified" by a data refinery. The manager might be interested in comparing the edge strengths between an especially valuable client and the finalists in the running for the job. Or the manager may actually be less interested in that one big client than in the potential employee's breadth of relationships across an industry, in which case it would be helpful to see if the candidate's communication patterns matched those of a so-called super-connector, regardless of how much she bragged about a specific contact. That communication profile would likely prove to be a better fit—not only because the candidate is acquainted with many people but because she's going to be happier in a job that requires lots of interaction with lots of different people. The refinery's recommendation would depend in large part on the balance between exploration and exploitation. The manager will want to decide if the most important goal in the choice of a new hire is deepening the company's existing business contacts or exploring new ones.

How comfortable would you be sharing an analysis of your professional communication patterns with a potential employer? Would you want to see the same analysis for the hiring manager in exchange, the way you get to see who is looking at your LinkedIn profile if you let others see that you're looking at them? What about the team's patterns as a whole? Such analyses could help you prepare for an interview, both by giving you ideas about how to present yourself as a strong addition to the team and by suggesting areas of concern you might want to broach during the interview. These characterizations could be a powerful tool for decision-making—about and by you.

The Ministry of Social Data Engineering

I know a man—let's call him Joe—who decided to try out Facebook to see what all the fuss was about. Joe is in his sixties, and he has strong feelings about the sanctity of his privacy. He didn't like the idea of revealing information about his personal life on the internet, so he signed up under a false name. He never befriended his real-world contacts, because he didn't want anyone to recognize him. And unlike Rebecca, he didn't attempt to make fake friends. His node was isolated in the social graph. Unsurprisingly, Joe didn't find anything very useful on Facebook when he logged in each morning. The news and information wasn't interesting or relevant to him. Joe's experience of Facebook was just average. But how could it have been any better? Facebook is not like the *New York Times,* which can deliver the same news, based on its editors' decisions, to anybody, irrespective of who they are. Joe didn't understand that Facebook's News Feed is based on an algorithm that requires you to give data to get data. Facebook is not a "turnkey" solution.

In this he's not alone. University of Illinois professor Karrie Karahalios surprisingly found that 62.5 percent of participants in a study on the Facebook News Feed apparently didn't even realize an algorithm was refining what posts they are shown. In her research, Karahalios let users compare the full universe of posts by their Facebook friends on a single day to the posts that appeared on their actual News Feed. Some people in the study were shocked to learn that posts from close friends and family members were hidden by the algorithm. They had assumed their contacts simply weren't very active on the site.

In an effort to provide more transparency about the data-refining process, Karahalios and her colleagues at the University of Illinois and the University of Michigan developed "FeedVis," an auditing tool that helps users understand how likes, comments, and posts shape what they are shown and gives them an opportunity to explore alternate feeds.[52] The first stage of awareness involved showing users their personalized News Feed compared to the chronologically ordered content shared by everyone in their network of friends, the "all stories" feed. The second stage involved showing users three sets of friends grouped by the percentage of content from each friend that appeared in their personalized Feed—"rarely seen" (less than 10 percent), "sometimes seen" (between 45 and 55 percent), and "mostly seen" (90 percent or more).[53] Finally, after reviewing the list of friends, the user could move specific content from hidden to shown, or move friends between the three categories, and see the resulting versions of the personally curated News Feed.

Quite a few of the subjects came out of the study feeling that Facebook captured their interest in content and friends more or less correctly based on their interactions, and they now understood that it was necessary to actively express interest in a friend—by visiting her Timeline or by interacting with her posts—to increase what they saw from her. Facebook itself could give much more feedback to users, for example, by letting them know what content leads friends to mute posts, which posts appear to infect other users with interests and ideas, and even how and when you as an individual have been affected by a contagion.

Given the amount of information people are sharing on Facebook, it really shouldn't be shocking that researchers are keen to use the platform as a lab for studying human psychology and the effects of social networks. One of the more curious questions is the extent to which effects that are known to occur in face-to-face encounters, such as how mood and emotion spread from person to person, also occur online. When researchers at Facebook and Cornell shared findings about how they had changed the algorithms of the News Feed to increase or decrease the number of posts with positive or negative words expressing emotion to see if emotional contagion exists on the site (it does),[54] the study was met with outrage: *How dare Facebook manipulate my feelings!*[55] Yet media and marketers constantly manipulate our feelings and select what information to show us with significant consequences—that's the essence of Greek tragedies, infomercials, and the majority of must-see TV.

If the researchers had said they had tinkered with the algorithms to show or hide posts talking about rainy weather, it's unlikely that people would have protested. But as it happens, in another study of Facebook, researchers who conducted the controversial contagion study decided to run a "natural" experiment on the spread of emotions by looking at the weather conditions in various cities. Why? Because they had discovered that people used more negative words on rainy days—and of course, they knew there was no way a person's mood could change the weather. When the researchers analyzed word use in status updates, however, it was apparent that the emotional effect of rainfall in one city cascaded through a person's social network, changing the emotional content of even those posts made by friends who that day had been blessed with sunnier, dry weather.[56] These studies on emotional contagion on Facebook reveal how easily and subtly we are influenced by our social network online. I believe in the scientific method and the value of learning from such experiments.

Some critics of the study claimed Facebook should have told users about the research before carrying it out. This approach, called "informed consent," made a lot of sense in a world where there were few experiments, small in scope and scale, and a researcher could sit down with subjects and make sure they understood the possible risks and rewards of participation. Now, *everyone* is part of online experiments *all* the time, and thus, the notion of informed consent needs to change. Requiring a website visitor to click "yes" on a consent dialog to confirm that he is opting in to data collections doesn't suffice. In the European Union, for example, cookie consents are required. Since not accepting cookies disables some web and mobile features, including personalization, most of us accept them almost as a reflex. This is not informed consent. Most of us also automatically accept software and website terms of service—like Apple's mammoth forty-four-page agreement—without reading a word, let alone understanding them. A detailed explanation of the experiment's protocols, like a detailed explanation of the algorithms Facebook uses to generate its News Feeds, would be unintelligible to the vast majority of people, even if they tried hard. This wouldn't meet the well-intended but unrealistically old-fashioned standards of informed consent either.

Worse, notifying users would jeopardize the experiment itself. If a subject knows that researchers are investigating a specific question ("How are people affected by the emotional content of the Facebook posts they see?"), her Facebook activity will probably change, but it won't be clear to the researchers *why* it has changed. In the case of the contagion study, she might become far more focused on spotting emotional content,

increasing sympathetic replies simply because she's noticing more opportunities to do so, or self-censoring comments for fear of revealing
intimate information to the researchers.

Instead, we need to insist that relevant experimental results are shared
with participants in an accessible manner and disseminate information
about the value of a study's findings to the company and to the public.
To provide greater transparency, companies need, at the very least, to
provide a page with a description of the experiments that have been run.
With more sophisticated experiments, particularly ones involving your
social network, there are more powerful options. Imagine that instead of
first reading about the emotional contagion study in the news, the users
whose Feeds were changed during the experiment received a message
from Facebook explaining the study and their role to them. The message
could include a post that wasn't shown in the user's Feed but would have
been if the person had been assigned to the "control" group. Ideally, users
would be able to apply the study's "treatment" options to their current
Feed and see the effects in real time, should they be interested. This sort
of disclosure would give users a tangible way to understand how they
are affected by the refinery's choices, as well as by their social network.
It would also allow users to express interest in participating in similar
studies in the future.[57]

Further, you stand to benefit from studies on the social graph and its
effects. For instance, what if Facebook alerted you to the fact that when
you read posts from one friend, your mindset typically improves and
you feel inspired, whereas when you got a mere glimpse of a post from
another friend, your productivity plummets. With enough data about
fluctuations in your mood and efficiency, Facebook could change what
you are shown to help you reach a set of goals you've set for the day. You
might install an app that lets you note your work productivity or your
feelings by asking you about what and how you are doing at random
times. Alternatively, you could wear an activity tracker like a Fitbit or an
Apple Watch that can supply regular readings of your vital signs. Or you
could give Facebook access to the camera on your phone or laptop to
figure out when exactly the smile of delight on your face morphs into an-
noyance at having "wasted" too much time reading your friends' posts. In
return for these data, Facebook could provide recommendations about
who to spend more or less time with, on- and offline.

Being able to observe and measure the spread of ideas and attitudes provides rich context for assessing the "national mood" about important issues such as the health of the economy or military interventions. Studies of contagion could also inform revisions to the law based on changing social norms. After the US Supreme Court legalized gay marriage in June 2015, Facebook gave users the option of applying a rainbow filter overlay to their profile picture to celebrate.[58] When I checked Facebook the next day, more than half of the people in my News Feed had already adopted the filter. I was amazed and delighted. But overall, only about 3 percent of all Facebook users did so.[59] I tried to understand what this meant. I started by looking at an earlier study of Facebook users who had changed their profile photo to a picture of the red "equals sign" logo in support of marriage equality two years earlier. In that case, I learned, users waited to change their profile photo until after they'd seen several of their friends had it. The number of friends with the logo was important, but so was the individual's susceptibility to others' influence.[60]

Users generally have little way of knowing in which order Facebook displays people to them. It could be based on an estimate of mutual interest, an advertisement for a new feature, a decision to highlight friends who, with more likes and comments, will create more content, some A/B experiment, or, perhaps, a political statement, such as the rainbow filter. Further, when friends visit a user's Timeline, they are shown a different subset of the user's friends than the subset shown to the user himself. Are those the people Facebook thinks the visitor might be most interested in? Facebook doesn't tell us, and we can't control in what order our friends are shown to us, let alone to others.

If Facebook wanted to influence a country's politics, it could prioritize posts that express a "preferred" opinion. And as Jonathan Zittrain, a professor of law and computer science at Harvard, has noted, Facebook has already conducted experiments in "civic-engineering," influencing people to go out and vote in the 2010 congressional elections. Almost all voting-age American users were shown an ad reminding them to go to the polls. One group was shown "social" get-out-the-vote messages that included the names and profile photos of friends who had already voted. Another, smaller group was shown an "informational" message, also reminding them that it was Election Day but without any mention of their friends. Both of these "treatment" groups were compared to a control group, which was shown no message from Facebook about voting.[61] The effects of the two messages were measured in three ways: by how many people clicked a button in the ad to search for their local polling place; by how many clicked a button to announce to friends that they'd voted; and by how many could be "confirmed" to have voted by finding a match to a voter's name, birthdate, and residence in state polling records. The researchers claimed that an extra 340,000 people went to the polls that Election Day as a result of having seen the social message. Surveying these results, Zittrain poses the most important question: What's stopping Mark Zuckerberg from throwing his weight—and Facebook's algorithms' weights—behind his preferred candidates, showing the most effective get-out-the-vote messages to those users most likely to vote for them?[62]

A reconstruction of the "social" and "informational" get-out-the-vote messages shown to Facebook users on Election Day 2010. Based on "A 61-Million-Person Experiment in Social Influence and Political Mobilization" by Robert M. Bond, Christopher J. Fariss, Jason J. Jones, Adam D. I. Kramer, Cameron Marlow, Jaime E. Settle, and James H. Fowler, *Nature*, vol. 489 (September 13, 2012).

Zittrain suggests that the law should make such political influence illegal, but apart from the difficulty of proving it, we haven't made direct mail or robocalls or targeted TV ads illegal; the courts have said that doing so is a violation of free speech, and I agree. Neither stifling communication nor embracing censorship is the solution. Instead, we must demand that the data refineries give us tools to detect and understand how our interactions are used to determine which information and recommendations are shown to us.

The Value of Trust

Put not your trust in money, but put your money in trust.[63]

OLIVER WENDELL HOLMES

Would you be willing to hitch a ride with a complete stranger? Would you be willing to stay at the stranger's home? Would you lend a thousand bucks to somebody you'd never met? Would you let them pick up your car from the repair shop or your kid from kindergarten? The concept of trust is central to an individual's answers to these questions. Trust is highly complex, and difficult to define and measure, but the social graph helps us to do both.

If you trust someone, you expect that she will behave toward you in a way that you can predict from her past behavior. Generally, you say you trust someone only if you think that she'll behave *positively* toward you in the future, that she has your interests in mind. Trust may in part be based on reputation, an encapsulation of a person's past behavior and expertise in specific domains. While reputation is a property of the person or node, trust is a property of the relationship between people, or, in the language of graph theory, the edge between two nodes.

Trust is not necessarily symmetrical. You might trust a particular person a great deal, and he might not trust you at all. Digital traces of our interactions convey information about trust between individuals. By analyzing the pattern of communication between people and the content of emails and chats, an organization can infer who trusts whom for what. Trust also propagates through the social graph. We rarely trust someone based solely on our own direct knowledge, ignoring reports from others. If I trust Ellen, and Ellen tells me that she trusts Mark, I'll trust Mark until he demonstrates to me that my trust is misplaced. If I lose some of my trust in Mark, it might affect my trust in Ellen—at least as far as taking recommendations about who to trust, but possibly in other areas as well. And the more people I trust who "vouch" for Mark's trustworthiness, the more I may trust him despite a lack of direct experience of his behavior.

Algorithms can augment and enhance these trust chains, creating transparency and providing new avenues for verifying and establishing both identity and reputation.[64] On e-commerce platforms like eBay, Taobao, Airbnb, and Uber, participants usually don't know each other and don't have friends in common whom they can ask about the reputation of others. Refineries must model trust from whatever data they can find—or that they can convince people to give to them. Sellers, hosts, and drivers who regularly use a particular platform have no choice but to leave a rich trail of data on it. On the other side of the transaction, buyers, guests, and riders might use a service once (or once before changing their identity). To build a trust ecosystem, for example, Airbnb relies on a range of data sources to verify identity and vet a person's trustworthiness, including user searches, ratings, reviews, interaction history, and other feedback, as well as external data.[65]

True transparency includes giving users information about the connection between a reviewer and the reviewed, such as a list of all published reviews and comments by and about a user. These details help people assess how relevant an individual review is to them. For instance, Yelp allows users to see a reviewer's top neighborhoods. The geographical distribution signals whether a person is reviewing places on his home turf or ones further afield—potentially including ones he's never visited. The company uses geolocation and other data collected by the Yelp app to compute a "trust rank" for each reviewer, which helps determine where his reviews appear in the site's listings.[66]

Yet, Yelp does not provide as much transparency as I think would be valuable to users when deciding if they can trust a review.[67] If a restaurant uses Yelp's reservation system SeatMe, the company can confirm that a person actually went to the restaurant he's reviewing. Why don't reviews get a "verified visitor" badge similar to the one Amazon attaches to "verified purchases"? So-called reputation management firms have been known to post fake four- and five-star reviews on Yelp for their clients.

There's a very good reason for doing so: Michael Luca, an assistant professor at Harvard Business School, found that a one-star increase in Yelp ratings garnered 5 to 9 percent more revenue for a business.[68]

Meituan-Dianping, a Chinese mash-up of Groupon and Yelp that boasts over 200 million monthly users, analyzes a rich set of data as it decides how to weigh customer feedback.[69] When redeemed, the site's coupons help to confirm that the reviewer actually set foot on the premises and purchased the service or product being reviewed. Meituan-Dianping could go even further, however, since it is backed by the two Chinese internet giants, Alibaba and Tencent.[70] Alibaba's transaction history, which comes from the Alipay app, can provide a sense of a merchant's reliability—a significant issue in China. Tencent allows users to link bank accounts and credit cards to their WeChat account in order to make it easier to pay for purchases through the app. So Tencent also has access to transaction data on top of messaging patterns. Using these data, Meituan-Dianping can rank and sort reviews and filter out likely fraudsters. But neither Meituan nor Dianping has historically told people what data are used to decide which reviews rise to the top, which drop to the bottom, and which are hidden. In addition, companies like Yelp and Meituan-Dianping could improve the service they provide users—and help them make better decisions about where to spend their money—by publishing the trust rank of reviewers and reviews. Data refineries can also provide tools to make trust a "searchable" commodity.

As a first step, data refineries ought to give users a simple switch to turn personalization on and off. Facebook has a hard-to-find switch that allows users to sort posts in the News Feed two ways: the "most recent" setting provides a simple chronological sort, while the "top stories" setting applies the magic sauce of its algorithms. These features should be easier to find, but there also should be further options for exploring different sort orders. Most users won't understand how ranking algorithms work in detail, but that doesn't mean they won't be able to try out different settings and form an opinion about what they prefer in a given situation. Ultimately, they are the only ones who can really judge when the algorithms are working well for them and when they aren't. Consider an example. If you want to find your friends' historical posts mentioning restaurants they enjoyed in San Francisco, would you want the first options listed to be the posts from a friend who is a recognized "foodie," racking up likes from you (and others) for her status updates reflecting on her latest great meal, or from a sports fanatic buddy who waxes lyrical over a bag of boiled peanuts and racks up just as many likes for his sense of humor? Recency and relevance go only so far.

Online retailers understand that, some of the time, customers want to see products sorted by price, while other times, they want them sorted by customer rating. Travel search and booking sites allow travelers to sort by fare, flight duration, departure and arrival times, number of connections, and specific airlines. Hipmunk, which was co-founded by Adam Goldstein and Reddit's Steve Huffman, created an "agony" function that assigns weights to price, number of stops, and duration of travel time and then orders flights based on this combination of factors. (Google Flights subsequently adopted a similar approach.) An algorithm that addresses trade-offs inherent in decision-making is good; letting users determine their own weights on the factors is better still. The travel management company CWT analyzed 15 million transactions and 7,000 surveys in an attempt to identify and quantify the cost of travel stressors, from lost work time to lost sleep time.[71] Perhaps you'd like to put a dollar value on having to get up in order to catch a cheaper early-morning departure. It's surprising that there are not more refineries already offering this level of customer agency, as it creates a win-win situation: the user learns his preferences by changing the weights and seeing which combination inspires him to make a purchase, and the refinery gets data that can help improve recommendations, both personal and general. Users' sorting and weighting options should be expanded, and not only in e-commerce. They should also be available on social network platforms.

On the other hand, as we gain access to more sort options, the patterns in how we live our lives can be discovered by people in our social network. If a query on Facebook is specific enough, its answer may be a sample size of one—you. Do you want Facebook to show your uncle, who's searching for the best places to visit in Amsterdam, that you've exuberantly liked every one of a friend's posts about a favorite "coffee shop"?

Social graph data will increasingly be utilized in the evaluation of people's trustworthiness before and during their interactions with many institutions. Several years ago, Allstate—which sells insurance to 10 percent of American households—hypothesized that its customers were more likely to file a false claim if people in their social network had themselves previously filed false claims in the past. This is a clever application of homophily: people with similar values—in this case, a proclivity toward filing a false claim—are more likely to be friends than not. Allstate receives millions of claims each year, and not every claim can be investigated deeply. In the past, the company had to rely on crude proxies, such as whether the physical neighborhood in which a person lived had a high percentage of false claims. If Allstate could instead access data about a customer's neighborhood in the social graph, these data would help staff flag up new claims that needed extra scrutiny for possible fraud.

Because property insurance companies are primarily "offline" businesses, Allstate needed to add an online data source. The insurer turned to data brokerage RapLeaf, which had a massive collection of email addresses and social network data, with most of the Facebook data—including users' friend lists—bought from apps that accessed people's Facebook accounts with their permission (but potentially available for purposes beyond what users ever imagined). First, RapLeaf used data mining to find out which online accounts actually belonged to the same person. Second, primarily based on its Facebook data, RapLeaf provided information of connections between people. The database allowed Allstate to identify customers whose friends were also Allstate customers, and Allstate then could determine at what level to investigate a client's claim based on his friends' history with the insurer. After RapLeaf became the subject of a withering profile in the *Wall Street Journal* for inadvertently sharing personal data combined from various sources with some of its clients, Facebook banned the company from scraping its site.[72]

Of course, Facebook itself is exploring ways to monetize its social graph data. In 2010, the company acquired a patent from Friendster that suggests how social graph data can be used to filter content about other individuals.[73] However, when Facebook filed an update in 2015, the patented idea that generated headlines was all about money. In the patent's words:

When an individual applies for a loan, the lender examines the credit ratings of members of the individual's social network who are connected to the individual. If the average credit rating of these members is at least a minimum credit score, the lender continues to process the loan application. Otherwise, the loan application is rejected.[74]

If your only real-world overlap with a Facebook friend is that you once worked for the same company, or occasionally played basketball together in a pick-up league, or knew from your mother that he was a third cousin twice removed, should you be considered risky business because he appears on your friend list and is a sketchy character? I think it would be more interesting if we could explicitly "couple" our personal reputation with that of the people in our social network. Here's how the basic concept works: I trust my friend Daniel Kahneman, who has a Nobel Prize in economics, among a few other trust-inducing accomplishments, to his credit. Perhaps I'd like 50 percent of my own reputation to be tied to his reputation—I'd assign a "reputation-coupling trust coefficient" of 0.5. This means that if Danny's reputation rating goes up by 1 unit, I would get a rating boost of 0.5. Conversely, if for some reason Danny's reputation rating went down by 1, my rating would go down by 0.5. Trust coefficients would allow me to curate an aspect of my identity—my friends, mentors, and inspirations, and their influence on me—with much finer detail than the typical, binary choice of indicating that a person is a friend or not.

If trust coefficients are openly published for other people to see, I'd definitely have to consider what my choices communicate about me. I might couple all of my reputation to "blue-chip" people like Danny, but because he has a well-established, stellar reputation, his reputation can't really go up much more, and I'm not likely to see much improvement on my own as a result. If my goal was to improve my reputation, I'd seek out people who were "rising stars."[75]

A mechanism similar to reputation coupling has been built into the business model of the German start-up Friendsurance, which brokers what the founder calls "peer-to-peer insurance."[76] To set up a Friendsurance plan, two (or more) people indicate they will contribute a specified amount—say, thirty euros—if the other reports that an insured piece of property has been lost or stolen. The customer pays lower premiums while keeping the same coverage, because each friend's commitment helps cover the higher deductible required for the lower-premium policy. Asking friends to pay on a claim also reduces the number of filed claims. People are less likely to submit a fraudulent claim "against" a group of friends versus a distant corporate HQ, either because they don't want their friends to know (say, if they've been reckless) or because they don't want their friends to be saddled with the bill. In a way, customers vouch for the honesty of their claims to their friends—and their friends vouch with their wallets for the veracity of the claim when the insurer has to pay the amount due above and beyond the Friendsurance deductible. In essence, Friendsurance hands over some of the work of assessing a customer's risk profile to his peers. Who wants to invite cousin Doug to join such an insurance plan if he has a reputation for losing a smartphone every three months?

Where trust coefficients and reputation coupling are adopted, subsequent design choices will significantly affect the social network. Is the amount of trust you have in others fixed or elastic? In the real world, your trust in a person might get strained or broken based on experience, but you don't have a fixed amount of trust to distribute among your friends. If my trust in my brother increases, I'm not forced to reduce my trust in someone else. My increased amount of trust in people also doesn't deflate the value of my trust—trust isn't like money, where printing more currency deflates the value of each unit. A data refinery implementing a trust coupling system might prefer to artificially limit trust, as some dating sites do when they limit members to sending only one message a day. Likewise, LinkedIn could give you a hundred "trust credits" to distribute publicly across your professional contacts instead of allowing users to endorse others in a specific area of expertise. Ideally, this would help to align your interests with the refinery's: as you assign and edit your trust, the data about how your trust assignments and levels change over time and in response to people's behavior and reputation would be refined to help you decide whose advice to seek when.

A refinery could also decide to let you see the distribution of trust across people and how it has evolved over time. This would allow you to see if someone has a habit of shifting her trust credits back and forth between contacts as a form of reputational speculation. People who don't like such behavior might decide to divest their trust in her. If the origins of the trust credits invested in you were published, other users would be able to see that you were getting trust from a very weak tie in your social network and could decide how much that mattered to them. It would also make a difference if you were required to accept a "trust request," indicating that you were okay that the person wanted her reputation to be tied to your own. Should such a market in trust credits operate somewhat like the stock market? If you buy shares in Microsoft, you are basically saying that you want your personal wealth to be tied to the fortunes of Microsoft. Microsoft has no say in whether you can buy shares in it or not.

Trust coefficients would provide useful data for decision-making—as well as for developing norms for online social behavior. If you trust someone enough that you want to tie your reputation to her, it probably makes sense to keep an eye on what she's up to.

The Larger Context

We take counsel from our friends and family. We notice what people around us consider to be appropriate and inappropriate. The new abundance of social data means that our relationships—who we interact with and how we interact with them—can be observed in rich detail. Will we be able to use social graph data to make better decisions? The goal cannot merely be to improve the response rate on marketing campaigns.

For the most part, Facebook, LinkedIn, and other data refineries that specialize in social graph data have been up-front about how they collect data: they provide a platform that encourages people to explicitly share information about their interactions and personal histories. But these platforms have their limits: we cannot share every moment of our lives on Facebook. That's why Facebook constantly explores new ways to improve its model of the world's social graph. It tracks users as they browse the internet, taking advantage of cookies built into the tools that allow readers to like content on another site and to share that like on Facebook with the same click.[77]

Facebook also links people who share a computer or mobile device, even on a single occasion.[78] It does this by creating a "fingerprint" for the device you are on, much like BioCatch authenticates a user through a "usage fingerprint" based on keystroke and mouse movement patterns. Facebook's device-print is based on many data sources, including the operating system's language setting, the list of installed apps, and the user's list of contacts (if the user gives Facebook access to them). Facebook uses device-printing to reduce fraud.

Of course, device-printing also allows Facebook to note when two users have at least once used the same device to sign in, perhaps because they live in the same household. These data can be used to improve the map of the social graph and to devise advertising campaigns, since many purchasing decisions are made at the household level. But how much do users benefit from Facebook detecting portions of the social graph that they haven't *chosen* to share explicitly with the company?

Data refineries must explain to users how the data they contribute will end up benefiting them—those twin aims of transparency and agency. This is partly why I have proposed the trust coefficient: it is designed so that people can improve their reputation by explicitly expressing their trust in each other. Some people are trust sinks; some are trust sources. Both sides are essential to a functioning society. Novel methods like this can do more than reward people for creating data; they can transform that data into a powerful tool for decision-making, influencing how we behave—hopefully for the better.

Decisions are always made in a context. There's little question that our social environment influences the decisions we make, but so, too, does the physical environment. Where we've come from and where we are help determine where we want to go next. We make different decisions depending on the time of day, the weather outside, our level of fatigue or happiness, just for a start. We also act—and make decisions—differently based on whether we are being observed, of course. When those observations are recorded, that also changes our context dramatically.

With the explosion in the number of sensors on the planet, the data refineries are in a position to point us in the most relevant direction. At least we can hope so. We're about to find out.

4

CONTEXT AND CONDITIONS

Making Sense of the Sensorization of Society

What Does It Mean to Live in a World Where Everything Is Recorded?

Wherever there is light, one can photograph.[1]

ALFRED STIEGLITZ

The sunlight is nearly blinding as it bounces off the squat, square, perfectly beige and banal government complex across the street. In the foreground, a police officer squints into the camera, shrugs, and shakes his head.

> MAN'S VOICE: Look, I'm out in public taking photographs. And beyond that, it's none of your business what I'm doing.
> OFFICER 1: Did you say it's none of our business?
> MAN'S VOICE: Yep. If I'm not being detained, you guys have a nice day.

At that, another officer pulls out a pad and the man is told he's being detained. Officers pat him down to ensure he's not carrying any weapons. When the search is complete, he gets a warning.

> OFFICER 2: Here's the thing: just make it easy for all of us. We'll get your name; we're going to make sure you're not someone who's out here trying to kill us.
> MAN'S VOICE: Is it illegal to take pictures of you? Is it illegal?

There's a long pause as the officer stares into the camera—at least, it seems that's what he's doing. It's impossible to know exactly where he's looking, as his eyes are obscured by his mirrored sunglasses. He tightens his lips and sets his jaw; the furrow between his eyebrows deepens. Finally, he answers the man: "No."[2]

The sun is just as bright in a second video recorded that day, but this time the glare glances off the front hood of a police cruiser. The dashcam observes the officer waiting patiently for the traffic light to turn green before he can reach a station wagon about to leave a parking lot. The officer, whose voice sounds familiar, reports his location to radio dispatch, then orders the driver to roll down his window. The officer informs the driver that he got pulled over because his license plate is partly obscured.[3]

The driver quickly informs the officer that he used to be qualified to drive commercial vehicles on his license, but that's been suspended—something he knows might cause confusion when his license number is radioed in to dispatch.[4] Sure enough, the dispatcher says the driver's license is invalid, and the officer arrests him, not merely for driving with a suspended license but for doing so *knowingly.* The day wasn't going quite the way Jeff Gray had planned.

Gray is a member of a citizen group that records videos of authorities in public and posts them at the website Photography Is Not a Crime. Earlier in the day, he had been conducting a "First Amendment audit," recording officers coming and going from the Orlando police department to see if they would challenge his right to do so.[5] He hadn't expected one of the officers to follow him from the scene and arrest him for a minor traffic violation because of it.

Gray didn't record the traffic stop or his arrest. However, the police car's dashcam was recording, and that audio captured the moment the police officer changed his frequency from general broadcast to direct car-to-car communication, which he used to consult the officer who had given Gray the warning across the street from the police department.

OFFICER 2: Hey, do you want me to go straight to BRC [the booking and release center] or do anything special?
OFFICER 1: [unintelligible]
OFFICER 2: I'm sorry?

OFFICER 1: Frankie's on his way over there, and we're going to find the L.T. [lieutenant] to see if there's anything else we need to do. You're not recording right now while you're talking?

OFFICER 2: I'm sorry?

OFFICER 1: Are you still recording yourself?

OFFICER 2: Uh, I only have same-car right now, but the mic is running.

When it came time for Gray to challenge his arrest in court, he was lucky: the "Sunshine State" of Florida has the strongest public records laws in the United States.[6] He could point to the note in a state attorney's office newsletter urging police officers to pull over drivers for an obstructed license plate only if it was impossible to identify the plate number. He could also refer to a Department of Motor Vehicles memo explaining why the driver of a noncommercial vehicle should not be arrested for having a disqualified commercial license.[7] Eventually, he could replay the dashcam footage, which made clear that his tag number was visible—and he'd also get to hear the police officers discuss whether to take him straight to booking or do something "special" to him.

As these Orlando police officers learned, because sensors have become so small and storage has become so cheap, today anything and everything you say and do might be recorded. The sign has flipped: the default condition of life has shifted from "off the record" to "on the record."

Consider the number of networked cameras that capture data about you as you go about your day. Surveillance cameras are mounted in offices, stores, public transportation; on city streets, ATM machines, and car dashboards. You or your neighbors may have installed cameras to watch over your front door; you may have a webcam watching over your valuables—perhaps even your children. Security cameras are virtually everywhere, installed both to provide a record if a crime is committed and to deter people from committing a crime in the first place.[8] Based on an exhaustive survey of the number of such cameras in one English county in 2011, it was estimated there were 2 million surveillance cameras in the United Kingdom alone—about one camera for every thirty people.[9] Generalizing this to the rest of the world, there are about 100 million cameras watching public spaces, all day and all night. Yet, this is only one-tenth of the 1 *billion* cameras on smartphones.[10] Within the next few years, there will be one networked camera for every single person on the planet.

Then think about the other sensors on our smartphones. There's at least one microphone; a global positioning system receiver, which determines your location based on satellite signals; a magnetometer, which can serve as a compass to orient your phone based on the strength and direction of the earth's magnetic field; a barometer, which senses air pressure and your relative elevation; a gyroscope, which senses the phone's rate of rotation; an accelerometer, which senses the phone's movement; a thermometer; a humidity sensor; an ambient light sensor; and a proximity sensor, which deactivates the touchscreen when you bring the phone to your face. That's a dozen or so networked sensors per phone, bringing us to a total of more than 10 billion sensors on mobile phones alone. And that's not counting cars, watches, thermostats, electricity meters, and other networked devices.

If technology continues to follow Moore's Law, doubling the computing power available at the same price every eighteen months, we will very likely be sharing the world with roughly 1 trillion sensors by 2020, in line with projections from Bosch, HP, IBM, and others.[11]

To record the Orlando Police Department, Jeff Gray used a standard video camera, a device that could be identified from many meters away. He did not try to hide his camera, since one of his motivations for recording the officers was to see if they would challenge his right to collect the data. In contrast, while the officer who pulled Gray over knew his patrol car had a live dashcam with a microphone, Gray was never notified during his arrest that the encounter was being recorded. Further, Gray always intended to share his video on the internet. The police department may never have shared the dashcam footage if it hadn't been forced to do so under the state's "Sunshine" laws.

Not all governments give citizens the right to access the type of records that helped Gray fight his arrest. Most organizations that collect data about a person do not share it with the subject. These records of our interactions will transform expectations about privacy. Even more fundamentally, they will also change the context and conditions of our interactions. We have significant issues to consider. Why do the laws currently treat photos and videos taken within public view differently from sounds taken within public earshot?[12] Which new types of sensors will be treated like cameras, and which like microphones? Why would a person's "right to record" depend on the type of sensor used? Should access to data be solely put in the hands of the person or entity that owns the sensor, or should all the participants in the event have access to the recording? If a person records an event involving another person, who has a "right" to decide how those data are used? If everything is recorded, will it encourage "better" behavior? And how will the *lack* of any recording be interpreted?

The complications of continuous recording can be seen in another case involving the Orlando police. In court, a driver successfully challenged a charge of driving under the influence of alcohol or drugs by noting that dashcam video of the arrest wasn't available. It didn't matter to the judge whether the camera was broken or the officer forgot to turn it on: the lack of video to "corroborate" the officer's arrest report meant the officer's word was no better than hearsay.[13]

As our world gets increasingly sensorized, we will need to come to terms with the trade-offs of collecting and sharing data about our bodies, our feelings, and our environment that others might put to some future, unknown use. Now is the time to set down the conditions for how these data can be used so that the rewards—to individuals and to society—will outweigh the risks. Small differences in the rules we set today may have tremendous consequences for the future. I believe it is essential to examine how sensor data can be utilized following the principles of transparency and agency.

A Personalized Point of View

Some of the issues of power asymmetry in the use of sensors can be seen in the public reaction to users of the Explorer version of Google Glass. As a social experiment, I wore my Glass pretty much all the time for nearly a year.[14] It was always there, plainly visible, right on my face.

The experiment came to an abrupt end at the Mexico City International Airport, where an immigration officer pulled me aside because wearing Glass meant that I might have taken photos in an area where photography was not allowed. The fact that my Glass was turned off, and only served as my prescription lenses at that moment, made no difference to him. I argued that most smartphones contain the same range of sensors as Glass, but my remonstrations led nowhere (beyond a seat in a small holding room for a few hours).

The immigration officer's reaction to Glass was not atypical. Why does a camera worn at all times bother people any more than a smartphone carried at all times? Quite a few of the people who became unsettled when they saw I was wearing Glass would probably have been comfortable with me holding my phone. I wondered if the difference was the ease of recording hands-free videos, or the difficulty for the other party of detecting when Glass was recording. Still, an attentive person might notice a reflection on the display prism—unless, that is, his attention was focused on some nearby spectacle rather than on my spectacles.

Further, while I was wearing Glass, people also seemed annoyed when they thought I was splitting my attention between our conversation and the display. I decided to "run" an informal experiment where I would pretend to look up information about the individuals I was talking to, or that I was receiving automatic "image search" results based on what was in front of me (including their faces). My companions were dismayed. They felt this put them at a disadvantage in the conversation. They were used to others having information at their fingertips, but Glass put it at the tip of my nose, where they had no way to see for themselves when I was focusing on them or on a screen.

Another possibility was that people were unsettled that I might share the conversation. I could upload a recording to the cloud, or send the videostream via my mobile phone,[15] for others to watch in real time.[16] What would stop someone from inviting a third party to surreptitiously listen in on a conversation? What would stop her from storing the conversation so that it could be shared with some interested party in the future?

Many people feel uncomfortable talking with someone who refuses to take off a pair of mirrored sunglasses, because they aren't able to see his eyes and get a better sense of what he is feeling about the conversation. Glass may not obscure the eyes, but it still challenges norms of conversation. The various reactions to Glass suggest that people have three main fears about living with ubiquitous sensors, and how they are either violating social conventions or forcing them to change.

First, there is the *fear of information imbalance,* of data being retrieved about others or the situation in a way that will alter the outcome of the interaction. When one side of a conversation has access to information and the other does not, the power imbalance can be unbearable. People may be worried about the "lemon" problem, whereby asymmetries in access to information cause them to get ripped off (as in the classic example of a used-car salesman hiding information from a buyer). There's also the issue of distractions from the immediate context, which heightens feelings of insecurity about whether the attention of your conversational partner is focused on you or something else.

Second, there is the *fear of dissemination*, of others sharing data with people, companies, or the web without permission. If a new person joins a group meeting in person, each conversationalist can shift the topic in response; the new "audience" is patently transparent. This transparency doesn't occur automatically with cameras, which is why organizations stick up warning notices. This allows individuals to decide how to act in view of the fact that there might be repercussions for having their actions witnessed and analyzed by the camera's owner or associates. Glass itself served as a warning notice, but it put people on alert all the time, even when the feed wasn't on.

Third, there is the *fear of permanence*, of others recording data and saving the data somewhere. In this case, the fear comes down to an uncertainty about how the data might be analyzed or used in the future. With no guarantee that the consequences of the recording will be positive, it might be best to assume the worst. In addition, laws differ from place to place about who is allowed to record what without permission. For instance, an individual or organization has the right to install a camera that records the movements of people visiting their property, but the people visiting the property don't have the same right. Regulation of privately owned cameras attached to drones, which can observe conversations from the air, will take years to be hashed out.

Perhaps the person with the most experience wearing a recording device is Steve Mann, a professor of electrical engineering and computer science at the University of Toronto. Mann has been wearing different versions of a "Digital Eye Glass" for more than three decades.[17] While a student in the 1980s at MIT, where Mann was a founding member of the Wearable Computing Project, he rarely removed his version of Glass and constantly experimented with applications for it, including transmitting a live web feed of everything he saw (in the early 1990s, when there were only a handful of live feeds on the web).[18] He also coined the term "sousveillance" to describe his video and audio recordings of organizations that had surveillance cameras on their premises.[19] Surveillance is conducted from above, sousveillance from below.[20]

Mann is an advocate of using wearable computers for personal empowerment. He believes an "always on" computer allows people to capture data they do not yet realize could be relevant in the future, even only a few minutes later. To demonstrate this, he has played around with methods to augment human senses and memory with wearables—for example, by zooming in on objects in the distance or cueing up super-slow-motion replays of information that the eye cannot process in real time.[21] In Mann's experience, wearables allow people to filter incoming data—for example, by obscuring ads they don't want to see.[22]

While such features are interesting, I believe the full value of sensor data will be unleashed only if they are shared and refined. In my year experimenting with Glass, I recorded many weeks' worth of video. However, I reviewed only a few minutes of the videos and never actually *used* them to help me make any decision or learn anything about my behavior. I wasn't able to efficiently search through and retrieve relevant parts of a video I had taken, let alone run the data through a refinery in real time to get feedback and suggestions for what to do. I had the tools to collect data but I didn't have the tools to find data that were relevant to my current context, let alone analyze the data to recognize patterns or generate predictions.

In the next few years, as work in artificial intelligence progresses and the refineries automate the process of labeling data, this will change. Companies are discovering the value of analyzing everything from where their customers walk in a store to how concentrated their employees are, and the technology will become affordable enough for most organizations. Increasingly, we'll all depend on sensor data to give us recommendations pertinent to our given situation.

More than twenty years ago, Eric Horvitz of Microsoft Research and Matthew Barry of NASA looked at when and how to optimize the display of information where time is of the essence in high-stakes decisions such as those necessary for safely overseeing an aircraft's flight from ground control.[23] They started with the assumption, based on a classic study in cognitive psychology, that most people are simply not able to juggle more than about seven "chunks" of information at the same time.[24] Worse, when a situation gets heated and there are lots of distractions—as might very well be the case in an emergency—this number could drop as low as two pieces of information.[25] Eric's early models, developed for engineers monitoring the Space Shuttle, identified which information had the highest expected value in a critical decision-making moment and gave this information more prominence in the engineers' displays.

Socializing sensor data can go further, by drawing attention to important things people may have missed. Imagine, for instance, that you could share a conversation with a refinery for analysis. The app Cogi allows you to keep track of the most interesting portions of a conversation, by storing the last fifteen seconds in the phone's temporary audio buffer. If you hear something interesting, you tap a button and the app permanently stores the recent audio and keeps recording until you stop it; if you don't tap the button, the buffer is subsequently overwritten. If several people use the app to record a conversation, they could compare what they found interesting enough to save. Over time, those saved conversations could be analyzed to determine which speakers, word choices, or topics received the most attention.

Attention and relevance vary based on your context. As we saw in Chapter 1 with the story of searching for an "ambiguous" jaguar—which might be a cat, a car, or a computer operating system—algorithms rank search results based on a variety of content categories, highlighting the information that best matches your intentions. Knowing your context helps refineries improve the relevance of their outputs to you. For instance, let's say you search for "jaguar" on your phone while standing in a zoo. If the app knows your geolocation, it can compare your coordinates to a map of the area and rank content about the cat higher in your results. If you're standing in the parking lot of the zoo, the app could use the phone's cameras to detect whether you might be curious about the newest model of a luxury car in front of you rather than exploring a facet of big-cat life after the day's visit.

Not all contextualized search terms are as innocent as a jaguar in the jungle, however. If a person searches for "jasmine" after a long night spent at a club, it's highly unlikely that he's looking for information about the flower in the hope of squeezing in some gardening time before dawn. He might be looking for the address of a twenty-four-hour Chinese food take-out that's on his way home, or—just maybe—he might be tempted to check out the live models on the adult entertainment site Livejas-min.[26] Is he wandering around downtown, or is he in his bedroom? A refinery can get him where he wants to be more efficiently, using current and recent geolocation data to personalize his results.

Taking context into account can also help us make better decisions for the long term—in Danny Kahneman's terms, "thinking slow" rather than "thinking fast." For instance, at least one bank considered offering a customer service code-named "no regrets" that looked at an individual's past transactions and current context. You walk up to an ATM in Las Vegas at 4 a.m. and ask to withdraw a thousand bucks. Instead of spitting out the bills, the machine prompts: "Are you really sure you want to withdraw that much cash right now? People like you who confirmed 'yes' in a similar situation tended to regret it later."

If the sensor is in *your* hands, you can choose the conditions when you share your context with refineries. But some of the trillion sensors that will record your life over the next decade will be controlled by banks, stores, employers, schools, and governments. There's a growing interest in using far more personal information than just where you are at any given point in time, and that interest encompasses who you're with, how you're feeling, and where your focus is—compared to where it ought to be. But who gets to decide when your "full" context matters? Before we turn to this fundamental question, we must first understand how context is extrapolated from sensor data that isn't always in your hands.

From Where You Are to Who You're With

At 04:00 UTC (Universal Time Coordinated) on May 2, 2000, the US government stopped adding noise to the signals of the Department of Defense's twenty-four Navstar satellites, improving GPS resolution by an order of magnitude, down to a few meters, enabling a range of personal navigation services.[27] The benefit of providing this level of precision to the general public has been enormous: it's estimated that GPS added more than $70 billion to the US economy in 2013, simply through business efficiencies.[28] The contribution of GPS to improved health, safety, and environmental stewardship is still to be tallied up.

Todd Humphreys, a professor of engineering at the University of Texas at Austin, argues that civilian GPS resolution could be even more precise. With funding from Samsung, he and his colleagues have pin-pointed a standard mobile phone's GPS receiver down to a centimeter.[29] Humphreys predicts that within a decade, we will attach miniature geo-location trackers to nearly everything we own, so that we can search for belongings much the way we search for information on the internet.[30] But the current resolution is more than high enough to find yourself—or allow someone to find you.

Geolocation trackers with the weight of a pen and the size of a stamp aren't science fiction; they already exist, and they run on a single, coin-sized battery for a year. They can be this light, this small, and this energy-efficient because they have been designed as beacons: instead of listening for regular signals from faraway satellites, they simply emit a unique ID via the Bluetooth Low Energy (BLE) protocol that can be picked up by devices within ten meters. A user can install an app that reports to the manufacturer's central database when his beacon's ID has been spotted at a place and time. Sometimes, a user is close enough to his beacon to find it with the app on his own phone, but most man-ufacturers offer the option of expanding the search by querying other phones with the app. People have reportedly used beacons to find lost keys, track down stolen property, and locate loved ones in large crowds.[31] In addition, Facebook and other big data collectors are exploring ways to spur beacon adoption by supplying free beacons to organizations. These beacons allow the Facebook app to note when a user approaches a Face-book beacon, to provide him with locally relevant content and to record his pattern of movements.

What stops a person from slipping a Bluetooth beacon into someone else's bag or purse? Nothing. Currently, the law doesn't make it illegal for a person to track somebody using a geolocation identifier (unless, that is, the person works for the government, in which case he'd need to obtain a search warrant). If you want to protect yourself from a sensor that's been attached to you, you are left to your own devices.

When I say "your own devices," I mean it literally. There's a growing business in privacy-preserving technologies such as portable Bluetooth jammers or GPS jammers, which produce noise on the same frequen-cies as Bluetooth or Navstar signals, effectively disabling all receivers within several meters of the jammer.[32] Although you can find instruc-tions for manufacturing jammers on the web, it's illegal to make, sell, or use jamming devices in the United States and many other countries. That hasn't stopped people from trying them out, however. In one case, a truck driver who didn't want his employer to track his movements during the workday deployed a GPS jammer in his company truck. The jammer worked—but it confused more than his employer's GPS: it also disrupted the air traffic control system at Newark international airport. (He racked up more than $30,000 in fines from this effort to obscure his whereabouts from his boss.)[33]

A jammer stops a GPS device from knowing where it is, but it's also possible to trick a GPS into reporting incorrect geolocation data. Todd Humphreys has built a GPS "spoofer," which sends fake satellite signals to a targeted receiver.[34] The spoofer makes the receiver believe that the device is somewhere it's not. If a person or vehicle uses a GPS navigation app, the spoofer could purposefully provide directions to an unwanted destination.

After hearing these tales of trackers, jammers, and spoofers, you might never again want to use any GPS or Bluetooth device, but even the simplest mobile phone conveys your geolocation. Your phone switches from cell phone tower to cell phone tower as you go through your day, creating a record of your movements. If you have a phone that connects to the internet using wifi, a hotspot provider can detect precisely which spots you have visited—and unlike GPS, wifi works indoors. This is the reason many retailers now provide free wifi: it is a way to observe how you move through the store.[35] (Wifi beacons compete with Bluetooth beacons as a method for tracking location.) This is an important sign flip. Knowing your exact location is more valuable to a retailer than making it difficult for you to look up product information, consumer reviews, and competitors' prices online. With that data, a retailer can even offer location-specific deals, whether that location is a specific branch with excess inventory or the aisle where you are currently browsing.

There is yet another very different source of data about where you have been: both photos that you've taken and photos in which you appear. To begin with, most photos shared online were taken from camera phones, and most camera phones have GPS. The metadata associated with the photo by default include the longitude and latitude where the photo was taken. While it is possible to delete such data from your own photos, you can't control the metadata of images taken by others. With billions of photos taken every day, chances are your location has been recorded.

Geolocation metadata aren't the only clues embedded in photos. A well-known landmark in the background, a street sign, or a restaurant's menu can give away your location. The length of the shadows on the ground can reveal the approximate time of day. Algorithms are being trained on video as well, so that a person pounding the pavement of a city street can be identified and tracked block to block by the characteristics of her gait, even using grainy video from low-resolution surveillance cameras.[36]

While some have advocated wearing dark glasses, hats, makeup, and stickers to confuse the machines,[37] it is becoming more and more difficult to escape facial recognition software. As we saw in Chapter 2, Facebook's DeepFace software can match your face to those appearing in images in which you've previously been tagged, including photos taken in dramatically different lighting and from various points of view. You might ask your friends to delete the tags they add to photos, but what about the machine-generated tags that you may not see? In addition, several companies are adopting identity-verification procedures that require users to share live streaming photos or videos of themselves.

Chinese social media platform Tencent was an early pioneer in this area. Tencent had noticed that the messaging service QQ had been overrun by characters who weren't exactly who they pretended to be. Quite a few prostitutes had opened QQ accounts to solicit customers, and for their profile photos they tended to use pictures they'd lifted off the web—sometimes even adding the legal sounding (and perhaps legally sound) but utterly useless disclaimer line "for illustrative purposes only" to them. Savvy Johns learned not to take a person's photo at face value, but the practice became so rampant that many users felt they could not trust any profile on QQ. In response, Tencent developed a program for dynamically verifying a profile using video. A Tencent-approved community manager would ask the user to turn on her webcam and perform a series of actions in response to real-time cues: *touch your right ear, shrug your left shoulder,* and so on. If the face on the video matched the uploaded photos, the profile was said to be "verified."

Tencent's solution involved enlisting a brigade of humans to issue commands and assess video, and there were still tens of thousands of accounts that simply couldn't be verified. With the swift evolution of facial recognition software, machines can do the job—and they can do it no matter the time of day or night. Payment processing company Worldpay has developed a "Pin Entry Device Camera" that can capture one or more facial photos as a customer inputs his card's passcode into a shop-based terminal. Worldpay plans to build and manage a central database of all those headshots and train facial recognition software on them in order to verify that the person using a card is authorized to do so; if the photo doesn't match up, clerks would be prompted to check another form of ID before the purchase could go through.[38] Likewise, in an effort to reduce the use of stolen credit cards or card numbers for online purchases, MasterCard has rolled out the Identity Check program. Card customers set up a biometric profile by uploading a scan of their fingerprints and facial photos. Then, at the time of checkout, they submit a fingerprint scan and a "selfie" video from their mobile phone, which are compared to the registered biometric data. If the images don't match, the transaction is denied. In early tests of the system, users were asked to blink in the video to prove they were a real, living human, to ensure against the situation where images as well as card details are stolen off the web.[39] Other banks and institutions are likely to create or buy access to databases of fingerprints and headshots to help protect customers and their money, and people who opt out of having their data collected for this purpose may be forced to forfeit certain financial protections.

Beyond the whorls of skin on the finger pads, humans have other unique biomarkers that can be used to confirm a person's identity, such as the pattern of pigmentation in each eye's iris.[40] Unlike the skin on our fingertips, the patterns on the iris do not wear down over time, which means the biomarker has a longer shelf life. And whereas scanning a fingerprint requires asking a person to touch a scanner or other collection surface, an iris can be scanned and recognized with a camera up to ten meters away. Biometrics researchers at Carnegie Mellon University in Pittsburgh have been able to capture an image of irises from the reflection on a car's side-view mirror, or from a person strolling through a room, and match it to previously stored iris prints.[41] Several governments, including India, with a population of 1 billion people, are taking (or plan to take) iris scans of every person who renews the required national identification card.[42]

However, your face doesn't need to be visible to identify you, or to pinpoint where you are. After your mobile phone, your car is the second-best proxy for you and your location. By law, your car's license plate number has to be readable, as Jeff Gray knows all too well. Vigilant Solutions, based in Livermore, California, combines images from tens of thousands of cameras that have been mounted in parking lots, shop windows, even outside private homes.[43] It's possible to reconstruct an individual's movements using place-based sensors, by stitching together the unique identifiers reported across a network of sensors to a central database. The photos from Vigilant's network of cameras are processed by optical character recognition algorithms to identify every number plate. Vigilant claims it adds about 100 million individual license plate identifications to its national database each month.[44]

In addition to its network of fixed cameras, Vigilant enlists a network of drivers to install dashcams in their cars and feed the data to its database. Many of these dashcams are in vehicles driven by investigators for "repo" companies, which hunt down cars whose owners have stopped making payments on loans.[45] By adding dashcam images to its network of place-based cameras, Vigilant is able to cover a much wider geographic area.

There are two ways to query a license plate database like Vigilant's. You can search for a particular license plate and learn where and when it was spotted, or you can search for a particular place and time and find which license plates were there. Police officers often search for plates at the location of a crime in order to identify possible suspects and witnesses. If a person's car was nearby, he was probably nearby, too. Unlike the rest of us, the police have access to state-by-state databases of vehicle registrations and can get the name of the car's owner from the plate number. According to documents uncovered by the ACLU, police departments themselves say the use of the database "is only limited by the officer's imagination."[46]

Reportedly, the primary customers for privately held plate databases like Vigilant's are law enforcement agencies, but in theory anyone could pay Vigilant for its services. The company's clients include car dealers hoping to repossess cars and insurance companies trying to determine the details of an accident. Private detectives use the database as well. If someone knows you, it's easy for her to get your plate number. All she has to do is look in the garage. Forget hiring a gumshoe to track a spouse to see if he's really staying late at the office every night. Just pop the plate number into the database and find out where his car has been—and find out what other cars have been there. And if you want to know who drives those cars, the database has a pretty good idea where a particular car frequently gets parked—likely revealing where the driver lives and works. What used to be an expensive, potentially risky data collection task has become cheap and safe.

Some US states have tried to pass legislation making it illegal to create a commercial database of plate numbers, but so far these efforts have been challenged successfully on free-speech grounds. Taking a picture in public isn't illegal, nor is storing the image in the cloud. Applying optical character recognition isn't illegal either. To protect people's privacy, what can we do? We could remove license plates from cars and replace them with a device, invisible to passersby and cameras, that transmits an encrypted code unique to each car. The authorities would have to install receivers in a variety of locations to catch the device's signal. Of course, that device could be hacked, just as fake license plates can be affixed to a car, and private companies could build their own sensors for detecting the signal. There are no perfect answers here.

Cameras aren't the only sensor that can pick up the unique characteristics of a person, place, or thing. The ambient noise captured by a microphone, including the one in your mobile phone, can capture enough data to discern the vehicle you're traveling in based on the vibrations of the engine, the rattles of the body, and the squeal and squawk of the tires.[47]

If audio analysis software is smart enough to distinguish your car from others, it's obviously smart enough to know if you're sitting or walking, regardless of whether you have your GPS turned on. If you've given a voice-to-text app, such as Apple's Siri or Microsoft's Cortana, access to your phone's mic, the app could use ambient sounds to characterize your context.

The big data refineries are also producing sensors for the home. The Amazon Echo propped up in my living room is always in stand-by mode, its seven microphones constantly listening. The user manual says that only after hearing the hotword "Alexa" does the device come to life, at which point it starts recording everything I say—responding to my queries or commands with information culled from the web, putting items I request in my Amazon shopping cart as a "to-buy" list. Similarly, Microsoft's Kinect system for Xbox gaming consoles and Samsung's smart TVs also recognize voice commands, including a request to be turned "on" from standby mode.[48] Google's Nest Cam includes a microphone and will alert you if there's an unusual sound in your home—say, "the voice of an intruder"[49]—while you're away.

Do these devices analyze everything you say, even when you aren't prompting them? It's safe to say that at least some of them do—and in fact, a developer at one of these companies has privately acknowledged it.[50] His company uses the data to improve its voice recognition software, especially when background noises are cloaking speech. In the quiet surroundings of your home, audio analysis could be used to construct distinct voiceprints for everyone in your household, indicating the pattern (and volume!) of family interactions. Google must learn the voices of regular household members in order to pick out the sound of a person who doesn't belong in your home. If this is the case, why aren't companies more transparent about the fact that they're collecting these data to improve the performance of the system? After all, Google isn't a space heater or baby monitor manufacturer; it's a data refinery.

If companies were more open about these audio data, you could ask to get more benefit from them. Personally, I'd like to have access to any and all recordings of my voice—they'd be a fantastic tool for tracking down information that I can't quite remember or discovering interesting patterns in my utterances that I wasn't aware of. To build better speech recognition systems, data refineries must create an index of sounds and words. That index could help me find anything I've said about a pet if I discover the pet is unwell and want to give the vet some extra context about the animal's behavior over the past week.

Outside the home, the "soundscape" communicates our physical context, as well. A blaring siren or car horn sounds much different if you're standing on the sidewalk, sitting in a nearby car, or gazing out on a street from inside a room. The clatter of dishes in a restaurant is unmistakable. So is the shrill ring of a referee's whistle, the crash of waves, and the echo of a tiled bathroom. If you're traveling by train around Tokyo, your location can be identified by the distinct tune played at each station.[51] When you are making a phone call, it's almost impossible to remove such distinct audio clues to your context.

Sensor data also contribute to the construction of the social graph. Consider two people who have agreed to a secret rendezvous. They realize an analysis of phone geolocation data could potentially reveal that they were in the same place at the same time on the day in question, so they agree to turn off their phones a few blocks before they reach the spot, and slip them into a "privacy case." When the unwelcome day of reckoning comes and their phone records are subpoenaed, is the fact that both phones became untraceable for the same few hours a signal that the two people were together? Perhaps so. Even more so if the phones were moving toward what seems to be a common destination.

At the same time, the social graph can help uncover a person's location. A German fugitive from the law wisely ditched his mobile phone and SIM card when he went on the lam in Canada. But though he had stopped using his old SIM card and phone number, he didn't want to abruptly stop calling all of the people he usually called. Any person's calling graph is distinct enough that Interpol could look for a new phone number popping up with a pattern of calls similar to the fugitive's previous one. After about a dozen calls, Interpol flagged the number as a potential match, located the new phone, and captured him.

Refineries that analyze sensor data will increasingly need to balance the benefits to the majority of users against the potential harm to people who may not even be aware that their movements are being inferred. Jetpac, which was founded in 2011 and acquired by Google in 2014, identified and categorized the content of photos to build a business directory searchable by characteristic. The company's software was trained on publicly posted Instagram photos—150 million of them[52]—from 6,000 cities around the world, many of them geotagged, hashtagged, or captioned.[53] If the photos taken at a place included a lot of mouths wearing lipstick, the app would say the spot was "dressy."[54] That information could help people decide if a place was a good match for them.

Jetpac decided it could create a list of the world's "top hipster bars" using its object recognition software. The company's data scientists looked at the ratio of mustaches in photos, thinking this could serve as a proxy for the number of hipsters hanging out in a place. The cities with the biggest hipster populations all appeared to be in Turkey. How could that be? Jetpac's data scientists realized that men in Turkey were much more likely to sport mustaches than men in the United States. They had to "normalize" the data to local conventions, creating different baselines for different geographic regions. This is a good example of the essential feedback loop between computers and humans in data analysis.

Other categories discovered through Jetpac's analysis of Instagram photos threw up thornier issues. For instance, Jetpac found it could actually create a listing of gay bars in Tehran based purely on the photos.[55] That might be a great service for an Iranian who didn't want to risk coming out to the wrong person by asking either friends or strangers, but the consequences could have been terrible for the gay community if the list got into the hands of the mullahs.[56] Yet, if Jetpac was able to develop this refining capability, what's to stop a government from doing so?

At MIT, Professor William T. Freeman and his colleagues have developed algorithms to measure a person's pulse, including the distribution of blood flow to exposed parts of the body, by detecting very small pixel-by-pixel variations in the tint of the skin. When the MIT group demonstrated its results, it was inundated with requests for the code, which they posted on the web for anyone to use for noncommercial purposes. One request came from a poker player who wanted to detect when an opponent's heart was racing, in order to make more informed bets about the person's bluffing.[57]

Indeed, cardiologists have found that the peaks and troughs of a person's heartbeat—called the "PQRST pattern"—are just as unique as a fingerprint or iris scan, and much harder to fake. MasterCard, the Royal Bank of Canada, and Halifax Bank in the United Kingdom have tested an electrocardiogram (ECG) bracelet as a tool for verifying identity at ATMs and during online banking and contactless payment transactions.[58] The bracelet is produced by the Toronto-based company Bionym and is based on patents for measuring, registering, and verifying heart rhythms.[59]

The data collected from the trillions of sensors on the planet are beyond our control. Pete Warden, Jetpac's co-founder and chief technology officer, has spoken eloquently about how image recognition software will involve a fundamental shift in the balance between privacy and security, as well as between privacy and free speech.[60] On the one hand, companies are searching for more secure ways to protect sensitive data, and increasingly they are asking people to use biometric data as a unique key in order to have access to particular services or customer protections.

On the other hand, much of our social data are created collaboratively, through our shared interests, activities, and relationships. Controlling the collection of data at the source to protect one person's privacy would necessitate something like a police state, with many others' personal expression miserably constrained.

Further, the three main options for protecting ourselves from the unwanted use of sensor data are imperfect. Cryptographic protections, where data can be accessed only by those with an electronic key, aren't suitable for much of the data being shared, such as the photos posted to Instagram. Social norms, which tell us when it's appropriate to share and use data, aren't going to protect us from bad actors. That leaves us with the protections afforded by regulations and laws. As seen in the twenty-year story of Louis Brandeis's invention of the right to privacy, the law reacts slowly to dynamic technological innovation. At the same time, the legal system's relative stability is an advantage when the goal is defining broad sets of data—such as people's race, sex, sexual orientation, and condition of disability—whose use is considered discriminatory and unacceptable. I expect societies will continue to add to such lists as we explore the uses of social data.

However, expanding that list is not enough. We need tools for detecting when discrimination might have been based on the use of social data. Every query to a database is a datum, which the refineries collect and analyze to improve their products and services; those data can be used to protect us, too. And this will be all the more important as algorithms are used to infer not merely our physical presence but our state of mind.

Baring Your Heart

Paul Ekman, professor emeritus of psychology at the University of California–San Francisco, has made it his life's work to measure the physiological effects of six basic emotions: anger, sadness, fear, contempt, surprise, and happiness. He began by studying the responses of people in five very different places—Argentina, Brazil, Chile, Japan, and the United States—to a variety of photographs of emotional situations. He expected that cultural context would color people's responses, but he was wrong. In experiment after experiment, he observed the same, distinct facial expressions to the photos: the furrow between the eyebrows associated with anger; the downward angle of the eyebrows and of the corners of the lips that characterizes sadness; the wrinkled nose of disgust; the creases at the corners of the eyes that accompany a genuine smile. (The polite but fake version—also called the "Pan Am smile," for its ubiquity among flight attendants—involves only the mouth.) In 1978, Ekman and his colleague Wallace V. Friesen distilled all of the observed expressions into the Facial Action Coding System (FACS).[61] Several machine-learning researchers have built software for facial recognition based on the FACS catalog.[62]

Ekman hypothesized that emotions are universal because they're an honest signal to others of our state of mind and relationship.[63] As he continued his fieldwork and experiments, he noticed other physiological indicators associated with each basic emotion, such as heart rate, breathing rate, blood flow, and overall muscle tension. Sometimes people experience multiple emotions in quick succession, so quick that it is difficult to catch the flash of the emotion unless you are paying special attention. These "microexpressions" often signal an emotion that a person wants to keep hidden from others or that the person may not yet be conscious of.[64] Because these expressions are so fleeting—appearing for one-fifth of a second or less—they are more likely to be detected by reviewing video than by the untrained eye.

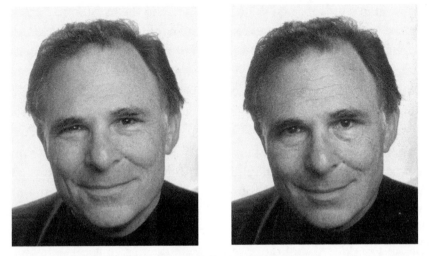

A genuine smile (left) compared to a polite one (right): When someone is truly delighted, the muscles around the eyes as well as the mouth are engaged, causing creases in the skin. Credit: Paul Ekman, PhD/Paul Ekman Group, LLC.

Ekman has served as an adviser to a San Diego company called Emotient, which has developed software to identify sentiments from camera feeds in real time. One of Emotient's first commercial applications, released back in 2007, was a "smile detector," available on Sony digital cameras, that takes a picture of a person in the frame as soon as the face appears to be smiling. Emotient's algorithms evolved rapidly. A single high-resolution camera could monitor an area with about four hundred people—say, in a lecture hall or a shopping mall—and simultaneously "read" emotional microexpressions as they play out on all their faces.[65] The company is also working on adapting its software for use in hospitals to detect pain on child patients' faces. In fact, studies indicate that computers do a *better* job than humans in focusing on the honest signals of physical distress.[66] An early Emotient–Google Glass app was marketed to retail managers as a tool for gauging staff morale or learning how emotions influence what customers buy—and from whom.[67] Emotient was acquired by Apple in January 2016.[68]

London-based Realeyes also draws upon Ekman's research to assess facial expressions in response to video ads. The screen may be a person's computer or one installed in a "public" space, as was the case for a campaign entitled "Stage Fright" for electronics manufacturer LG. The context was a men's toilet, which had LG monitors installed above the urinals. As the man stepped up, the ad on the screen was ripped away by a woman who appeared to be able to see into the bathroom. Realeyes cameras watched the men's faces shift from confusion and fear to delight. The analysis even showed that a portion of the men displayed disgust at the start and end of the video.[69] A rival company, Affectiva, was spun out of MIT Media Lab's Affective Computing Group's research to create an emotional alert system for people with autism who have difficulty reading others' facial expressions.[70] Commercial clients have asked Affectiva to measure the emotional response to ads; pollsters have used it to measure the response to political candidates during televised debates.[71]

Facial expressions are far from the only source of data about human emotions that is being collected and analyzed. The human voice also discloses emotions through pitch, volume (intensity), voice quality, duration, and speed.[72] To build one of the main catalogs of vocal expressions of emotion, researchers employed one hundred actors from five very different English-speaking countries—Australia, Kenya, India, Singapore, and the United States. The actors were asked to perform simple texts—things like dates and numbers—with various emotions in mind.[73]

Many researchers argue that such "posed" vocal expressions can't successfully train a machine-learning system to deal with actual human conversation in real time. That's because actors are taught to overemphasize their expressions. In recent studies, the huge archives of customer call centers have been used to build emotion libraries. The training data are created by the call centers, by getting their representatives to note a customer's emotional state during a call and then adding the label to the audio recording. Speech coded as irritated, resigned, emotionally heightened, or neutral—even for utterances as brief as "ah," "oh," "yeah," and "okay"[74]—has been used to train voice recognition systems. In some cases, voice signals are combined with data from a user satisfaction survey as a way to corroborate the detected emotion.[75]

Call-center companies like LiveOps and Mattersight use voice-detection software to match representatives with customers. Does the customer have a strong regional accent? Then route his call to a home-based rep in that area, for a more personal, local touch. Does the customer sound frustrated as she responds to voice prompts in the call center's option menu? Then route her to a rep who has a high success rate in resolving issues with difficult problems and customers. If a customer's voice is rising in volume and pitch despite the rep's attempts to calm him down, the call can be flagged for escalation to a manager. LiveOps adds further context to this audio data by scanning social media and other sources for customer complaints.[76] Someone who establishes an instant rapport with a call-center rep may be more inclined to give the rep an easy time about a complaint—or be persuaded to purchase a product or service. Mattersight claims that it can provide even more personalized service by matching customers to reps based on personality type. The company analyzes communication records for what is being said and how it is being said in order to profile customers into types such as "outgoing, sarcastic, serious, or shy," and routes customer types to reps who are better at handling each type, increasing customer satisfaction.[77] The matches are made personality type by personality type rather than call by call, and many of the company's clients are businesses that regularly interact with customers—for example, healthcare providers, insurers, and phone companies.

Algorithms can also give voice to those who cannot speak for themselves. It's often said that parents learn to distinguish the emotional pleas communicated in their baby's crying, but for most, it's less than a science. And no wonder: parents have a very small sample size to learn from. This highlights one of the differences in how humans versus machines build models from data of interactions with the world. Sebastian Thrun, who worked on Google's self-driving cars and co-founded the education start-up Udacity, points out that human drivers learn how to drive better based on personal experience, while Google cars learn how to drive better from mistakes made by all of Google's cars. Humans mainly learn from their own mistakes and successes, augmented by the mistakes and successes of the people in their social network; they also learn from the advice of experts. In contrast, machines can learn directly not only from their own errors but also from those of every other machine in their network.[78]

At IBM, Dimitri Kanevsky and his colleagues have patented a system that learns from data collected from babies' brain, heart, and lung activity alongside audio recordings of their wails and whimpers. Sometimes a baby cries for attention, sometimes for solitude, and a data refinery could help parents better monitor their children's emotional state and make decisions based on it.[79]

In the future, our emotions may be detected from other, more subtle clues than a person's facial expressions and the tone and volume of a cry. Some activity trackers like the Fitbit, the Withings Pulse, and Garmin vívo series record a person's vital signs, including resting and active heart rate, which can be correlated with the onset or escalation of certain emotional states. Heart rate can be measured through an infrared sensor, such as the one on the back panel of the Apple Watch, through the increased blush of the skin when blood pulses through the body. Many hospitals use infrared cameras to monitor patient heart beats because doing so is more accurate than relying on a device attached to the body that might get jostled loose. The Xbox uses infrared to track a player's physical activity level and to classify the level of excitement or boredom in real time.[80] This information is used to serve up new game challenges calibrated to the player's mindset.[81]

Emotions are even more difficult to hide on the biochemical level. A blood test can identify the biochemicals related to fear, stress, and fatigue, but so too can a sweat test. With funding from the US Defense Department, GE has built a wireless sensor that can be applied to the skin like a Band-Aid that it calls the "Fearbit"; on the skin-facing side, nanostructures have been designed to attract specific biochemicals and to alert a computer when their levels rise.[82] Sensors that can "smell" chemical compounds in the air are small enough to be integrated into a mobile phone. Versions constructed from graphene are already sensitive enough to detect molecules at a scale of a few parts per billion. One early study suggests that stress might even be detected on a person's breath.[83]

Combining different emotion sensors into specific contexts will have life-transforming effects. For example, graduate students in the Affective Computing Group at MIT's Media Lab have proposed a system called "AutoEmotive" that embeds several readily available sensors in cars to improve the health and safety of driving. Steering wheels outfitted with sensors for palm sweat, heart rate, respiration, and hand grip would provide key biomarkers associated with stress. A microphone could monitor voice pitch and volume for any utterances and determine whether they reflect momentary alarm or increasing frustration. An inward-facing dashcam could provide highly granular data of emotional microexpressions. If a driver exhibited high stress levels, a refinery could suggest a less nerve-racking route or more calming music for the car stereo's playlist. A driver's emotional levels could be displayed to her through changes in the color of the dashboard backlighting, so that she is able to reach better decisions based on biofeedback about her emotional state. Similar to the optimized display of data devised by Eric Horvitz for NASA ground controllers, AutoEmotive was envisioned to help people better manage moments of high stress, when they are more vulnerable to "tunnel vision."[84]

As we begin to consider how analyses of emotions can be used during decision-making, it's worth noting that not all psychologists agree about what exactly happens in the body when you're in a particular emotional state.[85] The biggest point of contention involves the extent to which emotional experience is subjective. How much do the situation and your personal history affect emotional feedback? If you're registering several hallmarks of fear—accelerated breathing and heart rate, sweating, and increased blood sugar levels—are you *afraid?* You may be momentarily shocked, chronically anxious, slightly nervous, giddy with anticipation, suffering the paralyzing effects of a phobia—or exercising after an afternoon candy break.[86]

Paul Ekman also notes the peril of making "Othello's error" when interpreting emotions. In Shakespeare's play, Othello sees fear and anguish cascade across his wife Desdemona's face when he accuses her of loving Cassio and subsequently informs her that he has had Cassio killed. He takes Desdemona's emotions as proof of her guilt: obviously, Othello thinks, she fears she's been caught and mourns her dead lover. Ekman points out that Desdemona did express fear and anguish in the moment, but not necessarily for the reasons Othello presumed. Instead, she feared her husband's irrational jealousy and was saddened by her inability to prove her innocence—and thus, mourned her own impending death.[87] As Othello's sorry mistake demonstrates, detecting the physiological signals of a particular emotion is much easier than identifying what has triggered the emotional response. Whenever we use emotional data to guide decisions, the lesson of Othello's error applies—whether the interpretation is being done by a human or a machine.

Facial expressions, voice cues, and other physiological data are honest signals, and emotion recognition systems can detect patterns imperceptible to most of us, however hard we try. Having access in real time to refined data about emotions could improve our lives immensely—but it also carries risks. Would you want to know your emotional state before, during, and after you meet someone for a first date or a job interview? Detecting your emotional state in either of these situations could have a profound effect on what happens next. If you went to a job interview and the interviewer told you she was using an emotion-detecting app, how would it change your emotional response to the interview? Would it make you more anxious or more confident about your performance? It's normal to try to hide some of what you're feeling in this context, but that wouldn't be possible if your face was being scrutinized for microexpression "leaks."

Earlier I argued that recordings of interactions should be available to all of the parties involved. If your call is recorded for "quality assurance purposes," you should also have access to it. But as more of our interactions get analyzed for emotional content, it's not clear if simply having access to the *raw* recording is a fair balance. If a company uses voice data to infer your mood and handles your call differently based on its analysis, what information should you have access to? What if your experience of your emotions differs from the interpretation made by the algorithm?

Further, if we want to get refined data about emotional states that can improve how we interact with family, friends, and colleagues, we'll need to do more than attach a sensor to the wrist or put a camera on the face. We'll need to find ways to calibrate sensor data, perhaps by creating and sharing explicit reports of what we were feeling, and attaching specific and personal labels to the physiological measurements taken by machines. Which of our moods and emotions are we comfortable disclosing in order to get insights about our behavioral patterns that can help us in our decision-making?

Where Your Focus Is (Sometimes, Literally)

Not only can audio and video recordings be employed to compute your location and emotional state, but they can also be used to compute the focus of your attention with surprising precision. It is actually relatively easy to identify the general direction and duration of your gaze in real time using a standard video camera. When your head turns, face and object recognition systems can figure out what or who came into your new line of sight. Researchers at Lancaster University in the UK and the Max Planck Institute for Informatics in Germany built a system, also using a standard camera, that can track the gaze of people passing an advertising screen and personalize offers based on their attention.[88] Knowing what grabs an individual's attention is a powerful tool, since in many cases we are not consciously directing our gaze but unconsciously reacting to stimuli around us.

Cameras can also detect small shifts in attention. When Eric Horvitz and his colleagues investigated better ways to display information to NASA ground controllers, they were concerned with the issue of *cognitive load,* the amount of effort people expend while processing information and solving problems. According to research by Danny Kahneman and Jackson Beatty, the relative diameter of the pupils provides an indication of a person's cognitive load during a task. The pupil dilates when a person is absorbing new information, such as listening to a sequence of numbers, and constricts when a person is reporting back the information. And the harder the task, the larger the relative change.[89]

Many cognitive processes are revealed by tiny eye movements. When you focus "sharply" on something, your eyes actually need to move around, since only a very small area of the visual field, less than 1 percent of the retina, has a sufficiently high density of the cone receptors that distinguish details. Further, the brain has to work around a blind spot where the optical nerve leaves the retina. The resulting eye movements, which occur between five and one hundred times a second and across a few angular degrees, are called *saccades*. The direction, amplitude, and velocity of saccades—and their tinier counterparts, *microsaccades*—expose the fluctuations in our literal focus.[90] In addition, the duration of a fixation may be viewed as a proxy for the amount of time the brain is processing information about part of a scene. Fixations signal attention.

Since the eye can see only about five to seven letters at a time with 100 percent accuracy, the process of reading requires a series of saccades. When we read, we fixate on words familiar to us for much less time. "Regressive" saccades, where the eyes return back and forth to information already viewed and processed, indicate that a person is confused about the information she's taking in. One gaze-tracking app, developed by Kai Kunze at Osaka Prefecture University in Japan, rates a reader's level of concentration on a scale from distractedly skimming to utterly absorbed. Kunze wants future apps to spot words that a reader is stumbling over and automatically offer a definition in a pop-up.[91] An app could also assess whether a person is "interruptible" based on her level of absorption in a text.[92]

Microsaccades are so small—a movement of less than 1 degree—that they cannot be easily detected in real time by a human observer. However, several companies, including the Swedish Tobii Group, have developed dedicated eye-tracking devices and software that can catch and analyze them. These eye trackers typically work by projecting engineered patterns of infrared light from a light-emitting diode (LED) on the subject's eyes. Although infrared light is not visible to the human eye, an infrared camera can detect the reflections off the corneas, and thus infer the location and orientation of a person's eyes.

Tobii's eye-tracking glasses can be used in the "field"—for instance, to discover what draws people's attention when they browse the shelves of a store, or whether and how preverbal toddlers are gaining perceptual and cognitive skills. Tobii also has a system that attaches to a computer screen, no glasses required.[93] The technology has had to overcome several challenges. Other light sources, such as sunlight or incandescent bulbs, can pollute the signals to the infrared sensor. Changes in lighting conditions, as well as sensory or emotional distractions, can affect pupil dilation, making it more difficult both to follow a person's gaze and to measure her attention.

For an eye tracker to accurately identify the person's gaze at the level of fixations and microsaccades, it must be calibrated. In an experiment or a work setting, users may be asked to go through a calibration exercise. But clever researchers have created methods for calibrating the device without the user realizing it—for instance, by displaying images on the screen that are designed to draw attention.

Tobii has explored methods for correlating eye-tracking data with other physiological clues of a person's cognition. These include heart rate, respiration rate, electrodermal response (the degree to which the skin conducts electricity), and EEGs (electroencephalograms measuring neural activity), all of which change when a person reacts to a stimulus—and strongly predict heightened engagement and interest. By combining and analyzing multiple streams of physiological sensor data, eye trackers can infer what in a person's view elicited an emotional response.

Refining eye-tracking data has great promise for improving individual learning and performance. Several studies suggest that novices can be trained to follow the same eye movement patterns that experts demonstrate in response to challenging situations. In one, the eye movements of students learning computer code via a computerized tutoring system were tracked as they reviewed a problem set. The beginning students tended to look at a small portion of each problem, going over the same material again and again as they tried to work out a solution, while the advanced students scanned a much greater amount of information as they devised their code. The scientists argued that showing the experts' gaze patterns to beginners would speed the learning process; the data could also be used to highlight important information that the beginner was overlooking.[94]

Similar eye-tracking analyses have been used to teach novice radiograph readers, the medical professionals who pore over X-rays to detect nodules and tumors.[95] The novices learned from the gaze patterns of both experienced readers and fellow novices, as novice readers don't tend

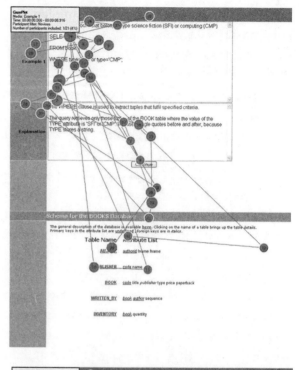

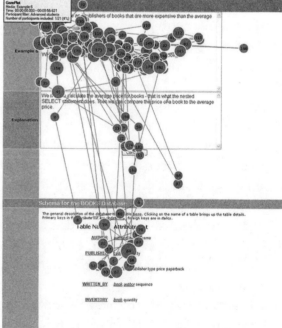

The gaze patterns observed when beginning and advanced database-programming students were given a coding problem to solve. Reprinted from "Eye Tracking and Studying Examples: How Novices and Advanced Learners Study SQL Examples" by Amir Shareghi Najar, Antonija Mitrovic, and Kourosh Neshatian, Journal of Computing and Information Technology 23, no. 2 (2015).

to uniformly miss the identical features on an X-ray. Such eye-tracking data can also be refined. By combining the gaze patterns with computer-extracted data from radiograph images, a machine-learning system was able to predict many human errors.[96] Ultimately, eye-tracking systems can help doctors make better diagnostic decisions.

Rudimentary eye tracking can be accomplished using the cameras built into many mobile phones and computers. Some smartphones are shipped with software that gauges where exactly on the screen a user is looking, with the option of having the phone automatically scroll down once he has reached the end of the displayed text. As gaze control systems for devices become more precise over the next few years, we will experience a significant shift in how we interact with machines akin to the changes that came with the invention of the mouse, the touchscreen, and voice interfaces. In 2015, Apple was granted a patent for using cameras and infrared sensors to measure when the eyes are blinking, and when and for how long they are moving.[97] These data can be used to counteract the Troxler effect, whereby fixating on an object, such as a cursor, for a relatively long time causes the brain to lose "sight" of it.

As we have seen, such data also give Apple and other refineries adopting gaze control systems access to a trove of information about a user's attention, far beyond what's on the screen. For example, because a number of neurological diseases and disorders—including Alzheimer's, autism, dyslexia, schizophrenia, and multiple sclerosis—affect eye movements, scientists are investigating the use of eye tracking in diagnosis and patient monitoring.[98]

Of course, eye trackers can also glean what isn't getting adequate attention. As a person spends more time on a repetitive task that requires ongoing attention, her eyes frequently drift from the central point of focus. Usually, this drift is the direct result of physical or mental fatigue.[99] Researchers are investigating the distinct eye movement patterns correlated with the moment just *before* a person "zones out," with the goal of devising eye-tracking systems that efficiently draw users' attention long before they are consciously aware of the risk of missing important information.[100] How often might that be the case? Harvard professor of psychology Daniel Gilbert created a smartphone app to sample attentiveness to real-world events and found that people reported being zoned out about 20 to 40 percent of the time.[101]

Again, such applications could transform education, work, and other fields by allowing organizations to observe and analyze focus at a granular level. Eye trackers might be utilized to pull individuals off assignments as soon as their attention begins to fade, or they could be used to evaluate how much compensation an employee receives for work tasks requiring complete focus. But this isn't entirely some nightmare scenario where Big Brother is watching every eye move. Eye tracking could improve performance of critical jobs where fatigue can have huge real-world costs, such as long-haul truck drivers and heavy-machinery operators.[102] Further, Gilbert found that it wasn't only task performance and memory recall that suffered when people zoned out; the majority of subjects also reported being unhappy when they realized their mind had wandered, even if their thoughts had drifted toward a pleasant distraction.[103] Being able to understand the conditions that lead to mind-wandering, or getting an alert when it appears that your focus has shifted, would be a great tool for increasing job satisfaction and overall happiness. Individuals can benefit from measurements of eye movement and attention, if they are given access to refined data that helps improve their decisions rather than controlling their activities.

This is especially true when sensors are employed to collect data about attention in arenas where individuals interact with one another. For the past decade, Alex "Sandy" Pentland's lab at MIT has been conducting experiments with "sociometric badges." The badges contain an accelerometer, to measure when and how fast a person is moving, an infrared LED, and an infrared sensor, to detect the light emitted from the LEDs in nearby badges, in order to infer whom the person is facing. They also use Bluetooth to capture proximity to other badges. By analyzing signals taken from the badges, Sandy and his group can construct a graph of interactions, such as those between employees in a workplace, mapping information about where they meet, who they meet, and for how long. The sociometric badges also record details about who sits next to whom in meetings, who garners the most attention in a group, and who nods their head in agreement when particular people are talking. Posture is measured, both in meetings and in solo work, since it can indicate engagement as well as fatigue.

In addition, the badges pick up characteristics of speech through voice data, such as tone, pitch, volume, speed, percentage of time spent speaking versus listening, and patterns of turn-taking and interrupting. Sandy says that in order to get more people to participate, the content of the conversations is not recorded; he also argues that a full audio recording is not necessary to identify meaningful patterns of interaction.

The focus is not on what people are saying but on how they're saying it. For instance, people tend to copy the conversational tone of the person they're speaking to if they want to fit in, bond, or avoid conflict, an often unconscious tactic called *mimicry*. A person's *influence* can be seen in how often others mold their speaking patterns to match him. Those who speak with *fluidity*—rarely interjecting their speech with ums, ahs, and pauses, or getting interrupted by others as they talk—tend to have a reputation as an expert. And the voice also expresses engagement and excitement, as speech speeds up and rises, a factor called *activity*.

Together, these sociometric data provide hints as to team cohesion and an individual's standing in the organizational hierarchy, regardless of what's printed on the person's business card.[104] Sandy believes that the signals captured by these sensors are far more honest than self-reports or outside observation.

In a study conducted for Bank of America, Ben Waber, a former PhD student of Sandy's who is co-founder and president of the consulting firm Sociometric Solutions,[105] investigated why some customer call-center teams were performing much better than predicted on measures such as staff tenure, experience, and training. The sociometric badge data revealed that the company's best teams frequently gathered informally and exhibited lower stress levels. Based on these findings, the researchers proposed an A/B test, scheduling some of the call center's teams to have simultaneous breaks and thus more opportunity for informal interaction. The performance of the teams encouraged to spend more time together went up about 25 percent.[106]

We've considered how numerous sensors are able to capture our feelings and our focus, but thus far, none have truly managed to decipher our thoughts. There are, however, sensors capable of observing some of what's happening inside the brain as a person makes a decision: functional magnetic resonance imaging (fMRI) scanners. Using fMRI technology, neuroscientists can observe blood flows and oxygenation to understand which parts of the brain are activated in response to sensory inputs at a temporal resolution of about one second and a spatial resolution of about one millimeter. When we're confronted with information that challenges strongly held beliefs, the parts of the brain that normally get fired up for "cold reasoning" tasks—nonemotional tasks such as an arithmetic problem—are inactive.[107] Further, fMRI scans allow scientists to see what parts of the brain are activated when a person is asked to make an assessment or decision—and in many situations, they have found that the decision-making process begins much earlier than previously anticipated.[108]

The strong magnetic fields needed for an fMRI scan are produced by superconducting magnets, and to become superconducting, the system must be cooled down close to absolute zero. As a result, there's no way an fMRI scanner will ever be installed on a mobile phone. However, researchers are exploring other ways to gain a glimpse of the neural activity in the brain. One experimental option involves the use of wireless, miniaturized near-infrared imaging (NIR) sensors to measure cortical blood flow. Although NIR devices measure blood flow differently than fMRI and the readings are not very detailed, NIR is far more portable. It may prove tempting to try to correlate fMRI scanner measurements to NIR readings that can be taken "in the wild."[109] Further technical innovations will provide additional windows into the inner workings of the brain.

As we saw with Othello's error, it's a huge leap from describing a person's physiological state to inferring what exactly triggered it in the complex environment of the real world. If scientists are able to calibrate phenomena recorded in the lab with phenomena recorded in the field, we as a society have to decide the guidelines for using the data created from new emitting and sensing technologies—from radio frequency identification (RFID) chips embedded under a person's skin[110] to pocket-sized nanopore units capable of sequencing an organism's DNA in real time[111] to a panoply of sensors we can't yet imagine.

Witness for the People

I've been telling people to change their behavior in the present, because they don't know how that recording will be analyzed in the future.[112]

BRAD TEMPLETON

A couple years ago, Dutch student Zilla van den Born set out on a very interesting holiday. For a school project, she told her family and friends that she was backpacking through Southeast Asia, then spent the next five weeks sharing tales of a pretend adventure.[113] She staged and photoshopped a series of pictures to post on Facebook: here she's snorkeling (in her apartment building's pool), there she's sampling the native cuisine (at a nearby restaurant), now she's paying her respects at a Buddhist temple (in her hometown of Amsterdam). She made sure to upload photos and make comments in the middle of the night, when it was daytime on the other side of the world. She went so far as to string Christmas lights around her curtained bedroom during Skype video-calls with her parents. Her family didn't suspect her deceit until she "returned home" and revealed her experiment to them. "I did this to show people that we filter and manipulate what we show on social media," van den Born explained. "My goal was to prove how common and easy it is for people to distort reality. Everyone knows that pictures of models are manipulated, but we often overlook the fact that we manipulate reality also in our own lives."[114]

While people can and do filter and manipulate the sensor data they share online, it's quite costly to create a fool-proof alternate existence, as van den Born's experiment shows. She was forced to spend all her time staging fake photos and researching topics for her video chats in order to keep her friends and family fooled. In addition, she had to hole up in her apartment for most of the five weeks. When she went outside—for instance, to visit the temple for her photo shoot—she took great pains to cloak her identity. She had no choice. Otherwise, she couldn't be assured neither her friends nor Facebook's (or another refinery's) photo recognition software didn't detect her true location. Most people don't have the time or energy for that sort of subterfuge.

The bar for falsifying sensor data is only going to get higher. In the future, an emotion recognition algorithm might observe that all of van den Born's vacation photos were showing that polite but fake Pan Am smile, leading her loved ones to ask if she is actually enjoying herself. And it's not that a person's friends and family will start from the assumption that they're being lied to. More and more data from many different sources are combined to automatically create information that will influence not only our interactions with our friends, but also with strangers. These honest signals about who, where, and how we are are becoming a significant part of our social data.

I began this chapter with the example of Jeff Gray, who was arrested after videotaping Orlando police. Many police departments maintain a private database[115] of dashcam and bodycam video recordings that are made available to the public only after a tortuous legal process. When the Los Angeles Police Department deployed 7,000 body-mounted cameras among its force in the summer of 2015,[116] it announced that a recording would be shared with the public only if a lawsuit cites the video as evidence. But that wasn't the worst asymmetry of the system. The bodycams did not automatically record everything. The decision to record—or not record—was left up to the officer. Further, a very small group of people—the department's very own officers—were given unbridled access to the database. They could pull up and review any footage collected by bodycams before writing incident reports, including instances in which their conduct was subject to an investigation.[117] This gives them the power to describe events in a way that would shield them from disciplinary action, by taking advantage of "blind spots" in the video. Why is there one rule for the police and another for the citizens they're pledged to serve?

The ACLU has tried to battle this blatant imbalance of power by providing a cloud platform that allows individuals to automatically upload their own recordings in real time in case they might be useful in the future. One of the apps gives users the option of alerting others in the area that an incident is being recorded, in case they are in a position to collect another point of view.[118]

Some localities, such as the Seattle Police Department, are embracing full transparency. Twelve officers in the department were outfitted with bodycams as part of a pilot program in December 2014. "We were talking about the video and what to do with it, and someone said, 'What do people do with police videos?,'" the department's chief operating officer told the *New York Times*.[119] Instead of dumping the videos into a private database, the department decided to upload them to YouTube.[120] In order to keep on the right side of current laws, the footage had to be somewhat redacted: an algorithm was developed to blur people's faces and the audio tracks were removed.[121]

Despite these redactions, the bodycam videos provided unprecedented access to data about the police department's conduct. If an entrepreneurial data detective wanted to, she could analyze the videos to uncover patterns in the city's policing, perhaps looking at how officers approach suspects, witnesses, and other members of the public. The data could be used to propose A/B tests to the police department to determine whether changes in training or procedures might improve the interactions between the police and community. Residents would have a powerful tool for improving their community.

Such applications don't protect us from the possibility that the data will be used against us, unfortunately. We cannot stop every click, view, connection, conversation, step, glance, wheeze, and word from being collected. But we can demand a set of rights with respect to our social data that ensures the fullest potential of transparency and agency.

5

SEEING THE CONTROLS

Transparency for the People
What Can You Demand to See About Your Data?

Not everything that can be counted counts, and not everything that counts can be counted.[1]

WILLIAM BRUCE CAMERON

We have seen the wide range of data that we now create and share on a daily basis, and considered the impact the outputs of data refineries have on our lives. We are not going to stop creating data; the vast majority of us are not going to stop sharing data either. For this reason, efforts to ensure that data are *for* the people must focus not on trying to control our data at their initial point of creation, or source, but on seeing, and exerting influence over, the controls of the data refineries.

We've also considered opportunities for increasing transparency and agency with respect to our data, taking into account that most of us will never be fluent enough in programming languages to review and decipher what happens to data inside the refineries. There are some simple ways to empower people, from giving customers access to their call-center recordings to letting users compare the "top news" version of their Facebook News Feed against the full stream of posts and comments from our friends.

Even with such tools in place, we will not be able to review every bit of raw data that is collected and analyzed without additional assistance, given how much data there is. We have to depend on the refineries to help us interpret and understand the implications of our data.

With all the data available about your characteristics, connections, and context, the refineries can make increasingly accurate predictions about what you want, whether or not you yourself know what you want. No matter how good the machines' recommendations become, we need to maintain the freedom to respond to them however we like, including to reject or shape them. This requires tools for understanding how the refineries arrive at their recommendations as well as tools to adjust some of the refineries' default settings to values we prefer.

Some refineries will be more focused on developing products and services for individuals sharing their data; others, on developing products and services for companies and organizations that want to identify and understand those individuals and their purchasing propensity (because this is where the money can be made). Your power lies in choosing to use those refineries which offer tools that increase transparency and agency for users—including tools that allow you to evaluate how much benefit you get from a refinery in exchange for the data you share with it.

We are only beginning to comprehend how social data might be used for or against us. For this reason, I believe it's more important for us now to define a set of standards to help us evaluate refineries rather than suggest a specific toolset to be implemented by them. The following six rights provide a framework for this.

Two rights to increase refineries' transparency:
1. The right to access your data
2. The right to inspect data refineries, *comprising*
   a. The right to see a data safety audit
   b. The right to see a privacy efficiency rating
   c. The right to see a "return-on-data" score

Four rights to increase users' agency:
3. The right to amend data
4. The right to blur your data
5. The right to experiment with the refineries
6. The right to port your data

These rights will give us the means to "read" data and the refineries' characteristics, and then to "write" our own instructions for interacting with the refineries.[2] As Austrian-British philosopher Ludwig Wittgenstein said, "The limits of my language mean the limits of my world."[3] If we don't have the concept for something, we simply don't *see* it. In our case, to understand the refineries and to guide our interactions with them, we must learn a new language.[4] If we do not have tools for evaluating the refineries' analyses and recommendations, we will be hard-pressed to imagine how our data could be interpreted or employed differently. Merely getting raw access to your social data is not empowering. Instead, it is empowering to see how you might use these data.

Most important, the transparency and agency rights will need to be translated into actionable tools. When you exercise your rights and use these tools, you will necessarily create more data, which can and should be analyzed by the refineries since this feedback is important for the refineries to improve their products. Every interaction with a refinery is a new data point.

We'll consider agency rights in the next chapter. But for now, let's drill down into the two types of transparency that we need to demand: the right to access your data and the right to inspect data refineries. The first right involves letting you see and interpret what data is collected by and about you. The second right involves making the refineries and their operations more transparent and letting us see characterizations of how they generally handle and use data.

The Right to Access Your Data

Access is the foundation of any data right, whether the right is focused on transparency or on agency. And as we saw in the Introduction, having access to data collected about you is already standard in a number of countries, including the United States and members of the European Union. However, the way we currently think about "access to data" is woefully inadequate. It doesn't take into account the qualitatively new aspect of social data, wherein data about you are entangled with data about others.

Consider a category of data that you already have access to: your financial transaction data and credit history. Some governments have given individuals the right to access these data and correct mistakes, since the data are used to determine people's access to lines of credit. In the United States and the United Kingdom, the big consumer credit bureaus, which collect and analyze data about individuals' debt and bill-paying behavior, are required to provide you with a copy of your credit report once a year, upon your request. You are encouraged to check the facts and notify the bureau of anything that is incorrect—for example, if you spot a cluster of applications for credit using your name and address that you didn't actually make, which would be a sign of attempted identity theft. Your financial behavior and situation are summarized as a credit score based on your history of paying bills on time or late; your history of paying off short-term debts quickly or accumulating high or revolving balances; the age of your credit accounts; the number of times you have applied for new credit; and the mix of credit cards, loans, and mortgages in your name. The bureaus show you which activities in the past year have positively or negatively affected your score, and specify how heavily they weigh each category in their descriptive analysis. You might learn that 30 percent of your credit score depends on paying on time, while only 10 percent depends on how your debt is distributed across credit cards versus other, longer-term loans. If you receive a report that indicates you are an "above average risk" for credit because you tend to pay your bills late, you can try to improve your score by paying your bills on time or early.

You probably think of your credit score as a single number: your FICO score. But your credit score can differ from one bureau to another, because each bureau collects its own data about you. The *New York Times* counted at least forty-nine variations of the FICO score, depending not just on which bureau collects the data and how the data are collected but also the type of credit you're applying for.[5] Further, according to *Fortune* magazine, nobody has "one" credit score, even at a single bureau, because "each institution"—meaning each bank considering whether to issue you a new credit card, loan, or mortgage—"can tinker with the parameters."[6] Such one-way mirrors limit your ability to see these data the way those who are making decisions about you get to see it.

True transparency would allow you to see how different creditors can and do play with the weights assigned to these categories of credit data—that is, to see how the institution views your credit history. With that type of access to refined data about you in place, you would be able to consider which banks to contact first about a loan application.

The right to access your data should include the ability to see your data in context. Two of the most powerful contexts are your past and your peers. Meaning emerges from seeing the difference between how you were versus how you are, and how you are versus how others are. Access to raw data alone, without any tools for analysis, comparison, and interpretation, is meaningless.

Think about how you might benefit from being able to compare how you walk today versus how you walked in the past: Gait recognition software can track you as you walk across a corporate campus. The same software could detect changes over time in how you walk that could be an early symptom of chronic back pain or a serious muscular dystrophy—so early in the process that you might not yet be aware of a potential medical problem. I know I'd want to be able to get an early warning like that.

You also need to be able to see data about you in comparison to others in order to be able to get value out of it. But how much discretion should you get in choosing whose data you can use as a benchmark? Should you be able to compare data about yourself to data for other patients in the same medical practice, the customers of your bank branch, or the employees in your department? If you want to compare yourself to others in a relatively small group—say, a dozen people at your workplace—you may be able to infer information about the other individuals based on the distribution, and others may be able to infer information about you based on it as well.

In fact, much of the data about you is entangled with data about others: "your data" is not necessarily yours alone. Even superficially straightforward data about you—such as the profile produced by data brokerage Acxiom—is entangled with others. Recall that the unit of analysis of Acxiom's profiles is the household, not the individual. Advertisers traditionally thought in terms of the household unit because that's the level of data that was available. They explained this choice by pointing out that many purchasing decisions were made at that level. However, not everyone in a household wants the other occupants to see ads that might reveal sensitive information about them—like that secretly pregnant teenager whose father saw that she had received coupons for baby clothes and cribs and complained to his local Target about its misguided marketing.[7]

Social data are even more intertwined than the address shared by members of a household. You comment on a friend's Facebook post, investing time and energy creating and sharing data, revealing your personal passions and preferences. But then, for whatever reason, the author of the original post changes his mind and decides to delete it. What should happen to your comment? Should a response to data attached to someone else be under the control of that person? You should be able to continue to access any data you've created jointly, and be able to see it in its original context. That doesn't mean, however, that you can *use* other people's contributions without their permission.

A significant portion of our lives is experienced, communicated, and even constructed digitally, and as we interact with others and the world, we literally share in data's creation. What rules should govern access to your digital "legacy"? This isn't an idle question: between 1 million and 10 million Facebook users died in the past year,[8] and there's been a great deal of debate—and confusion—about who gets to have control of accounts after a person dies.[9] Some accounts have actually been deleted at the request of one close family member. When that happens, all the co-created data on the account—the manually tagged photos and the conversations—are lost, without any respect for the many people who shared ownership in them.

In 2015 Facebook began to offer users the option of naming a "legacy contact" who, like the executor of a person's estate, is granted very limited ability to review and change the deceased's account. She can select a different profile photo, write a special post pinned to the top of the Timeline, and accept new friend requests from friends and family.[10] Access to data beyond that is not granted, and for good reason: access is about being able to use data, and there really isn't much use to anyone else in receiving recommendations and rankings that have been personalized for the dearly departed. And if many new data were to be created on the account, it would cease to be a memorial and instead reflect the character and characteristics of the account "manager."

Defining "your data" gets even trickier when you consider data collected by sensors. As a society, we have come to the conclusion that a person taking a photo in a public space doesn't have to ask for permission from the people who walk into his camera's frame. The photographer might not know the identity of everyone in the picture, but Facebook's DeepFace facial recognition system often does. DeepFace uses Facebook's vast library of photos tagged by users and their friends to identify the people. Facebook's algorithms are sophisticated enough to automatically suggest tags for the faces in newly uploaded photos—though it reveals these "computed tags" only to those users who are friends with the person tagged.

A few governments have argued that these tag suggestions are a breach of privacy. Indeed, after the European Union raised objections to auto-tagging images, Facebook voluntarily turned off the service in European countries.[11] But why are human-suggested tags allowed while machine-suggested tags are verboten? Either can be removed from search results by the person who has been identified. And human tags are just as likely to help or harm a person as computed ones.

Does Facebook try to compute tags to identify every single face in uploaded photos, regardless of who posts them? It must. It cannot possibly pre-filter which photos should be kept out of the algorithms before the faces have been recognized. This creates a conundrum about what to do when people fear that tags might be used against them. A government could ban companies from ever computing tags, but that sort of wholesale regulation would reduce the benefit people get from data they share with the refineries. A better option is to allow people to learn about the risks and rewards of computed tags by *showing* the tags to them.

Let's say someone you don't know has posted a photo on Facebook of an event you attended. There you are in the photo with a bunch of people. Facial recognition software identifies that one of the faces might be you and suggests the corresponding tag to your Facebook friends viewing the photo. Yet, if no one accepts the computed tag, you might never know about the photo.

If you ask Facebook for all the images you are tagged in, it should show you the photos regardless of whether a human or computer created the tag, and whether the poster has given you permission to see the image or not. Because computed tags are probabilistic, you will also see images in which Facebook identified you but with a low likelihood. If you want to see every image you might possibly be in, you might have to sort through a lot of images. To make it more manageable, you need to be able to rank the images by likelihood and to vary the minimum likelihood that you are the person tagged. Such tools for discovery are especially important because multiple photos, videos, and other data could be stitched together to infer your movements through space and time, much like Vigilant Solutions can track a car's journey over the course of a day from a series of license plate spottings. The right to access your data needs to include access to any content a refinery associates with you, wherever the data came from.

What about other people who appear in a photo or video? Should you be able to see everyone's face? Should you also be able to see the tags computed for people who are not your friends? You were at the event, after all, and you could find out who the people were, by asking the event organizers, the photographer, or others (or perhaps by using Google reverse image search). That's true even if all the faces in the image were blurred or obscured by software—similar to how the Seattle Police Department handled its YouTube channel of bodycam footage. However, the economic constraints on discovering strangers' identities have a benefit: they provide an obstacle to our data being used against us. Imagine the outlier scenario in which a person attends an event, strolling around the rooms in order to get caught in as many photos as possible. Then, once he was alerted that images of him had been identified by a refinery, he could use any public information visible in or attached to the photos to track down the individuals who had also been there—including people he wants to target in some way, whether as potential clients (a nuisance) or as stalking victims (a crime). Giving people the power to set the rules of who can see their name attached to a photo when a computer tags them does not simply change the costs of obtaining that information; it also signals a scope of use. Generally, we should include rather than exclude data while always respecting the individual. Each person should get to choose whether to allow tags identifying her to be seen by others, and who can see those tags.

The right to access your data is clearly complicated by the questions of who "owns" data and what "owning data" actually means. Historically, creators and subjects may have conflicting interests, as seen in the case of tags. But more fundamentally, our current concept of ownership evolved in the physical world. If I buy an apple, I own it: it's solely mine to do with as I please. I can slice and dice it; I can eat it; I can give it or sell it to somebody else. But only one person can own the apple at any given point in time. And of course, once you start consuming a bite of the apple, there's no turning back. In contrast, a byte of data can be consumed by more than one person simultaneously, and it does not get eaten up. We need a new concept of ownership for data. Data can be owned by more than one person at the same time. In fact, ownership of data is not about having sole decision-making authority in determining the data's destiny—to buy, sell, donate, or destroy the bytes. Instead, ownership of data is the ability to access the data, with potential to use them.

Once you've considered these dimensions of access, you can see why getting a raw data dump just isn't good enough. The right to access your data requires significant deliberation about what should and should not be revealed to others, and thoughtful development of sophisticated algorithms, user interfaces, and software that can partially conceal people's identity and provide nuanced options for communicating who has a share in what data and for how long. Many of these innovations—whether in computer code or in the social code—are nontrivial. Yet that should not stop us from demanding them. Our ability to see and use our data depends on them.

The Right to Inspect Data Refineries

How can you decide which refineries are giving you a good return, at a comfortable risk, for your data? For full transparency, you need to see more than data about yourself; you need to be able to see data about the refineries.

I argue that you need to be able to inspect the integrity and health of a refinery's social data ecosystem, measuring the refinery's "hygiene" in terms of its resilience against security attacks; its efficiency of data use, or how quickly privacy gets "burned"; and the return you can expect for your data. In the realm of health, we understand that maintaining good hygiene isn't a guarantee that you won't get sick. That's also true for this trio of measures, which aim to make the refineries more transparent.

Consider the example of scoring the hygiene of a restaurant, an inspection required in many localities. It would be possible to institute a clear-cut, binary system, where a restaurant is open if it has met the minimal standard during inspection, or it's shuttered because it hasn't. While public health inspectors can indeed close a restaurant, they typically assign a hygiene score on a scale ranging from "poor" to "exemplary."[12]

Having a spectrum of inspection ratings—rather than a simple pass or fail grade—allows government authorities to balance two very distinct imperatives for members of the diverse community they serve: public health and economic vitality. A person with a compromised immune system who has to be especially careful about exposure to pathogens would go only to restaurants with the highest hygiene rating. The authorities have to consider the negative outcome for this person, even though she is an outlier. At the same time, some customers would probably be happy with the trade-off, accepting slightly-less-than-perfect conditions in return for, say, incredibly cheap prices or amazingly inventive dishes.

Hygiene inspections can't prevent rare but potentially extreme dangers. Even people with exceptionally robust immune systems can get sick after eating food prepared when a Typhoid Mary is stirring things up in the kitchen.[13] A semi-regular inspection would include ensuring that the restaurant's workers are trained to wear gloves and not to come into work when they are sick.

All of these concepts of a hygiene score apply to the trade-offs involved when creating and sharing data. There are negative and positive aspects, and there are unexpected and expected outcomes, for every decision we make, including the decision of which refineries to use to help us make decisions. In this framework, an unexpected outcome isn't one you haven't planned for, or even imagined; it's an event that is rare or improbable, but still possible, like Typhoid Mary showing up for work at your local eatery. An expected outcome is one you can and should plan for, like having to pay the bill at the end of your meal. Outcomes, both unexpected and expected, can be either negative or positive. Typhoid Mary and the restaurant bill are both negative, though it's much easier to calculate the expected cost of a meal versus the risk of getting seriously ill.

In the world of data, one of the most significant unexpected negative outcomes, or risks, is a security breach, wherein your data are accessed by people who intend to abuse that data and potentially harm you, financially or in some other way. Just one of these rare events can affect millions of people simultaneously. A common expected negative outcome, or cost, is the slow erosion of privacy as information about you gets processed again and again by refineries. As others repeatedly query a refinery, the probability increases that some specific data can be associated with you. Some loss of privacy is unavoidable, but how much of your privacy is used, or "burned," depends on the refinery's policies and procedures. This can be captured in a "privacy efficiency" rating.

The familiar expected positive outcome, or benefit, you get in exchange—which most of us rely on, day in and day out—is characterized by a "return-on-data" score. Refineries differ in how well they use your raw data and revealed preferences for ranking and matching. The right to compare refineries on these three measures—the safety and security risks of your data, the efficiency with which privacy is used, and the aggregate return on data—allows you to choose which refineries you want to use.

	Negative	*Positive*
Expected	"Privacy efficiency" rating	"Return-on-data" score
Unexpected	Data safety audit	Serendipity

You will notice that I do not suggest any specific measures for the unexpected positive outcomes of using a refinery, what I have called "serendipity" in the matrix above. Serendipity is the moment you meet your soul mate on a dating site, land your dream job through LinkedIn, find a photo match for an undiagnosed health condition,[14] or discover the answer to some other once-in-a-lifetime question through social data. Though I am certain refineries will increasingly guide us in making such crucial, life-changing decisions, the happy, rare outcomes of recommendations and rankings—a joy to behold in your life—they are too subjective and idiosyncratic to be aggregated into one number.

Now let's look at the three measures for inspecting the refineries.

The Right to See a Data Safety Audit

It seems every few months there's news of a massive data breach. Every technology has upsides and downsides. Most technologies that provide a powerful new way of living come with risks attached—all the more so when humans maintain some role in running the operation. Driving a car might end in a wreck; sharing data with a refinery might leave you open to a security breach or hack.

Marc Goodman, the author of *Future Crimes* and an adviser to the United Nations, NATO, and Interpol, stresses that security breaches shouldn't be brushed away as extremely unlikely events. Between 15 and 20 percent of the world's GDP involves organized crime, activities like drug trafficking, human trafficking and prostitution, and data trafficking and intellectual property theft. Increasingly, cyber operations are providing these criminals with significant revenue streams.[15]

The most high-profile breaches—such as the transaction data stolen from retailers Target[16] and eBay,[17] the financial data from JPMorgan Chase,[18] the employment data from Sony Pictures,[19] the patient data from health insurer Anthem,[20] and the voting data from the Philippines Election Commission[21]—get big headlines, and cause big headaches.[22] Afterward, there is rarely a clear public accounting of what exactly went wrong, or an open discussion about how the company could or should have improved its security. Were the data intercepted in transit from one hub to another? Could the weakness have been identified internally? How can you determine whether a refinery is "secure enough" to share your data with it?

Often in the case of a security breach, companies argue that they were powerless against a sophisticated attack. Sometimes that post-mortem assessment is reasonable. After Sony Pictures got hacked, for instance, a spokesman said "any suggestion Sony Pictures Entertainment should have been able to defend itself against this attack is deeply flawed and ignores essential findings and comments made by the FBI."[23] The head of the FBI's cyber division testified to the Senate that "the malware that was used . . . probably would have gotten past 90 percent of the net defenses that are out there today in private industry, and I would challenge to even say government."[24] The custom malware used by the hackers was like Typhoid Mary: an unexpected, very negative outcome for a company that had reason and capacity to invest heavily in digital security but was still left vulnerable.

Conducting data safety audits ought to be considered a necessity for every company that refines social data, and the results should be made available to users. Based on past performance, however, users will have to demand these safety inspections for them to become the norm. For the most part, companies do not have an incentive to share the results, because they fear publishing a safety audit would make them *more* vulnerable to hacks. Sharing a low safety rating, let alone specifying a refinery's security vulnerabilities, they say, would be the equivalent of erecting a billboard in front of a house advertising that the door is kept unlocked—and inviting burglars to visit. However, criminals tend to choose their targets for their value, not their vulnerabilities.

Sony Pictures had hired a pioneering cyber security expert, Kevin Mandia, to protect the company's assets.[25] Many companies handling sensitive information, whether it is multimillion-dollar Hollywood releases or millions of customer credit-card numbers, hire security consultants. The security interests of companies and users are aligned; neither wants to have data stolen by criminals, and neither wants to pay the hefty cost of an incident. But currently, most people are given very little information in order to judge the vulnerability of their data at a specific company. They have even less ability to compare one company's data safety practices to another's. This is why we need data safety audits performed and published across refineries.

One component of data safety is adopting secure standards for communicating with users and analyzing their data. The Electronic Frontier Foundation highlights the "inherently insecure" nature of the HTTP protocol, which sends data in an unencrypted manner and unfortunately remains the default for most websites. Refineries ought to be employing HTTPS, which establishes an encrypted connection between clients and servers, making it much harder for an outside attacker to intercept the communication.[26]

The audit would also look at how employees gain access to data. A refinery that requires two- or multi-factor authorization, whereby a person inputs a second, one-time passcode supplied by a mobile phone app or dedicated device, has a stronger commitment to data safety than one that does not. Logging and analyzing every access would increase the security rating of the company. Not only would such a log help investigators trace any anomalies to the point of origin, it would also encourage greater compliance and diligence among employees. As we have seen, when people know they are being recorded, they change their behavior.

However, many security breaches start not with a software weakness but with a human weakness inside a company—an employee who is disgruntled, disaffected, inadequately trained, or simply too busy to do a thorough job. Users deserve to have more visibility into the safety of the data inside a refinery, including a certification of the integrity of the employees handling their data. Financial institutions are required to conduct a background check on all job candidates, including an investigation of whether the person has committed fraud of any sort at a previous workplace. Data refineries should also vet potential employees and assess potential employee risk. Developers at a refinery may have broad access to people's raw data, and they may be asked to write or edit code that few others review line by line. If in the past the refinery could have observed that a developer was slack in following security procedures, or submitted code that turned out to be egregiously negligent or fraudulent, the refinery has to be held accountable if it did nothing about it.[27]

Indeed, some of the biggest breaches have involved sloppy data handling practices rather than nefarious attacks. Take the case of a government hard drive containing the health and military discharge records for 70 million American veterans.[28] After the drive failed, an employee sent it to the outside contractor who had originally supplied it, hoping it could be repaired. When that didn't work, the contractor sent it to a third party for recycling—with the data still on it. Initially, the agency in charge of the records claimed that the privacy clauses in its contract with the vendor ensured the data were protected. Criminals don't care about such legal niceties. Both the data handling and the response were unacceptable. Any quantification of the risk of a data breach should include a thorough review of employees' knowledge of safe data handling, just as a restaurant inspection reviews employees' knowledge of safe food handling. This emerges out of a company's culture, not out of individual job hires.

Data can also be breached by robots, which are often used to extract information from the web by crawling and scraping a customer-facing site. Good data safety practices include setting up systems to detect abnormally active accounts and shut them down. For example, a user that stays logged in 24/7 and moves from page to page every second is not likely to be a human. Robots and their operators are becoming smarter and smarter, by now avoiding such easy-to-spot patterns of behavior. In this arms race, refineries that use machine learning to identify unauthorized data scraping would receive a higher safety rating.

Even with sophisticated monitoring in place, robots will be able to get data. Users of PatientsLikeMe, a social networking site for people managing medical conditions, learned this the hard way.[29] The data people shared on the site's chat forums were quite sensitive: their clinical diagnosis, current health condition, prescribed and unprescribed medications, side effects, and prognoses. Many swapped advice about how to handle the physical and emotional toll of living with chronic illness such as multiple sclerosis, HIV/AIDS, post-traumatic stress disorder, and depression. It was a wonderful example of the power of sharing data—the ability to find others dealing with similar issues, learn from their past experience, and benchmark the progress of one's treatment against others'.

While some people used a pseudonym on the site, not all did, and a number of them shared email addresses and other personal identifiers in their profile pages or comment signatures. While this made it easier to connect directly with fellow patients, it also made it easier to link the pseudonym to a person's real name and identity. So you can imagine the dismay when PatientsLikeMe revealed that its forums had been accessed by robots surreptitiously scraping data for the data firm Nielsen, which was conducting market analysis for an unidentified pharmaceutical or medical equipment manufacturer.[30] PatientsLikeMe shut down the robot accounts, but some 5 percent of the site's posts had already been copied. A regular data safety audit should assess how likely it is that a company's procedures will catch robot accounts and data scraping swiftly.

Such initiatives ought to be part of a larger commitment to finding security holes before they get exploited. Since 2011, Facebook has offered a bounty to anyone who discovers and reports a programming bug or vulnerability to the company. More than two thousand bugs have been found, with more than $4 million paid out to hackers who discovered the bugs—a small percentage of Facebook's overall security budget.[31] Each "white-hat" hacker's reward was based on Facebook's assessment of how significant the discovered risk was, and whether Facebook was already aware of the problem. The biggest single bounty to date totaled $33,500, paid to a Brazilian man who was able to hack into Facebook's servers through a bug in the code used to handle user requests to reset forgotten passwords.[32] Not every data company will have the resources to set up a full-fledged security department. However, a competitive bounty program can close security holes efficiently and cost-effectively.

The consequences of a hack are especially terrifying when you consider the "Internet of Things." The huge amount of data analyzed by computer systems in planes, trains, and automobiles, as well as the network of computers embedded everywhere from homes to hospitals, puts people at *physical* risk. In Chapter 4, we considered how a GPS spoofer might be employed to lead people to an unwanted location. In one eye-opening test case, engineering University of Texas professor Todd Humphreys used a spoofer and a remote controller to take over the navigation of a yacht without the crew's knowledge.[33] In another, a duo of hackers proved that they could take over a Jeep Cherokee's "steering, brakes, and transmission" via the car's networked entertainment system.[34]

Such demonstrations are changing how companies think about digital security. In 2015, the Mayo Clinic hired a team of a dozen white-hat hackers to see if they could break into the network that controlled hundreds of the hospital's life-saving medical devices. The results were startling and sobering. The devices were incredibly vulnerable—so vulnerable that the hackers, many of whom were celebrities in cybersecurity, didn't have time to investigate all of the security failures in the week allotted to them. Some of the equipment was still set to use the default factory password, which, for someone interested in breaking in, was about as good as having no password protection at all.[35] After reviewing the team's report, the Mayo Clinic updated its purchasing policies and procedures, requiring all medical devices to follow a stringent security protocol. However, that protocol is far from standard in the healthcare industry.[36]

Too often, data safety monitoring decisions are made through a simple cost-benefit analysis. It's the mindset of the Sony Pictures executive who, in 2007, before the company's big hack, said he had not wanted to "invest $10 million to avoid a possible $1 million loss."[37] The breach ended up being much more costly—$15 million in "investigation and remediation costs" alone,[38] and a potentially bigger hit to Sony's corporate reputation. One way to bring down the costs of vulnerability detection and white-hat hacking programs is to create an independent industry organization to conduct audits across the industry and certify hackers in some way. At the same time, if users insist on a higher standard of data safety, the costs to the company of not enrolling will also increase.

These high-profile breaches summarize the five elements of data safety that need to be transparent to a refinery's users. First, as with a hygiene inspection, there are minimum requirements that must be met in order to be considered "open" for business, such as having up-to-date software with all known vulnerabilities patched. Second, data safety is about more than secure code; it's about people, and creating a company culture that respects users and their data. An audit by an outside group can certify the refinery's overall health standards and provide a rating for the security procedures and practices, including whether people are trained in safe data handling. Third, a team of white-hat hackers would regularly try to break into the refinery's networks and computers to check for any hidden vulnerabilities. Ideally, the auditors would also assess the refinery's response times to abnormal activity and suggest concrete improvements—a service for both the refinery and its users. Fourth, data safety must be assessed using consistent standards and tests across all refineries. Fifth, there should be a capacity to assign weights to potential harm when certain categories of data are breached. If your connected car is hacked while you're driving, the resulting injury could very well be far more devastating than a fraudulent transaction on your credit card.

As the auditors go through the data safety checklist, reviewing and testing a refinery's performance, they would add points for sound practices. Users would be able to see the refinery's most recent summary score, and put the score into context by having the option to look at previous audits. If a refinery's audit has improved, it might signal an investment in security infrastructure or indicate employee training that has paid off over time. A worsening score might reflect a recent vulnerability or a lackluster commitment to training new employees. Being able to see the trend can be as helpful as seeing the most recent report.

Finally, publishing a bad data safety audit or risk rating should not relieve a refinery from any legal or ethical obligation to compensate users for harm they have incurred if a breach occurs due to negligence. The expense of such events must be shared between the companies getting these data and the people who are giving them. Otherwise, the companies may see little reason to improve security if their competitors have a low safety rating (or a high rating, but terrible products and services)—all the more so because future harm to an individual may not be traceable to a specific breach or other security failing. This is an area where the government or courts could impose fines or reimbursements to users if companies do not compensate them voluntarily.

As data refineries become integrated into more and more aspects of our lives, it is essential that much more information about data safety is communicated publicly—and well before security breaches occur. Indeed, because social data are increasingly being used to establish and communicate a person's identity, reputation, and state of mind, the threat of a security breach is incredibly personal.

The Right to See a Privacy Efficiency Rating

A security breach is a catastrophic, unexpected event, but there are also regular, expected costs of using refineries, including the gradual erosion of your privacy. As we've seen, you need to give personal data to obtain personally relevant products and services from a refinery. Privacy is also a *resource,* consumed by refineries in the process of creating outputs from your data.

As with any resource, the consumption of privacy can be more or less efficient, and the process of using it can be managed and budgeted. According to Cynthia Dwork of Microsoft Research, what's imperative is quantifying the amount of privacy lost when the data are used. The purpose of what Cynthia calls "differential privacy" is to set up data systems so that any individuals with data in the system will experience no direct negative consequence from sharing their data. Cynthia puts this in the form of two questions: "For a fixed bound on privacy loss, which technique provides better accuracy? For a fixed accuracy, which technique provides better privacy?"[39]

A refinery has to be designed to manage the privacy loss across its users against the benefits they receive for sharing data about themselves.[40] Again, it helps to think of a refinery as an ecosystem, which is best maintained with an eye to the health of the entire ecosystem, not the health of particular individuals within it. The trade-off between accuracy and privacy isn't for one person alone, but for everybody. As you choose which refineries to use, you should be able to see whether they tend to use up privacy quickly or slowly, inefficiently or efficiently.

The speed and efficiency of privacy use is similar to a concept from engineering and environmental science called "burn rate."[41] An engineer can build a wood-burning stove that burns a lot of fuel, very fast, without much heat being generated to the surrounding room. It's still a functional oven, but it's not very efficient: the raw material is quickly used up to achieve the desired outcome—a warm room. Adding more and more logs to the stove might keep the room warm enough, but the heat transfer still remains far from optimal. Data may no longer be a scarce resource, but privacy still is—and getting scarcer by the minute. Privacy, like wood, can be easy to burn up without getting much benefit.

Modern wood-burning stoves are certified to run within a range of overall efficiency—between 60 and 80 percent—calibrated against the maximum theoretical efficiency of 100 percent. The privacy efficiency rating would be calculated in a similar way, with 100 percent efficiency indicating the ideal case of the lowest possible privacy loss for a result with a fixed accuracy, and with the data used being only those that were absolutely necessary—for instance, a navigation service requiring a person's current location and destination in order to provide directions to him.

A refinery constantly makes decisions about which user data to access as it looks for ways to improve its products and services. The databases of clicks and purchases that Amazon uses to make recommendations to customers do not need to have a record of the identity of each individual customer. What matters are the trajectories that customers take from one product to the next, not the fact that it was Veronica in Omaha who clicked on the product and then on another. Thus, if someone peered into these databases, she would not find information about specific individuals, reducing the chances of customers being harmed by these data.

When I was working with the dating site Fridae, we analyzed thousands of notes that users had jotted down about other members, little annotations ranging from "sent me 5 messages; need to write back" and "met him—not my type" to "graduated with honors in chemistry" and "looks much older than 29." These annotations were visible to the user who made them but not to any other users. We were interested in what types of information got captured in the notes, and whether any of it could be incorporated into the site's design. Our analysis revealed the notes helped users remember who they had already messaged or met with no luck, so that they could avoid the effort—or embarrassment—of contacting those individuals again. But before we analyzed the note content, all usernames were stripped out. This reduced the amount of privacy we had to burn in the process of improving Fridae's services. No one on the team needed to know the predilections of a particular user in order to notice patterns in the notes and consider new features or fields for the site.

If efficiency is of no concern, it is easier to build a very powerful machine. A car engine designed to compete on the Formula 1 circuit can gobble up a lot of gas. And, more generally, for several decades car makers weren't particularly worried about how much fuel a car used, because gas was cheap and seemingly limitless, and car buyers were more interested in other things, such as the car's looks, performance, safety, and price. The oil crisis of the 1970s radically reweighted the costs and benefits assigned to various aspects of engine design. Governments mandated that cars be more fuel-efficient, and consumers counted pennies at the gas pumps.

Fuel efficiency—measured in the United States as miles driven per gallon of gas—can range dramatically depending on the demands on the engine. "City driving," with its many stops and starts, and lower speeds, tends to be less fuel-efficient than driving at a consistent high speed on a freeway. The weather and other drains on the engine, such as the air conditioner, also matter. The US Environmental Protection Agency boils down the wide range of driving conditions into a single fuel efficiency rating by testing five driving scenarios in a laboratory. Every car is subjected to the same checklist. According to the EPA, "Testing vehicles in controlled laboratory conditions establishes a level playing field for all cars and ensures that the test results are consistent, accurate, repeatable, and equitable."[42]

Regrettably, fake efficiency ratings can be quite believable. That's true of any efficiency rating that summarizes mechanisms or conditions that people do not or cannot experience directly. Say you're staying in a hotel and your room feels too warm. You've adjusted the thermostat, but the temperature doesn't seem to have changed in response, so you ask for an engineer to come to your room to look at it. When she's done tinkering with the box, the display shows a lower temperature. If the room continues to feel too warm, you might wonder if she merely "fixed" the display instead of fixing the thermostat, and might demand that a thermometer be brought up to verify the temperature.

Much of the time, however, people do not have the computational or sensory capacity to question the credibility of a measurement. And in some cases, machines are so complex that it is possible to configure them to appear to perform far more efficiently in some conditions—including when the machines themselves are being inspected. Volkswagen's engineers took advantage of the fact that cars were tested by the EPA for nitrous oxide emissions in a lab, a condition that could be detected by a car's sensors. After the engineers couldn't find a way to get a good fuel efficiency performance from a line of diesel engines without exceeding emissions standards, individuals at the company developed the software to lower emissions when the car was being tested. It was only after researchers at West Virginia University attempted to measure emissions on cars during road tests that the cheating was uncovered.[43]

Data refineries are at least as complex as a car. Most of us will have a difficult time judging the credibility of a privacy efficiency rating, even after we make the effort to understand what data must be given in order to get particular products and services. But communicating a refinery's use of privacy could be as easy as communicating a car's efficiency. Instead of estimating the number of miles that can be driven per gallon of gas, the aim would be to estimate the number of queries a refinery can answer per unit of privacy loss.

In practice, this would require defining a battery of tests for assessing privacy efficiency, much like the EPA creates a set of standardized tests for fuel efficiency. The tests would probe a refinery to learn the average number of interactions after which an individual is identified with a certain probability. Bigger numbers—more queries conducted before a loss in privacy occurs—would signify a more efficiently designed refinery.

Several people, including Cynthia Dwork and British entrepreneur John Taysom, are exploring methods for improving data privacy while maintaining data utility, and their work indicates that it is possible to develop tools like this for calculating a refinery's use of privacy. John has patented a few interesting inventions for reducing the amount of privacy that must be burned to deliver products and services.[44] He also argues that we cannot depend on the refineries to inspect themselves, nor should we rely on government agencies to do it for us. "Companies don't live very long when compared to people who expect to live to one hundred, in the developed world at least; and governments don't have a great record for securing personal data—and they are subject to change," he has said. "Neither looks to be the right governance structure for data that may be relevant for one hundred years, and potentially even across generations, as is the case with genetic data."[45] As with data safety, we need an independent body of data experts to evaluate and communicate privacy efficiency for us.

In many respects, we're in the very early stages of understanding how to measure and manage the loss of personal privacy in exchange for data products and services. The future may involve a number of surprising innovations. For instance, when environmental scientists study climate change, they look at the burn rate of the planet's total carbon resources. That burn rate is calculated not simply in terms of how much carbon is being consumed each year but also in terms of how much can be used each year without tipping earth's ecosystem out of balance. To encourage less carbon use, companies in some countries are given a quota for their annual emissions. A company that uses less than its carbon budget can sell its unused credits to another company that has used too much; if a company has used too much and can't find carbon credits to buy, it has to pay a fine to "offset" its overuse. This raises the cost of manufacturing for the company, nudging it to decrease its carbon use or deliver a dramatically better product than its competitors for the extra cost to the pocketbook and the environment. Organizations and individuals can also voluntarily offset their carbon footprint by paying money toward tree-planting and other efforts.

We may someday allow data refineries to trade in privacy credits, too. Such schemes will be possible only after we develop tools for objectively measuring and clearly communicating how privacy gets used, and learn how comfortable we are with various burn rates.

The Right to a "Return-on-Data" Score

How can you estimate the benefits you can expect to receive in exchange for your data? Conceptually, the return on data and the privacy burn rate both convey information about a refinery's efficiency of data use. The privacy burn rate measures the expected cost in terms of how much of your true identity is exposed as you use the refinery. The return on data measures the expected benefit in terms of the value received compared to the data shared; it helps you decide whether the products and services you get are worth the effort of giving your data to the refinery.

Too many refineries ask for too much of our information before we can evaluate whether or not they're useful. It's as though you've met someone for a first date and the person has shown up with a list of twenty questions for you to answer, but doesn't tell you anything about himself: the date probably won't go very well. However, this is how many data-collecting companies start their relationship with you. Instead, there needs to be a way for people to assess the potential benefit of using a refinery before they give data to it. The return-on-data score provides a means for scrutinizing this aspect of a refinery's usefulness.

The perception of what a user gets from what she gives is subjective. For some people, sharing a photo of their toddler on Facebook feels like a big disclosure; for others, it's no big deal. For some people, there's a huge value to being able to make the acquaintance of a friend of a friend who shares a passion for J. S. Bach's cello suites; for others, the new acquaintance may feel like a big nuisance demanding time and attention. While it's only after a person has shared data with a refinery and tried out its products and services that she can really get a sense for the personal return on her data, she should be able to decide whether to start to use a refinery based on the average return on data for its past and current users. The return-on-data score averages what people get—the value received in information products and services—divided by what they give—the investment made by sharing their data.

How, then, is the return on data measured? We could start by seeing whether the data the individual provides have any effect on the refinery's outputs. If there is no effect, the marginal return on these data is zero. Most of the time, there will be some effect, and that's where things get a bit tricky.

Let's start by looking at how to compute the denominator—a user's investment of data in the refinery. A return on investment is usually calculated in dollars and cents: for every dollar you spent on a project, portfolio, or company, how many dollars did you make? As we saw in Chapter 1, however, you cannot easily point to a string of data that you have shared with a refinery and assign a price to it. Investment of data does not lend itself to a straightforward arithmetic tally of dollars and cents, nor of bytes and bits.

The investment of data in a refinery, however, can be captured through measures of user effort, or attention. Measuring attention is more complex than just measuring the time spent at a refinery. For instance, having a page open in a browser does not indicate whether a person is actually looking at the page unless there is some activity: clicks, swipes, searches, comments, uploads, and downloads (unless, that is, the person has allowed the device's built-in camera to send a video stream to a refinery so that he can be observed directly). Some refineries require new users to fill out a few profile fields before they can access their services. If those data are necessary—sharing an address to get an item shipped—there is some return for them. But some data are collected simply because marketers have been trained to believe they need demographic information about their customers. Filling out surveys that have zero impact on what you see has zero value for you.

Another consideration in measuring effort is to look at how data are created and shared. Creating data explicitly for a refinery—answering a survey or uploading a profile photo—is more work than sharing clicks, swipes, and searches. Explicitly checking into a location on Facebook is more work than turning on geolocation sharing. However, your check-in tells Facebook more explicitly that you may want to get recommendations based on where you are. More generally, in calculations of a user's investment, explicit data should be given more weight compared to implicit data.

This weighting mechanism also reflects the fact that connecting to a site or app using Facebook Log-In or similar services reduces the investment required to obtain personalized recommendations and matches when trying out a new refinery.[46] Facebook shares relevant data with the app—your profile photo with ride-sharing platforms Uber or Lyft, so that driver and rider can recognize each other; your friends' music choices, so that Spotify can populate your playlist, saving you the effort of recreating data that have already been shared elsewhere.

In some cases, as with the house- and room-sharing service Airbnb, a site or app may require you to link your account with a social network. In fact, Airbnb assures customers that it accesses a broad range of personal data, including a government-issued ID, online ID, profile photo, email address, and phone number, in order to verify users' identity and establish a feeling of trust between users. For Airbnb, online identity encompasses having a network of friends; it's much harder to fake hundreds of mutually confirmed friendships on Facebook than to fake a personal profile. Here, we can see that the minimum amount of social graph information needed to approve a host or guest is relatively high, but it still doesn't require handing over every bit of data about you. Additional data from your profile could also be used to improve Airbnb's services. Love pets? Like to work out every morning? Airbnb could probably find a match of host or guest by analyzing your interactions with your Facebook friends. But this isn't as efficient as letting guests and hosts explicitly indicate which of their interests are important in making a decision about whether to accept a guest or book a room.

Now let's turn to the numerator: the value the user gets from the refinery. This value can come in the form of better communication, better matches, and better decisions. Quantifying improvement can be difficult. Time spent on a site does not always indicate benefit, let alone joy; you may be desperately trying to find the customer service phone number of a company. Savings in time may or may not indicate that users are happy with what they get, or that it is useful for them. A different approach counts the number of monthly active users—that is, how many people visited or used the site or app in the last thirty days—as a measure of a refinery's usefulness. But the number of visitors may also simply reflect the company's latest marketing campaign.

A more robust calculation looks at several dimensions of user engagement data that are already regularly measured and analyzed by refineries: *recency* of use, *frequency* of use, and *variety* of use. How long ago did a user last visit the refinery? How often, on average, does a person visit the site or use the app? How many different things does the user do at the refinery? Recency depends on the type of services the refinery offers. If users on average have visited Google within the last six hours, it doesn't mean you receive far more benefit from it because you have been searching it in the past six minutes. It simply reflects bursts of search activity compared to other activities, including all those hours spent sleeping. It's only in being able to compare the data on recency of use to similar search sites that recency becomes a useful metric. However, if a person used a dating app the day before, the app is more likely to suggest him higher in the ranking of potential matches than if he last used it a month or a year ago. Increased engagement can provide greater benefit. Frequency of use—how many times a person uses a refinery per day, week, or month—can also be compared over time. If people on average visit a refinery less often today than a year ago, that suggests less return on data. Finally, variety of use demonstrates the range of products and services that a refinery successfully offers to people based on the data it's collecting and analyzing. Ideally, the return-on-data score would give a user the ability to look individually at the recency, frequency, and variety figures, and see how putting different weights on each factor changes the scores for different refineries.

Once the denominator and numerator are calculated, taking their ratio gives the return on data for the individual. To summarize the return on data across all users, the average of these individual ratios would be taken, regardless of how often each person uses the refinery. (If we were to first add up the benefits across all users, and then divided this by the investments across all users, more active users would be given more weight in the ratio than less active ones.) If a refinery's aggregate return-on-data score is less than 1, it indicates that users typically get less from the refinery than they give to it. That does not sound like a deal, let alone a good one. However, the return on data is more than a binary signal. You might also decide that the return in decision-making value just isn't high enough compared to the *type* of data you are being asked to share.

Observations of user behavior can and should be supplemented with qualitative data that can reveal users' motivations. For instance, asking users to review their experience with the refinery, much like a customer satisfaction survey aims to quantify the benefit of a product or service and the likelihood that a customer will continue to buy or use it, can help to put high-frequency visits in context. A refinery knows how often a user comes back to a site or app, and may infer the purpose based on clicks and queries, but it doesn't know precisely why. A simple survey question might offer additional insight: *We noticed that you visited our site on 3 different occasions today: Did you come back because you found what you wanted but got interrupted, or because you didn't find what you wanted but felt the recommendations were good enough?*

One methodology, Net Promoter Score, might be particularly attractive to refineries, ensuring that refineries' interests are aligned with users'. Individuals are asked to rank their likelihood of recommending the company on a numeric scale from 0 to 10, with the aggregated scores placed on a spectrum from −100 (where everyone asked is a "detractor," unlikely to recommend) to +100 (where everyone asked is a "promoter," likely to recommend).[47] Asking a user "How likely is it that you would recommend our company/product/service to a friend or colleague?"[48] would naturally lead to an option to share that recommendation with the people in the user's social network. In this case, users' interests and refineries' interests can be aligned: the feedback is channeled into growth in the refinery's user base.[49]

Over time, individuals will learn how much value they can expect not merely in comparison to the investment they put in but also, taking the bigger picture into account, in comparison to the safety risks and the privacy costs associated with a refinery. We must be able to see and review estimates of the unexpected risks, expected costs, and expected benefits across refineries so that we can decide which ones we want to work with.

In Plain Sight

When you drive, you want to have the car's key performance indicators—the engine malfunction light, oil pressure light, fuel gauge, and speedometer—within easy sight, so that you can keep an eye on how the car is operating while at the same time scanning the surrounding environment and steering yourself to your destination without incident. The dashboard instruments distill and communicate this important information in ways that allow you to make decisions based on a quick glance.

I believe that for true transparency, we need to have a similar standardized dashboard to distill and communicate the three inspection metrics of a refinery's health and hygiene.[50] Before creating an account, first-time users would get to see the inspection metrics. Thus, the metrics would need to be conspicuously displayed on the refinery's home page or app description. For existing users, the metrics could be integrated into the user settings page—for instance, on Google's existing Dashboard. I expect "refineries of refineries" will emerge, similar to shopping comparison sites, to collect the data, compute the metrics, and show them to users side by side. Clear, intuitive visualizations are needed, such as mapping the inspection results onto a spectrum from green to amber to red, where the ratings of the best-performing refineries are displayed in green and the worst-performing in red.[51] Again, this requires that an outside body be established to inspect the refineries, since the ratings will have to be analyzed in order to produce these benchmarks.

My hope is that people will consult the dashboard when they are deciding whether to share their data with a new refinery. The dashboard will also allow people to better assess their own personal experience with each refinery—and make decisions about whether to continue using it or to try out a new refinery that pops up on the scene. The more a person uses a refinery, the more concerned she might become about privacy burn and want to compare her current refinery to competitors. She should also be given the option of receiving an automatic notification when a refinery's rating on one of the three metrics falls below a certain level, or into the "red zone."

The exact formula of how the metrics are computed will change as our understanding of data and data refineries advances. As with laws and regulations, what matters most are the guiding principles; the details will evolve as we learn how best to use refined data and exercise our transparency rights. However, nothing will happen if we sit back and wait for the data refineries to create a dashboard for us; we must demand that they provide this tool for judging the aspects of their performance that are relevant to us.

Much like a single user's data has very little monetary value to a refinery, a single user's demands for transparency may get very little attention. But the social data revolution is composed of a billion of us. A million or a billion users' demands for transparency are not easily ignored, even more so now when a billion of us are not limited to writing letters but have access to amazing tools—many of them built by the refineries themselves—for discovering, communicating, and organizing people and information. We can take advantage of these tools to discover fellow users who want to adjust the balance of power and seek better data safety handling, privacy efficiency, and return on data.

Together, we can put pressure on those refineries that fall short. We can vote with our data, choosing to interact with refineries that have a transparent record of serving users' interests and avoiding those that obfuscate, siphon our data for others to use, or simply provide too little in the way of transparency or value for us, the users.

If that does not work, we can even form virtual boycotts, banding together in an organized campaign to stop sharing data with low-performing refineries until we see tangible improvements in their performance. If the refineries do not respond to our demands, as a next step we can pressure our governments to create regulations that require such refineries to be inspected regularly and publicly post the results, much like US airlines are required to publish statistics about flight delays.

Now, we can look at dashboards all day long, but unless we *do* something in response to the information shown to us, we will be limited in how much control we have over the benefit we get from the refineries. To ensure that we can act on the information, the four agency rights—the right to amend, right to blur, right to experiment, and right to port—are essential.

6

TAKING THE CONTROL(S)

Agency for the People
What Should You Demand to Do with Your Data?

All that is required for this enlightenment is *freedom;* and particularly the least harmful of all that may be called freedom, namely, the freedom for man to make public use of his reason in all matters.[1]

IMMANUEL KANT

A DATA REFINERY is a machine. However, it doesn't run without some human direction. So while a company may be perfectly transparent about its internal mechanisms, that doesn't ensure the data of you and by you are also used for you. The people in charge of designing the machine may tell you (and might even themselves believe) that they know best how to set the bells and whistles for users. But how can you know that the refinery is no more than a pinball machine, with the users reduced to nothing more than a ball—a toy to be dropped, bumped, flipped, spun, and held captive to the whims of the people who actually have their hand on the controls of the refinery? If the people playing with the balls get a commission or bonus each time a ball rolls over or bumps into an ad or other piece of paid content, you can bet the machine will be designed to optimize the chances of doing just that.

This is why transparency about how the refineries work is not enough; we must also have agency—the ability to freely decide how our data are used by the refineries. We must demand a seat at the controls of the refineries.

This applies to how we interact with data refineries, too. Even a mundane problem like the labeling of incoming email as "spam" or "not-spam," which we happily delegate to computers, can be improved by giving users more agency. No one wants to return to the days when offers for cheap Viagra or promises of unclaimed inheritances filled your inbox. Still, more than once you've probably found a message you were waiting for in your spam folder—or, more annoyingly, learned that a message you wanted someone else to receive has landed in his. Spam filters give you the option of marking an email as not-spam, in order to move misdirected messages to your inbox and adjust the rules applied to your emails going forward. This feedback improves the performance of the system for you.

Spam filters try to find a setting that balances false positives—the number of messages that are incorrectly labeled as most likely being "spam"—and false negatives—the number of messages that are incorrectly labeled as "not-spam." Most of the time, the spam "scores" are assigned to incoming messages based on sender data and metadata for all of the emails that pass through the provider's servers, allowing machine learning on the network level. To help improve the system, however, your email provider could offer an analysis of why a message was put into your spam folder. Further, you could be given the option to drill down into the rules and adjust them to better reflect your preferences and the pattern of your communications.

On the one hand, you could set aggressive parameters for filtering messages to spam if you don't want to spend much time deleting spam manually and aren't worried about missing messages that are routed incorrectly. On the other hand, if you want to be certain you don't miss any messages and don't mind spending extra time reviewing junk, you could set the parameters more leniently. If you have a lot of friends and family in Nigeria, you may not care that the country boasts a spam rate of 90 percent.[2] Why not give humans more areas for offering feedback to the machines, giving users more say in how their messages are classified? In order to do this, email providers would need to expose the dimensions they utilize in spam analyses, and allow users to have some control over how their messages are processed by letting them adjust the corresponding parameters.

Increasing user agency requires shifting more power over data and the refinery's processes into the hands of individuals. There are four main ways a refinery can give you more control: the right to amend data; the right to blur your data; the right to experiment with your data and the refinery's settings; and the right to port your data. The right to amend increases your agency through the power of self-expression, while the right to blur does so through the power of self-determination. The right to experiment increases agency by expanding freedom of exploration, while the right to port does so by expanding freedom of movement. Developing tools based on these four rights will improve the information products and services of the refineries, creating a post-privacy economy in which you can put data to work for you on your terms.

The Right to Amend Data

In the earliest days of record-keeping, about six thousand years ago—when the Sumerians invented cuneiform[3]—the ruling class of priest-kings was largely given responsibility for creating, drying, storing, and preserving the clay tablets that contained the civilization's permanent records.[4] The tablets registered who owned what; who owed what for taxes, rent, fees, loans, or trades;[5] and what laws governed these possessions and exchanges. With so much at stake, there were forgeries and fights over exactly what had been "set in stone." The people of Sumer decided that these tablets had to be locked up, and often entrusted the local temple with the job. However, this meant the priests controlled much of the data: they decided who was granted access to the official record stored in the temple—and who was denied. Everyone else had to hope the priests had recorded the information correctly and would not be tempted to corrupt the data under their care. Unfortunately, the priest-kings and other elites weren't always correct, or trustworthy. Maintaining the data was a way to concentrate power.[6]

Pete Warden, the co-founder of image recognition start-up Jetpac, has made the point eloquently that today we're dealing with yet another period of overzealous protection of information.[7] We see a problem—the potential harm done by incorrect data—and imagine the solution is to ensure that all data are correct. But because there's so much data today, it's no longer possible to protect every bit and byte from tampering. The Sumerians tried to do that for a population of about 1 million and yet, after granting the power to control the record to a small number of people, discovered that data were still prone to corruption. It's also not possible to have humans police the truth for every piece of information. The East Germans tried to do that for a population of about 16 million and, after enlisting 1 percent of the nation's working-age people in the Stasi, discovered that manual data verification does not scale. However, we can now take advantage of machine learning to confirm that data are what they claim to be and sort data by relevance to individuals.

We need to let go of the goal of maintaining only the "correct" data and give users more ability to make their own mark on the record. The right to amend is about the power of purposefully *attaching* data, creating and sharing new data related to existing data and thereby creating connections that can be analyzed like any other data. The same algorithmic machinery of rankings and recommendations that was created to surface relevant ads can help surface the information relevant to an individual in a given situation, including data attached to other data. Given the vast amount of data available, the capacity to analyze large amounts of potentially inconsistent data, and the economics of modern communication, we no longer need to collapse the world into the binary of true or false. Thus, the right to amend adopts a probabilistic worldview.

The right to amend provides far more user agency than the EU's right to be forgotten. Take the case of Greg Lindae, a private-equity investor who asked that a 1998 *Wall Street Journal* article about a Tantra workshop in which he had participated be removed from Google results for his name almost as soon as the EU directive was adopted.[8] The directive was big news, and the newspaper's editors decided to track down the person who had made this too-sexy-to-resist request and write a story about him. Ironically, the clicks on the new story almost certainly increased the ranking of search results for "Tantra" or the "EU right to be forgotten" that mentioned Lindae by name. (Only when you searched for Lindae's name using a computer based in the European Union would Google suppress the links that Lindae had requested be removed.) Lindae acknowledged that the right to be forgotten was unlikely to become a global standard, and it was more important to him to be able to add some commentary about his original quotes. "If it adds a little more context . . . that is not a problem," he told the *Journal*. "That is actually better."[9] The vast majority of us won't ever be in the position of having the *Wall Street Journal* or another authority "amend" our data for us. We need to have the right to amend, no matter how sexy (or unsexy) our data may be.

The right-to-be-forgotten directive provides no clear standard for where information falls on the spectrum between public interest and personal privacy. As a result, the organizations responding to requests might "overwrite" information that people might consider useful, maybe even essential, when making a decision; it challenges other individuals' "right to know." Further, thus far the only way to determine the validity of a request seems to be to employ humans to evaluate each one on a case-by-case basis. It's as though we're back in Sumer, asking the priests to decide which clay tablets to keep and which to destroy.

Most of the requests made under the EU's right to be forgotten concern information that was posted by others. That's because most platforms already allow users to remove data they have created and shared themselves if they decide later that they no longer want it to be visible. But as we saw with the right to access data, many if not most data are created in relation to other people, and would be more accurately described as "co-owned." If a person deletes part of the conversation, whether about politics or products, she orphans the responses to her points. She changes the data's context.

People are most motivated to amend a record when they are likely to benefit from the change. A homeowner may have more of an incentive to correct a mistake in her county property assessment than a government clerk—but only in some contexts. If the homeowner believes the assessor overstated some features of the house, she may want to correct these to lower her tax bill. If she's about to put the house on the market, she might be happy to let the higher valuation stand, since it could improve her chance of fetching a higher sales price. The assessor doesn't have much incentive to reconsider the valuation, since that will cost extra time and perhaps the admission of some mistakes. Only if the house was undervalued and the assessor was paid on a commission basis would it make sense for him to revisit it.

The right to amend is especially important when data might harm you. Your phone's geolocation data might suggest you were in New Jersey at a certain point in time when you were actually in Manhattan, because your phone connected to a base station on the other side of the Hudson River.

Then, something comes up and you need to prove your whereabouts on that date. You could seek out other data, like a video recording, that shows you were in New York and attach it to the geolocation—to ensure that others are aware there is contradictory data. In the future, data that are beyond your control—for example, video footage taken from a camera mounted in a public space—might be used to determine your eligibility for a job or loan. You cannot stop such data from existing, but you can insist on having an opportunity to amend other data to them.

Additionally, for any data about yourself you should be able to create a "pinned" amendment—a rebuttal, explanation, or disclaimer—that is highly visible to anyone seeing the data and which is prioritized over amendments to the data made by others. In addition, because data about you may simultaneously be data about others, you ought to have some way to express how important a pinned amendment is to you, to help refineries determine how to rank and surface amendments to other users. If there are no costs to pinning or prioritizing an amendment, social data platforms might get cluttered by them. This problem can be solved by introducing artificial costs, where each user is granted a budget of points to allocate among their amendments.

Amendments can also be given more or less weight based on the amount of validation they receive, including a confirmation of the data source and feedback from other users. As we saw in Chapter 2, Reddit allows users to judge the merit of posts by voting content up or down, and identifies usernames who may be trying to game the voting system by ring-fencing votes that appear to be coming from the same user or a coordinated group of users as, for example, evidenced by similar IP address. Upvotes and downvotes are data amendments. However, an internet troll can hurt or destroy the reputation of an individual, or an online community, often for no other reason than to upset users. One way to maintain a healthy ecosystem is to require that every amendment comes with an identity, whether in the form of a real name or a persistent pseudonym. A persistent identity doesn't guarantee the truth of an amendment any more than the oath in a courtroom guarantees the truth of a witness's testimony, no matter how sincere a person seems when he promises to say "nothing but the truth." Further, tying amendments to a person, with the goal of increasing accountability and reducing negativity, does not work in the case of whistle-blowers, whose lives might be at risk if their true identity is revealed. Recent examples are WikiLeaks for government secrets, the Panama Papers for tax evasion,[10] and LaborLink[11] for factory conditions.

The metadata of an amendment, such as when and where it was created, can be utilized to validate it. Video and audio recordings contain a background hum reflecting the frequency of the electric current. In the United States, Canada, and China, the standard frequency for alternating current (AC) is fifty cycles per second, or fifty hertz, while in the United Kingdom and Europe, the standard is sixty hertz. In both cases, however, the frequency also varies very slightly in response to changes in the load put on the power grid, enough that these variations can be mapped to specific places and times, down to the minute. In the continental United States and Canada, there are four main power grids, each with its own distinct "frequency signature" in response to load demands.[12] By comparing the fluctuations in the background frequency hum of a recording to the idiosyncratic fluctuations in the frequency across the grid, it's possible to verify that the recording was probably made on a given day and time, and in a general location.[13]

This example, whereby a recording contains information about its provenance that cannot be erased, resembles the concept of the blockchain, the digital ledger system developed for the crypto-currency Bitcoin.[14] Essentially, a blockchain is a permanent history of all the past interactions and transactions involving some data that is embedded in the data. The entire history is thus always transmitted with the data; it cannot be pulled apart, tampered with, or erased. The blockchain records the current holder of each Bitcoin and ensures that a single Bitcoin cannot be used in simultaneous transactions, even while many Bitcoin users choose to attach pseudonyms to their "wallets." The system has been set up so that every transaction is recorded publicly through a decentralized, distributed process; anyone can read and write to the blockchain. The design relies on the basic fact that once a bit of data is shared with others, it can't be deleted in an existential sense, since there are copies floating around, saved on machines across the web. Every transfer and change is transparent and can be traced back in time. Users can also embed notes in the blockchain, putting a transaction in context.[15]

A blockchain can be set up privately, whereby a select group of individuals or an organization—called a "consortium"—get full read/write access to the history,[16] which might be an attractive option for medical data, with only the patient, physicians, and authorized family allowed to amend the record. A fully public blockchain is more transparent and trustworthy, since transactions of data are authenticated across the entire network of users. People will notice if someone tampers with anything that matters. In contrast, a consortium can process transactions more quickly, because fewer actors are involved in authenticating and saving the transaction. Thus, it is also easier for the parties to collude, so people may need to be more vigilant about changes to the data. Whether public or private, a history of all interactions embedded in a blockchain creates unprecedented accountability, especially in the event that your data are ever used against you. The blockchain helps ensure that amendments are attached to the person who created them in an enduring fashion, the technological equivalent of super glue as compared to a paper clip.

As we saw in the previous chapter, explicit data will be weighted more heavily than implicit data when calculating a person's investment of data in a refinery, reflecting the greater amount of user effort. Amendments are explicit data, but they can be attached to any data, implicit or explicit. By amending implicit data—noting that the metadata on a photo is not quite correct, for example—you increase its weight in the calculation of the return on data and signal that amendments like it are more relevant or interesting to you.

Finally, for the right to amend to become a reality, refineries must commit resources to support the right of users to amend data. It may be tempting for a refinery to funnel user attention into areas where there is money to be made, such as paid advertising. Allocating virtual real estate for displaying amendments and building the architecture for surfacing them are necessary, initial steps to serving the interests of users.

The Right to Blur Your Data

The second agency right, the right to blur, gives users the power to determine the level of detail of the data they share. The blurrier the data you give, the less personalized the services you can get from a refinery. Nonetheless, you should have the right to assert your own terms—and decide what level of personalization suits you at different times and in different places. Today, we can measure attributes about people to an amazing precision, such as knowing geolocation, via GPS or beacons, on the order of a meter. But this doesn't mean we want or need to share that level of resolution with the refinery; indeed, we should be able to determine the resolution of the data we share. Giving us a binary choice between supplying the highest-resolution data and not getting a refinery's services made sense when only very coarse data were available, but it is not appropriate anymore.

Sometimes we need or want high-resolution geolocation, sometimes we don't. You will share your exact location without a second thought when you want to have something get to you in a timely fashion. If you refuse to give your exact address to Domino's for delivery, you're not going to get your pizza. Yet, in many cases, we can get what we want where we want while sharing less precise information, and the price to be paid is completely palatable. You can ask a taxi driver to take you to an intersection near your destination rather than giving the specific address; the cost is just a few minutes of walking. In most towns, you can give Google Maps an address a few street numbers up or down from your intended destination and you will get perfectly functional directions.

Although it is possible to manually change or blur data in this way, we can take advantage of technology to do some of the work for us, taking high-resolution data and reducing the number of specific digits or characteristics that are passed downstream. Eric Horvitz of Microsoft Research has proposed a model that allows people to set the spatial resolution of the geolocation data their phones transmit to a refinery anywhere from a meter up to "Planet Earth."[17] Eric suggested that the granularity settings could be a function of your situation. You might want the highest resolution while looking for your car in a parking lot or for a specific item in a store. You might prefer a lower resolution if you're strolling through a shopping mall during work hours. If you're meeting a new client for coffee at the mall, you may want a higher resolution. An algorithm could learn your preferences, based on variables like time of day or geolocation. In addition, granularity might not always be measured in units of physical distance. If you're in a sparsely populated area, instead of blurring your location to a radius in miles, you might want to blur it to a radius that includes the closest one thousand mobile phones, so that you are not as easily identifiable. Being data literate includes learning which level of precision you need to give, but not more, in order to get the outputs you want from a refinery.

Geolocation is not the only area where data resolution can be dialed up or dialed down. The relationships between people, their preferences and sentiments as reflected in clicks and swipes, how relevant something is to a given situation, the extent to which a place is considered private or public: all of these are more complicated than toggling an on/off switch. Life is not binary; neither are data.

Many personal characteristics—including age, weight and height, ethnicity, religion, employer, industry, and occupation—could be blurred. LinkedIn, for instance, allows you to blur what level of identity details people see about you while you browse others' profiles—and the system is designed such that, should you choose to show only blurred details about yourself, you get to see only those details at the same level of resolution about the people visiting your profile: the resolution you choose to reveal determines what you see about others. If you are a woman or an ethnic minority submitting an application for a job, you might want the option of blurring your identity by having only the initials of your first name displayed to the person screening the incoming resumés. Economists have actually found that applicants with "ethnic"- or foreign-sounding names are less likely to be invited for an interview compared to those with "white" or native-sounding names.[18]

Blurring also gives individuals more control over their data in commercial settings. When you buy an item, the retailer has to know the specific SKU (stock keeping unit) of the product you bought, and the detailed characteristics of a product say a lot about you as a consumer. For more personally sensitive purchases, you might request that the precise item is described only by a blurrier category of "Massage Tools" or "Wellness and Relaxation," or perhaps to the sub-department of "Health and Personal Care" or "Health and Household." Blurring the exact SKU to the level of product category would protect you from potential embarrassment in the event of a hack—or an accidental disclosure to someone sharing your computer, if you forget to log out of your account.[19] Of course, blurring product data would affect the product recommendations you see, since the link from your shopping history to the SKU would no longer exist—but getting less personalized recommendations in this scenario might be precisely your preference.

To consider how the right to blur might work pragmatically, you must acknowledge that you have to first create data, sometimes very precise data. When civilian GPS was much less specific, you couldn't get useful directions for navigation. To make a call on a mobile phone, you have to connect to a base station, the location of which the carrier of course knows. You can reduce the resolution of data only after that point—that is, when you decide to share your data with some other refinery and apply some restrictions to its subsequent use.

In some cases you can change the resolution of the data at the point of creation. However, blurring data at the source is irreversible. It may make it impossible to take advantage of future products and services, including some you may not yet have any inkling that you'll want or need. For example, if you blur parts of your identity, you may not be allowed to make a digital payment—and it may not be obvious what parts of your identity are required for authentication.

You might also decide to blur data but later discover that high-resolution data are pertinent to a decision you need to make. Say you regularly stayed with a friend who lived on a block that was a known hotspot for buying illegal drugs, and you decided to blur the address to a radius of a few miles so that you aren't inappropriately associated with that block's reputation. Later, you want to use a refinery to see if your environmental exposure puts you at a higher risk of getting cancer. Several buildings in that area have since been detected to have had higher-than-reasonable amounts of lead or another carcinogen, but if you've blurred the address, the refinery won't be able to assess your risk accurately.

The choice to blur data will often come with consequences, and you will not always be able to predict in advance what those consequences might be. Amazon's Kindle records where I start and stop reading a book, and how many minutes I spend on each page. A student may not want his teacher to see that level of data, depending on how it affects his grade in class, even if it would help the teacher personalize a lesson plan for the material where the student seems to get stalled. You might decide to share highly granular reading data with Amazon or another book recommendations site to get pointers to authors you might enjoy, and then find an FBI agent at your front door because you spent a long time on an article about how the Boston Marathon bombers built their pressure-cooker bomb—very close to an actual scenario.[20]

It will take time to become familiar with how blurring various aspects of various situations might affect us and our future decisions. As we build a mental model of blurring, we would benefit greatly if refineries were more transparent about the marginal increase in value of their products and services in response to a marginal increase in data resolution. It will also help if users were given the agency to adopt others' finely tuned blur settings as their preference, overriding the refinery's defaults. Imagine being able to replace the default settings on your phone or computer with blurring settings developed or recommended by the Electronic Frontier Foundation, the American Civil Liberties Union, or a similar organization. The organization could offer a few profiles for different user types, clearly defining the blur settings and outlining the advantages and disadvantages. After exploring different settings, you would be able to decide which one works best for you and possibly fine-tune and personalize the settings further.

How can we create an environment that encourages more open but "owned" expression—more amendments to data—when data involve sensitive categories of information? For instance, a person might fear sharing a political comment under his real name if he knows it's counter to his employer's opinion, or avoid admitting to heavy drinking or illicit drug use in the patient annotations to his medical record.

In the 1960s, Canadian economist Stanley L. Warner faced exactly this problem while gathering field statistics for his research.[21] He realized that individuals often have valid reasons for withholding information about themselves, and no amount of pleading about the social good of sharing, or explaining how the person would benefit, would persuade everyone to be completely honest. If you posed a provocative question like "Do you use marijuana?" or "Are you HIV-positive?," there's no way of ascertaining what percentage of people might have lied when they answered (short of conducting an impromptu blood test).

Warner figured that some people would lie, and that he wouldn't know whether certain subgroups of people were more likely to do so. If people living in some neighborhoods were more likely to give a false negative answer, then his data would be skewed in ways that he couldn't fix. To add a layer of protection between themselves and their answer, he suggested introducing random noise to the data—which was a method for blurring them.

Here's how it works: Before a person provides the answer to the question, he flips a coin. If the coin turns up heads, he answers the question honestly, with a "yes" or "no"; if it turns up tails, he answers yes, irrespective of the truth. Only the subject knows whether his answer was honest or dictated by the outcome of the coin toss. If the subject is later confronted with his affirmative answer, he can rightfully claim that the coin toss dictated that he answer "yes"—and no one could ever give him trouble for his answer because they had no way of knowing if he was lying or telling the truth. The elegance of Warner's method is that while it protects the individual, it still provides decision-makers with the data they need. In fact, the data can be more "truthful" than it would have been had no noise been introduced.

Blurring can be applied to both a person's raw data inputs and a refinery's outputs. By randomly jiggling individual points around, we can blur our personal data while still reaping the benefits of aggregating and analyzing data to make predictions and prescriptions.

The Right to Experiment with the Refineries

Data refineries are constantly experimenting with their design, settings, and ranking algorithms. And, as we saw earlier, they also run experiments on their users. If refineries can experiment with us, we should be able to experiment with them.

While the right to amend is about free expression and the right to blur is about self-determination, the right to experiment is about exploration, letting users play with the possibilities. One of the key functions of a data refinery is to determine the order in which products and services are presented to users. The ranking of results is based on parameters such as recency, with the latest options placed at the top of a list; geographical proximity, with the nearest options to you placed at the top; or social proximity, with the options with stronger connections to you placed at the top. I like to think of these settings as "knobs" or "sliders," which can be set to higher or lower values much like the controls on a sound mixing board can be used to alter the balance of inputs from different microphones when a musical performance is recorded.[22]

Unfortunately, the refineries' knobs aren't always visible to the user. Why are these settings so often tucked inside a black box, out of users' sight or reach? It's not for some prosaic reason, such as laziness or greed, or some unwavering devotion to the principle of simplicity in interface design.[23] There are sound business reasons for not revealing the knobs, including the fact that knobs cost money to create, that they might expose proprietary secrets, or that some of the knobs might open a company up to lawsuits. In addition, refineries are not in the business of custom programming. They aren't going to add knobs for whatever a user might dream up. But refineries ought to give users the ability to access and adjust the settings of the knobs that do exist. However, there are also epistemological reasons for keeping some knobs out of users' sight. It is often difficult to find a word to describe what a knob does that people will instantly understand—and therefore feel comfortable using. Nevertheless, as Viktor Mayer-Schönberger and Kenneth Cukier point out in their groundbreaking book *Big Data,* predictions and prescriptions can work without people understanding exactly *why* they work.[24] While these are legitimate concerns, they are also excuses for limiting user agency. I believe that it's only by playing with knobs that people gain an understanding of what a knob does, what a knob means, and what settings work best for them.

By experimenting with the settings of the knobs, you can build a mental model of how the refinery works. If one of the knobs varies the weight given to recent data relative to older data, you could turn it back and forth to see how this affects the information being surfaced. Plus, a knob is a far more dynamic tool for understanding a refinery than the on/off switch of the FeedVis program developed at the University of Illinois to allow users to gain an understanding of the Facebook Feed.

Travel search site Hipmunk's "agony" function ranks flights by analyzing a combination of price, number of stops, and travel time. While the availability of this knob is a step in the right direction, users who do not quite like the results sorted by agony have to resort to sorting flights solely by price, duration, or take-off or landing time, or try filtering out specific airlines or travel arrangements—like having two or more stops—that they know they are not interested in. Wouldn't it be more efficient for everyone if users could experiment with the weights put on each ingredient in the agony equation? The next step is to let users apply different weights to each term in the agony function. This would be in Hipmunk's interests, too. If a user's weights don't match with Hipmunk's, the company's innovative options for comparing flights—clustering similar itineraries together so that customers aren't overwhelmed by choices that are basically equivalent, and placing results on a timeline that visually communicates time in flight, features on the flight, such as wifi, and time during layovers—will not provide as much benefit to them. Let users experiment with the settings and find the flights they really prefer.

Or consider the sort of data collected at Amazon. The company has a record of every purchase you have made, and where you had it shipped. In addition to using click and purchase data to make personalized recommendations for you, Amazon could analyze how far away you live from others who have previously considered the item. You might want to get recommendations based on items purchased more frequently by people in your city, county, or state, especially if you are looking for a product that meets the requirement for a local area—like a low-water-use version of a device if you live in drought-plagued California.[25] Amazon collects other categories of data that might be worth playing with, including the type of device used when browsing. If you're on a mobile phone, you may find what you are looking for faster if you are able to increase the weight put on products that have been ordered from phones rather than from PCs. This might require joining the device fingerprint to some contextual data—for example, observing that you are currently connecting to the internet through in-flight wifi.

Refineries might argue that exposing their knobs, including their corresponding default settings, will reduce their competitive advantage. Indeed, some organizations may resist giving users the right to experiment with the knobs that control the rankings and recommendations offered to them because portions of their business are based on withholding information. A few years ago, a twenty-two-year-old entrepreneur named Aktarer Zaman set up Skiplagged, a flight search site that uncovered cheaper fares between two cities than the airlines' published prices. The site took advantage of the fact that airlines sometimes discount multi-leg flights that include a hub that is a popular destination in its own right. For instance, I might want to fly from San Francisco to Denver on a particular day, and the cheapest fare I can find is $750. The same airline might be offering a flight on the same day from San Francisco to Phoenix via Denver for $500—and in fact, the first leg is exactly the same flight. I'm being charged a 50 percent premium for traveling six hundred miles less, because there's less demand for a flight to Phoenix than there is for a flight to Denver. Zaman called this "hidden city" ticketing. United Airlines sued Skiplagged for "unfair competition," when all Zaman had done was make this by-product of the airlines' yield management systems transparent to customers.[26] Having access to the knobs—not just to the data—will allow us to explore and expose similar situations where the interests of a refinery may not be aligned with our own interests.

Most important, as we gain the tools to experiment with refineries' settings and see how outputs change, we will gain knowledge of personal preference functions: how we feel when we consider different possible outcomes, and how this influences and improves our decision-making. As psychologists Daniel Kahneman and the late Amos Tversky showed in their landmark studies of decision-making under uncertainty, people often fall back on heuristics, or simple mental rules, to find satisfactory solutions to a problem when there are just too many variables to efficiently identify the optimal option. Originally, Danny and Amos noted three common heuristics: *availability*, the ease with which an idea or thing comes to mind; *representativeness*, the desire to give more weight to something that seems more typical of a category; and *anchoring*, the tendency to judge things in relation to a baseline.[27] Since their seminal paper, published about half a century ago, a whole cottage industry has sprung up, with hundreds of variations on the theme of heuristics. However, only through experimentation can we gain a better sense for how these heuristics affect us—and with today's refineries we can explore our assumptions about our current situation and preferences, and what we might face in the future by turning the refineries' knobs.

Here's a practical example. It's tough to advise a person about how much money he needs to save for a comfortable retirement because so many uncertain variables enter into the calculation. How strong will the economy be in five or ten years? How much will energy prices increase, and what sources of energy will be available? What level of health care will the person need for a condition that may not yet be diagnosed? All of these factors will affect the future retiree, but he has very little information about them. Even if an oracle gave him all the answers, he would not have much influence over them. But what he can do is run different scenarios, watching how the distribution of possible outcomes shifts based on the decisions that he actually has some control over. Playing with the parameters of the model, such as economic conditions and portfolio allocations, lets him see how the probabilities of various outcomes change, as well, potentially making him more comfortable choosing an option far from his initial anchor. We need to ask the refineries to create and share tools for such "what-if" analyses.

What-if analyses are useful in many areas of life. Imagine you are a high school senior staring at acceptance letters from, say, Harvard and Stanford. How do you decide which to pick? In 2014, LinkedIn launched its University Pages service, which analyzes the massive database of resumés on the site, to see where graduates of a university go to work and what their career paths are. This refined data can help guide a what-if decision-making process focused both on the initial settings (which university to consider) and on the outcomes (what career is probable). If a student has a career goal in mind—working at Google, McKinsey, Monsanto, or the World Wildlife Fund after graduation—she can look up whether graduates of the university have an unusually high probability of working for a particular employer. She can see which universities are top feeder schools for specific industries, including intriguing subfields such as NGO management consulting, TV screenwriting, or ceramic engineering. She can experiment with filters, drilling down from an academic major to discover specialties that might be an especially good fit if she wants to increase her chances of landing a job with a certain employer.[28]

As with so many decisions, retirement planning and college choices require trade-offs. Often, however, people do not know how much they want something until they're forced to give it up. It's in seeing trade-offs that we come to understand what outcomes are less or more desirable to us. By experimenting with the knobs, people are in better position to understand their trade-offs in advance. The right to experiment opens new vistas for informing—and understanding—our decisions.

The Right to Port Your Data

As with the rights to amend, blur, or experiment, the right to port data is focused on increasing agency. In the previous chapter, I argued that the right to access data is about more than seeing your bits and bytes; it is the right to see those data in a way that makes sense to and for you—for instance, in comparison to aggregates and benchmarks. For meaningful transparency, you have to be able to *interpret* your data. Under the right to access, you could request a copy of your data from a refinery,[29] but in most cases, you would not be able to do much with it unless you had another refinery at your disposal. For meaningful agency, you need to be able to *use* your data freely—to whatever scope you like, and with any recipient of your choosing. This is the fundamental purpose of the right to port.

When a physical thing is exported or imported, it must moved from its place of origin to its destination. When data are ported, the data continue to exist where they were created. Take the familiar situation of a student who wants to share her undergraduate grades with several graduate school programs or potential employers. There's no question that the record of her grades will remain at her college after her transcript is sent out. Yet even this simple example draws attention to the complications inherent in porting data for use elsewhere. First, the recipients need to be able to verify that the transcript has come from the student's university, and that it hasn't been tampered with. Further, the student might want to ensure that the transcript is sent only to places of her choosing. She can think about her grades and decide whether or not it is in her interest to release her college record to each recipient. That way, she can also put any poor grades in context in a letter or interview—an amendment to the record. Posting the transcript for anyone to see, or sending it to anyone who requests a copy, diminishes the student's influence over the data-review process.

For a long time, this process has been done manually, with students getting transcripts in sealed envelopes and sending them out to their chosen recipients. For this task, the manual system works, because the scale of data was relatively small; about a million students newly enroll in graduate programs each year, and request a small amount of data created over a fairly long period—the summary of a college career of work in four years of grades—to be shared with a handful of recipients.

Porting on the scale of the data created by a billion people through the mere click of a button or swipe of a screen requires a more sophisticated technological solution. In addition, when one of the main functions of a refinery is to analyze and summarize reputation, it has to be very careful if it allows people to introduce data whose provenance is unknown. A ratings and review system, like the ones developed at eBay or Amazon, would be vulnerable to fraudsters importing cooked-up data indicating that they have a stellar track record with customers at another site. If users could no longer trust the reputation data at the refinery, trust in the refinery, and the entire ecosystem, would be at risk. Ported data has to be authenticated and verified to be functional.

Verification could be accomplished using encryption keys, which are already used by many people to lock and unlock electronic communications. You get a pair of keys that are used in tandem: a private key that is not shared with anyone and a public key that is posted for anyone to see. Let's say you want to send a message to someone, and the recipient needs some assurance that the data actually came from you. You would encrypt your data with your private key and the recipient would be able to verify that the data came from you by applying your public key to it and unlocking messages that make sense.

The same tactic of matching keys also solves another problem, the situation where you want to send a message to someone but ensure that no one else can read it. You would encrypt your data with the recipient's public key, and after that, only a person who knew the recipient's private key could decrypt or unlock the message.

It is also possible to combine both approaches, verifying the sender's identity and restricting who can read the message. Encryption should be used for any ported data.

Just as college transcripts can be printed and sent individually, porting could be done individually, by sending individual emails. But while the print-and-send process is perfectly fine for college transcripts, it does not scale. Verified data must also be transmitted in a format that can be plugged directly into a recipient refinery. Thankfully, a protocol for such data sharing already exists: an application programming interface, or API. APIs allow developers to access a refinery's data in an automatic fashion, without having to submit a series of queries to the refinery and translate each of the results one by one. APIs allow travel search sites like Hipmunk to access the flight and fare information of dozens of airlines within seconds. APIs let developers create new products and services that require combining data from multiple sources.

When an API "call" is made to a refinery, the data are a snapshot for that specific moment in time. When you do a travel search at Hipmunk, for instance, the site doesn't continuously re-rank your results in real time as the airlines sell seats and change fares. You understand that an available seat might disappear while you are evaluating your options, and if the search results were constantly shifting before your eyes as new data were shared and analyzed, it might prove hard to make a booking decision, since you may be forced to constantly reconsider your options.

Together, these tools help to ensure that data are not locked inside a refinery. You get more value out of your data if you can combine, compare, and contrast them with data from other sources. That's especially true when you consider that some of the most important social data being created involve trustworthiness and reputation. Ride-sharing platforms such as Uber and Lyft rely on user ratings and reviews to build confidence in their services. Reviews and ratings serve to "vet" both drivers and riders. The average rating of the driver is a key metric for assessing the quality of customer service. In 2015, if an Uber driver's average rating fell below 4.6 on a scale of 5, he was at risk of having his account suspended.[30] Another important metric is the driver's acceptance rate. Each ride request gets sent sequentially to one driver at a time based on the best match of location, and each driver gets about fifteen seconds to accept the hail. If he does not accept within this brief window, the ride is offered to the next match in the system. If his rate of accepting hails falls below 80 or 90 percent, he receives a warning; after too many warnings, he will be temporarily locked out of the app. If he rejects three hails in row, the app will stop sending him matches for about ten minutes, because it infers that the driver isn't available, and if he is matched with a hail, the requesting passenger will just end up waiting longer for a ride. Finally, if a driver tries to game the rules by accepting all hails sent to him and then canceling them, it is even worse: he is at risk of having his account suspended.[31]

The ride-sharing platforms also offer incentives to drivers to work based on their data analyses. During periods of peak demand, the platforms want to have as many drivers available as possible to avoid long wait times for pickups, so they have created incentives for drivers to spend as much time as possible working on one platform. Lyft has tried to make its platform more attractive by taking no commission on rides after a driver completed sixty rides per week while also accepting at least 90 percent of the rides matched to him.[32] Likewise, to qualify for Uber's guaranteed hourly earnings scheme in 2015, a driver had to not only accept above 80 or 90 percent (depending on the city) of rides offered to him; he had to be online with the platform for at least fifty minutes of the qualifying hour—usually during peak hours like rush hour and late nights on weekends—and complete at least one trip per hour.[33] So although Uber does not prohibit the driver from being available on another platform, these rules effectively mean that he would lose his guaranteed income on Uber if he was.

Such compensation schemes make worker lock-in a real issue. As a driver builds up a great reputation on one platform, he has to make a choice: Does he keep using that platform, or does he try out a competitor, which requires building his reputation from scratch? If his reputational data are locked in to one platform, his ability to find work is increasingly locked in to the platform, too.

The right to port challenges this status quo, shifting power from the organization to the individual. Albert Wenger of Union Square Ventures has argued that workers in the on-demand economy—including drivers for Uber, Lyft, and other ride-sharing companies—should have the "right to an API key," a token that provides permission to access a designated portion of a user's data through an API.[34] The goal is to level the playing field of information as users bargain with refineries over what data they give for what they get. Users can move their information to new "marketplaces"—perhaps to a site developed for drivers who are so highly rated that the ride-sharing companies are willing to pay a premium to have them on their platform. Being able to copy reputational, transactional, and other data from one company to another will improve all on-demand workers' ability to negotiate their terms.[35] The right to port data can ensure that reputation travels with people, just as it does in the physical world.

In addition, the right to port forces companies to focus on creating better products and services rather than just hoarding data. It is now apparent, if we look back over the first twenty years of customer-facing companies on the web, that those companies which relentlessly focused on collecting more and better data tended to be more successful than those focused on developing better algorithms. Data trump algorithms. Indeed, companies that want to improve personalization have an incentive to accept ported data, since adding and joining data from other sources often improves the quality of personalization.

However, data must flow in both directions—out and in—for the right to port to benefit individuals. Users will have to make a stand, taking their data to refineries that allow portability. They will have to demand portability from the big, early data players—the Googles, Facebooks, and Amazons—which have an intrinsic advantage over newer companies that are just starting to collect data. From a user perspective, the right to port ensures that your data are not held hostage to a specific refinery, letting you explore what another refinery might make of them.

For a thousand years people fought for the right to move their bodies freely. We now must fight for the right to move our data freely. In the social data revolution, mobility is key to agency.

Influencing the Machines

The four agency rights invite users to be in charge of their data and the settings that affect the refineries' outputs, rather than turning to "the authorities" to regulate exactly how, when, and where people's data can be used. However, it is important to be clear about what humans do well compared to what machines do well. I believe we should let people do what people are good at, computers do what computers are good at, and not confuse the two. Learning what to control and what to let the machine control comes through experience.

To see what I mean, consider one of the first examples of a technological development that required people to relinquish some of their control to a machine. In the 1960s, several big automakers and engineering companies looked into the possibility of an antilock braking system (ABS) for cars.[36] Similar systems in planes—where a pilot's braking mistake could affect hundreds of lives, and airlines were eager to reduce the chance of an accident—had already made aviation safer. However, car sales reps, engaged customers, and even some industry experts were incredulous: *Customers will never let a few transistors make a life-or-death decision about how to handle a car in a skid,* they proclaimed. In 1978, parts-maker Bosch manufactured the first standard-feature ABS for the top-of-the-line models of Mercedes-Benz and BMW.[37] Time after time, safety tests showed that the computer was both more reliable and more precise at controlling brakes during a skid, while people were better at controlling the direction of the car. Combined, the two systems—machine and human—made driving safer. Based on decades of evidence, governments determined that *not* having ABS installed in cars was unsafe for drivers.[38] A sign flip had occurred. Today, every new car in the United States and European Union has ABS.

Since the development of ABS, we've grown very comfortable delegating quite a few driving tasks to cars' onboard computers. However, we haven't handed all decisions over to the machine—only the ones where a computer can do a better job than a human can. Think about "cruise control." Early cruise control systems allowed a driver to maintain a car's speed without having to adjust the pressure applied to the accelerator pedal. The computer didn't take in any data related to the surrounding environment and wasn't set up to make changes to the speed. Such changes were solely the driver's decision, based on her assessment of local regulations and road conditions.

More modern "adaptive" cruise control systems have evolved to give the computer a role in analyzing the environment. Some systems warn the driver, or override the speed setting, based on incoming sensor data; for instance, the speed will be reduced if another car or obstacle is detected to be too close to the front of the car. This ensures that the car begins to slow at a prescribed "safe" distance, rather than depending on the driver to be alert to the need to turn off cruise control before there's an immediate hazard. In traffic sign recognition and alert systems, BMW, Mercedes-Benz, and other car manufacturers combine inputs from infrared distance sensors and a windshield-mounted camera that are processed by image recognition software and, in some cases, compared to a geolocation-tagged database of statutory speed limits. The next stage in dividing the labor of driving between humans and computers is automatic emergency braking (AEB) systems.[39] In early studies, AEB has been shown to reduce the incidence of rear-end crashes by nearly half; a front-collision warning system—which alerts the driver but doesn't engage the brakes—reduces them by about a quarter.[40] Still newer technologies allow car computers to communicate directly with each other, exchanging information about each car's location, velocity, and direction of travel, as well as about its "intent"—the car's goals, whether to travel at a target speed, change lanes, or find a parking spot—before another driver observes or infers them. Each of these driving innovations is a milestone on our journey toward self-driving cars.

Today, computers have responsibility for many aspects of driving safety. But would you want to be at the wheel of a car in which the automatic cruise control could automatically increase the speed of the car because the sensors indicate it's safe to drive faster than the speed you've set? A computer can discover our preferences and adjust the corresponding parameters, but we need to set the weights we put on the possible consequences of our decisions. This will become ever more important as social data gets fully integrated into commerce, finance, employment, education, health care, and governance. By demanding tools for making refineries transparent and exercising user agency, we maintain control of what matters: seeing how data shapes our decisions, while always retaining the power to make those decisions ourselves.

RIGHTS INTO REALITIES

Applying the Power of Transparency and Agency
How Will We Experience Data for the People in Our Lives?

The best way to predict the future is to invent it.[1]

ALAN KAY

IT'S ALL WELL AND GOOD to talk about rights, but they're meaningless if their existence has no effect on our daily lives. We face big questions about the possible and acceptable uses of data. What types of data should retailers be permitted to use when offering you a personalized deal? Should lenders be permitted to see your Facebook friends before deciding if they should give you a loan, or would that be the twenty-first-century version of "redlining," of treating applicants differently based on where they live? How can you know that fitness data provided to an employer-based healthcare provider will not get analyzed as part of other decisions regarding you and your job? As extensive data are collected about students, can we optimize the design of classrooms to actually ensure that no child is "left behind"? Sharing data lets us make better decisions, and make decisions more intelligently, but we should constantly strive to understand the potential upsides and downsides of sharing data, and how to take advantage of our transparency and agency rights.

Buying on Your Own Terms

When people shop, they usually compare prices, product specifications, ratings, and reviews for the goods and services they are considering.

Social data have significantly reduced traditional information asymmetries, but being transparent about customer purchasing patterns can also improve how people make purchasing decisions. At Amazon, we wanted to know which type of data most helped people decide which product to buy: browsing data ("Customers who viewed this item also viewed . . . "), purchasing data ("Customers who bought this item also bought . . . "), or a combination of the two ("Customers who viewed this item eventually bought . . . "). We found that customer satisfaction increased when people had more data about the relationship between clicks and the eventual purchases of others.

Sensor data will help companies to become more transparent about products. For several years, New Zealand–based Icebreaker assigned a unique alphanumeric string to every piece of clothing it makes. By entering the "Baacode" on the company website, customers could see information about the specific sheep station at which the wool fibers in their garment were shorn.[2] When I looked up my sweater, I learned that the wool originated at the Branch Creek Station, where Ray Anderson keeps nine thousand sheep on more than sixteen thousand acres. The station has been in the Anderson family since Ray's grandfather returned home after service in World War I.

Getting an introduction to the source of my clothing was warm and fuzzy marketing, but the Baacode served another purpose: it allowed Icebreaker to track where fakes and clones of its brand were showing up around the globe. Once fraudsters figured out that customers were looking for the Baacode, the fakes started getting a similar type of code so they would appear legitimate. However, if a Baacode entered on the website turned out to be a duplicate or unassigned, the data scientists at Icebreaker got down to some detective work, trying to map possible sources for the counterfeit goods so that the company could contact vulnerable suppliers and retailers about the problem. In the past, fakes needed to be as similar to a branded product as possible to ensure they weren't spotted; now, being too similar increases the likelihood that they will be discovered.[3]

I expect that in the future, many products—as well as product components—will come with unique identifiers, whether individual barcodes, QR codes, or RFID tags. A number of companies are exploring ways to track items, starting from the earliest stages of manufacturing; food packaging can also be tagged. QR codes, which can be scanned with a camera phone, are being used to track freshly caught fish from the pier to a wholesale market, allowing chefs to support local fishermen.[4] They have also been trialed as a way to confirm that the medications in a bottle at a drugstore match the ones the pharmaceutical company says should be in it—an effort to combat fraud.[5] Further, identifier data can be joined with data from sensors placed at each stage of the process. This would allow customers to confirm that food or pharmaceutical products have consistently been kept at safe temperatures. Customers might choose to buy products only from those companies that share explicit information about where their components came from and how they were assembled. One company, Applied DNA Sciences, is selling a liquid form of DNA, extracted from plants and reassembled into a unique genetic string, that can be applied to the surface of items and registered in a central database. If a stolen item is recovered by law enforcement officials, a chemical test will detect the unique DNA and provide a pointer to the legitimate owner. Because the amount of DNA is so minute, the technology is also being tested for use against counterfeit medicines.[6]

Customers will increasingly have a choice between buying traceable products from transparent companies and buying products with an inscrutable history. Transparency has its price—but so does a lack of transparency. Whether or not a product is subject to regulation by a government body, you ought to have access to information about the item, such as the origin of its raw ingredients, the conditions on the production line, and its journey to the store shelf. Likewise, as you consider sharing data about your purchase and use of a product—including registering your purchase to get a warranty—you should be able to see how the company might use those data. You may consider it a fair deal if you are informed of product defects or recalls, or if the company will help you find the product in the event that it is lost or stolen.[7] You may also feel okay about the transaction if the company promises that you'll only get recommendations for products of genuine interest to you, rather than those being pushed by the marketing team. You may not like the deal if the data are mainly used to send you irrelevant ads, let alone sold to others to target you.

Adding visibility into the lifecycle of products—before purchase, at purchase, during use, and after use—can change consumption patterns.

If companies enabled unique identifiers to track products throughout their use, they could reward customers who allowed such tracking by suggesting products that are a better fit for their patterns of use or rewarding people who recycle them. MIT's Trash Track project developed tags, made out of mobile phones with limited functionality, that were attached to trash to see how much ended up at a recycling center versus a landfill. The phones were programmed to "wake up" a few times each day, detect the current location, and text the information to the researchers' central server.[8] One of the project's goals was to understand how fines and subsidies changed the rate of recycling in a community. Another goal was to increase recycling rates simply by making people's trash more visible.

Phone data could be used in other novel ways. As noted in previous chapters, your phone company necessarily knows where you have been and whom you have called. Sometimes, under the auspices of trying to save you money, a telco will suggest a different plan based on your calling, texting, and data usage patterns, but that's the extent of what you get for your data. Yet telcos could create quite useful services from these data.

Taking a page from Alex Algard's company Hiya (formerly Whitepages Caller ID) and spam filters, telcos could tell you when an incoming call is likely coming from a telemarketer or scammer. Like Skydeck, they could offer a "friend relationship management" service that warns you when you are at risk of falling out of touch with someone based on an analysis of your calling patterns. Telcos could even provide health alerts based on phone use. If a person is suffering an acute episode of clinical depression, his mobile phone use changes, as do his movements, captured through his phone's location: he visits fewer places, leaves for work and other regular activities on an irregular schedule, and spends more time on his phone, but not making calls.[9] He could ask to receive a notice when such patterns emerge, to help him be more aware of his mental state, or ask that a trusted friend or doctor gets a message to check in on him. The return-on-data score could help spur innovation in these areas and others. Reflecting the extra value they deliver to their customers, telcos that provide these new types of services would get higher return-on-data scores compared to those that stick to mundane phone services.

These examples demonstrate how the rights to access and inspect will help customers make better decisions. Yet customers will get even more power when they are granted the rights to amend and port data, because these rights also present opportunities to find better matches, including the ability to negotiate personalized terms of purchase. To see how this might work, let's look at air travel.

For decades, customers had very little access to information about how airfares were set. The price, dates, flight numbers, and other details were fixed; a paper ticket and flight coupons were printed; and a flight coupon was handed over to the gate agent to get on each plane. Once the ticket was issued, changing it was time-consuming and often expensive.

Airline scheduling and revenue management today are handled digitally, and almost all tickets are issued electronically, too. Since the advent of online travel refineries such as Skyscanner, Kayak, and Hipmunk,[10] customers have come to expect that they will be able to compare the price of tickets across airlines and routes, see how fares have changed, and get predictions of how they might change in the near future. They can sort through the thousands of flights available, experimenting with putting more or less weight on other aspects of travel, such as the length or duration of a flight, with Hipmunk's agony function or similar services. Airlines have even found a way to take advantage of travelers' anxiety over changing prices: you can pay a fee to hold a fare for a few days. Still, all the various ranking options come down to finding the ticket that is the best fit for you at the time of purchase. Given that airline tickets are no longer printed on paper but take the form of electronic bits, we no longer need to freeze the terms of purchase.

The right to amend could be the foundation for a new model for buying and selling air travel. Imagine that you could amend your ticket with information about the flexibility of your travel plans. Say you have bought a $350 ticket for the first flight of the day between Boston and San Francisco, departing at 6 a.m., but you are actually quite flexible that day. You amend your ticket to let the airline know that you would be willing to take any later flight if you get $200 cash back. A few weeks later, another traveler goes online to make a reservation. She would love to be on that early flight since it would allow her to see a friend in San Francisco before the business lunch she needs to attend, but at that point, both the 6 a.m. and 7 a.m. flights are sold out. All she can do is buy a ticket for a later flight and amend it by stating she would be willing to pay an extra $300 to get on the 6 a.m. departure. Once the airline's system detected the match, the airline would assign your seat to her, collect her extra $300, put you on the later flight, and send you $200 while keeping the remaining $100 as additional revenue. Amendments to tickets you've purchased would have to be as legally binding as the tickets themselves. In some cases, you would also need to specify the terms of how and when an amendment might be used.

Data rights would also affect the balance of power between customers and airlines when it comes to frequent flyer programs. Too many of these loyalty programs are engineered to lock customers into a specific airline or alliance.

For example, because you live in Dallas, one of American's hubs, you might fly American a lot, and let's say you've reached gold status in its frequent flyer program. You then move to Houston, a United Airlines' hub. Your status on American—including possible access to airport lounges, priority check-in, as well as free upgrades and other privileges—doesn't do you much good when taking United. If you could port your American Airlines status level, its expiration date, and potentially your entire flight history to United, then United might choose to match the benefits you have on American in hopes of gaining your business.[11]

Make no mistake, our transparency and agency rights are not just a way to make customers feel better about the data they share with companies. They represent a fundamental shift in mindset, turning customer relationship management inside out.[12] Companies stand to benefit from thinking creatively about how to deliver new products and services to customers on more flexible terms, but most important, data for the people shifts power into the hands of customers.

The Future of Finance

Exercising our social data rights will change not only the way we spend our money but also how we manage it. In the past, the loan officer in a small town often knew everyone's business, George Bailey–style. Today, you're likely to be asking a too-big-to-fail multinational to judge your creditworthiness. When you apply for a loan, you might not want the loan officer to check your detailed transaction history or your Facebook Timeline to find out what you've been up to. However, with the plethora of data available, some of these data may in the future be helpful to you when you apply to a bank for credit. The decision of what data you want your bank to see (and not see) will be up to you—though if you choose not to share some data that the bank considers necessary, you'll have to live with the result. Regardless, sharing many kinds of personal data will be particularly important for people who have very little credit history—for instance, when they are just out of school.

Consider the situation of recent college grad Miguel, who really needed a new mattress to support his bad back. Miguel didn't have hundreds of dollars at his disposal. His credit card was maxed out, and he was pretty sure that paying the over-limit penalty interest rate of 39.9 percent wasn't going to help him get a good night's sleep. So when it was time to check out at Casper.com, an online mattress retailer, he opted to "Pay with Affirm," a short-term credit option developed by the fintech start-up Affirm. He was instantly shown how much he would pay each month on a three-, six-, or twelve-month schedule. As soon as Miguel picked a plan and made his first payment to Affirm, Casper Sleep got paid in full and the mattress was shipped to him—no more layaway and no monthly interest to worry about.

Affirm CEO Max Levchin co-founded PayPal and was its chief technology officer. With Affirm he aspires to reinvent consumer credit much like PayPal reinvented online payments. He believes that social data can give more people access to credit. To do a better job of estimating credit risk for people with scant financial history, his company draws on far more than the five categories of information used to come up with Miguel's FICO score. Among the data analyzed are web browsing behavior, activity on Facebook and Twitter, frequency of mobile phone calls and text messages, and even the operating system of the mobile phone.[13] Affirm also looks to see if the applicant has been active in an online community such as GitHub, where software developers share their code and collaborate with others. Contributors to the site generally have an authenticated identity and reputation feedback on their work. For some applicants, Affirm will ask for temporary read access to a checking account in order to analyze purchasing and income patterns.[14]

Other fintech start-ups serve "underbanked" customers. Upstart has focused on offering credit to people in their twenties and thirties who want to refinance credit-card debt. The company does not rely solely on an assessment of current income and expenses, instead examining the university you attended, your major, the classes you took, the grades you got, and your SAT scores to predict your salary growth over the next several years and figure out the likelihood that you will repay its loan.[15] Similarly, ZestFinance has claimed that it collects thousands of data points to determine when to extend credit to poor people and those without bank accounts. Among other things, the data scientists have found that people who use only capital letters, rather than using both upper and lower case, on their loan application forms are less likely to repay a loan.[16]

In each of these cases, fintech companies are using social data to determine whether they should make loans to people with poor credit scores or limited credit history. In China, where one in five adults had a credit score as of 2015, social data are playing a key role in the creation of the consumer credit sector.[17]

Until quite recently, most Chinese citizens had to turn to friends and family when they needed to raise extra cash. In 2016, around 200 million new credit-card applications were completed. The approval rate for applicants is around 30 percent, not only because people lack or have bad credit history but also because the central government limits the amount of credit each bank can extend.[18]

One credit rating license that Beijing granted went to Sesame Credit, the pilot project being developed by Alibaba. More than 650 million people use Alibaba's e-commerce site each year, which gives Sesame Credit access to a wealth of transaction and communication data. For example, through its payment system, Alipay, Alibaba reportedly handled $14 billion in gross sales on November 11, 2015—Singles Day, or 11/11, a "festival of shopping" for single adults popularized by Alibaba—making it the biggest shopping day in history so far. Nearly 70 percent of the sales were conducted via smartphone,[19] and Alibaba could look at geolocation data recorded by the Alipay app to identify where shoppers spent the day. When people share a meal, the Alipay mobile app has a payment option to "go Dutch" on the bill. This gives Alibaba real-world information not only about where people are eating but also with whom they are eating, in calculating Sesame Credit scores.

As more transaction and social graph data become more important in the decision of whether to approve or reject a credit application, people will need to have access to these data as well. You should be able to see an analysis of the data sources and how they affect your credit score, much like FICO tells you what percentage of its score is based on whether you pay your bills on time. How much weight is put on a semantic analysis of your tweets, which could reveal that you are worried about losing your job? Are your location data considered, to see where you spend your time, noting with approval that you clock long hours at the office—or with concern, too many nights at your local bar? Is the refinery analyzing your social graph for indications that some of your friends are a credit risk, akin to how Allstate flagged claims for investigation in cases where some of your friends may have filed false claims themselves? If connections with certain people are making lenders turn down your loan application, you should have a right to know which ones they were. Just as Facebook should show you the photos that it thinks you're in, the bank should show you the data that it uses to make a credit decision.

Once you've reviewed the data, you can decide whether to change your behavior or change your data, by amending or blurring them. You could amend data with additional context, as you might in order to explain a bad grade on your college transcript, or, in past decades, to explain a missed payment in an interview with the loan officer at your local Building & Loan. After seeing the effect of each person in your social graph on your application's chances, you might decide to unfriend a person who is dragging down your social data credit score, much like a person might sever ties with a disreputable character in town. This can get complicated if a data refinery considers the reputation of friends of friends of friends, the use case mentioned in Facebook's patent for using social graph data in a variety of sectors, including finance.[20] You might agree to let a financial institution review your Facebook social graph for your loan application, but only if you have the right to blur the resolution of your friends.

In some circumstances, your social network might make it easier to get a loan, because your friends are responsible debt payers or because, à la Friendsurance, they are willing to effectively "co-sign" a certain amount of your loan. Exercising your right to experiment with your social graph will give you a good sense for which of your data you want to port to a potential lender.

Porting data is not only important when you need to borrow money. When you want to invest your money, porting data can level the playing field for you. One pioneer in the investment sector is SigFig Wealth Management, founded by Mike Sha, who was in charge of payment products at Amazon when I was there. After he left Amazon, Mike wanted to see how investment decisions might be improved by bringing together and analyzing the data that individual investors had access to across brokerages.[21]

Not so long ago, financial brokers were trusted and respected for their advice. Brokers would sit down with their clients and try to understand their long-term financial goals, and suggest an investment portfolio to them. The fees charged for these services were rarely broken out, so customers had very little leverage to negotiate. It was clear to Mike that brokerages were unlikely to disclose more than the law required. "It's not like you can try calling them and ask them what they charge," Mike told *Business Insider.* "We've talked to people who work with brokers or advisers and they have no idea what the fee structure is in other firms."[22] Data about the performance of individual brokers was particularly hard to come by. It often seemed that financial advisers were experts in the art of smoke and mirrors, not the magic of transparency. How, then, could retail investors ever hope to get access to the information they needed to make good investment decisions? Mike's idea was to apply the principle of "give to get" to this problem.

He asked customers to give SigFig read-only access to all of their accounts in exchange for unbiased investment analysis and an assessment of their financial position. The algorithms detect inefficiencies and suggest ways to improve investment mix. SigFig even works with brokerages that don't support data portability, by simulating the user logging in to her account and screen-scraping the data—with the user's permission, of course. This can be viewed as porting data without the collaboration of the brokerage, yet it's just as powerful. More than 800,000 customers at over 100 financial institutions have already given SigFig access their accounts, totaling more than $350 billion.[23] This amount of data allows the company to deliver an unprecedented level of transparency to its users, more than any brokerage could or would do on its own. SigFig calculated how much investors were actually paying in fees and shared this information with them. It also analyzed the performance of each individual's portfolio and compared it to exchange-traded funds (ETFs) and other low-cost alternatives. This information empowers customers to ask for a better deal or service from their brokerage, or switch to a competitor.[24]

SigFig and its customers helped force open brokerages by giving individual investors the means to port their data.

In China, too, customers are taking advantage of technological tools to create more transparency around financial decisions—including the process of applying for credit cards, which is complicated by the secrecy surrounding the amount of credit each bank has been given by the central government. After working at FICO and Acxiom, Darwin Tu moved back to China to establish 51credit.com, which helps applicants navigate this opaque procedure. As with SigFig, people must give 51credit access to their data—in this case, the information typically required for a credit-card application. By analyzing these data and comparing them to previously approved and rejected applications, 51credit can steer people to banks where they have the best chance of getting a card approved.[25] In effect, Darwin and his team "reverse-engineered" the decision-making process at the banks, creating transparency where none had existed.

If banks do not increase transparency and agency for customers, people will seek out tools to pry them open.

Fair Employment Agency

While he was the chief information officer at investment bank Dresdner Kleinwort Wasserstein, J. P. Rangaswami came to a sobering realization: employee bickering was taking up far too much of his time.[26] His email inbox was filled with complaints about other departments, managers, and team members. Some of the concerns were legitimate, but others seemed to be nothing but the typical office politics.

J. P. didn't have time to sort through all this information and determine which emails needed his attention and which didn't. As CIO he definitely could have set up some system on the company intranet that would let people rate each other's credibility and contributions, but that might have a negative effect on morale. Instead, he had a much simpler idea: he gave all of his direct reports access to his inbox and outbox.[27]

J. P. noticed an immediate drop in the number of emails in which people complained about their colleagues. The move wasn't universally popular, and some staff left the company in the months that followed. Knowing that others would read their emails changed how employees behaved. Then J. P. got curious about what the people working for him were clicking on; he wanted to understand their thinking, or, in his words, "get inside their heads."[28] He discovered that people were much more interested in his outbox than his inbox—that is, what he was saying rather than what others were telling him.

J. P. did this in 2001, three years before Gmail and Facebook were launched, and more than a decade before the appearance of Slack, a work communication platform that makes every memo and message accessible to everyone in the company.[29] Powerful tools for amending data are needed to navigate the vast amount of information now accessible to employees. Threads and posts gain traction as people post their reactions to them using a well-designed annotation system, including emoji, which are more expressive than up- and downvotes, or the even more simplistic like button. In the future, communication platforms like Slack could recommend a few emojis for employees to choose from based on a real-time semantic analysis of a draft post or on a camera-based emotion recognition of their facial expression.

Today, businesses can inexpensively measure employees' output—keystroke by keystroke, video frame by video frame—and analyze both their job satisfaction and performance. Assume a company has enrolled its employees in a sociometric badge–style program. Managers would be able to see how workers interact with each other and how productive they are in different environments; it may become accepted practice to have sensors monitor alertness, mood, even overnight sleep patterns. Access to these data might help employees decide when and where they should do certain types of work. The system could recommend what sort of project was the right match for a person's current energy level. Then again, a manager could elect to pull an employee off of a big presentation based on that same data. To know if it's worth it to you to participate in such a data collection and analysis program, you would need to be able to see the return-on-data score—calculated from your perspective as an employee, not the perspective of your manager.

As companies explore new data sources, workers should demand to see the equation their company uses to evaluate performance and determine compensation, including a complete list of all the inputs and their weights. This transparency will give workers a better opportunity to align their time and effort with the company's priorities. If a company combines data from multiple sources—communication patterns in email and phone calls; sociometric badge readings; colleague evaluations, ratings, and surveys; and others—it will be much harder for people to fake their accomplishments. Analysis of these inputs will let managers and workers alike see how ideas propagate through the organization, revealing informal expertise hubs as well as communication bottlenecks. Being able to access and port data may also make it easier for people to detect when managers' actions differ from what the system suggested, highlighting possible biases and discrimination.

As employment data are shared with external data refineries, we will also gain a better understanding of economic trends affecting our careers. LinkedIn can characterize the health of specific companies and industries from the data shared by 400 million users. In one striking example, data scientists at LinkedIn noticed a lot of activity on the website on September 14, 2008—a Sunday. Given the highly unusual pattern for a weekend, they worried the site was being hacked. The security team was called in. After some investigation, they tracked down the source of the traffic: all of the requests were coming from Lehman Brothers employees, who were frantically reaching out to connections, updating resumés, and downloading contact information. LinkedIn's team suspected the data meant that Lehman Brothers' attempts to make a deal to avoid bankruptcy had failed—news that was not yet publicly confirmed.

It's a bad sign when employees are downloading all their contacts. An employee exodus is another bad sign. If a company consistently loses talent to its peers, its fortunes might not be as bright as those of its rivals. Such information is currently available only to corporate clients. For individuals, LinkedIn already shows the most popular employers for graduates of a particular university through University Pages, so it could go a step further and show the most popular employers among people who previously worked at a particular company, following the example of Amazon's recommendations, by showing what percentage of people who previously worked at one company now work at another.

Social data can also be used to optimize not just who is working for a company but when they work and whom they work with. For example, scheduling shift workers is a perennial challenge in retail (as well as in other sectors). Many variables influence the number of people visiting a store at a given time or on a given day, from the weather (a cold stretch or heavy downpour) to marketing (a hot sales promotion or big TV campaign). Greg Tanaka, founder of in-store analytics company Percolata,[30] and his team have developed models to generate predictions of store traffic and determine how many staff are needed to attend to customers. Optimizing staffing levels is key. "One in three customers leaves because they can't find a salesperson to help them," Greg explained.[31] Consistently overstaffing is not economically feasible, given how tight margins are in retail. Interpersonal dynamics cannot be ignored. A team can be more (or less) than the sum of the individuals working together on a shift, affecting productivity, morale, and the overall atmosphere in the store.

While good managers have a sense for the heaviest sales days and hours, predictions based on personal observations are not as good as Percolata's models based on data from cameras and microphones it installs in stores. Video and audio measure not only the number of customers but also their level of engagement with products, from sensing the overall noise level to identifying which aisles or products seem to attract the most footfall. The company also captures mobile phones' fingerprints,[32] the offline equivalent of internet browser cookies. These data help the store learn how frequently customers visit and which parts of the store they go to. Further, by assembling teams of people who Percolata has predicted to have high sales performance when they are working together, stores have been able to increase revenues by 10 percent without increasing staffing costs.[33]

One surprise for Percolata was the challenge of matching workers to each day's shifts. Greg suggested that staff members share their personal calendars, streamlining the system for contacting workers when a shift was predicted to need extra staffing on short notice. He gave workers the ability to blur the details of the entries in their calendar, sharing only the blocks of time when they were free or busy. However, only a few participated. Why? Was it that they didn't want to share the data with their manager? As Greg talked to workers, he discovered it was something much simpler: it turned out that many of them did not use an online calendar, and if they did, they didn't keep it up to date. They needed an incentive to create the data about their availability in the first place.

This is where the right to amend could be effective. A person's willingness to take a shift is not usually binary. A worker may be interested in working the busiest hours, particularly when she may get a sales commission. The worker could note the times when she is definitely free to work and get assigned to the shift automatically if more staff are needed. If she were possibly free to work over a stretch of hours, she might amend that stretch with a bonus or a higher rate she'd need to be paid to accept the shift. If the company wanted to stick to existing pay rates, she might instead amend her calendar by distributing a budget of points across the possible hours for the coming week to indicate her preference for working them over others. Managers could reward top performers by giving them extra points for a week. In either case, workers get more negotiating power and managers get more efficiency. Once again, increased agency improves the entire ecosystem.

The right to experiment with work data will also be helpful as people strive to advance in their careers. LinkedIn University Pages let students experiment with different educational scenarios to see each one's probability of leading to particular career outcomes. Imagine extending that service to help you understand the trade-offs for your future earning potential or promotion timeline of gaining different skills—as identified through an analysis of resumés or skill endorsements—or of working in various departments or companies. Being able to experiment with how the wording of your resumé affects its ranking in search results would also be a powerful service, leading to better matches on the job market.

Discovering talent takes time and money, which is why companies are increasingly relying on social data to do the work for them. When Gam Dias, the CEO and founder of data strategy company MoData, was looking for a data scientist, he realized that if a person posted consistently good answers about a topic on the Q&A website Quora, chances were that the individual really knew what he was talking about. "People sign up. People read. People post. People upvote. People comment," Gam said. "Quora is a knowledge economy like no other that I can think of, communicating post quality, popularity, and influence, and uncovering an implicit network of knowledge and influence around a topic."[34] He found several contributors with a great reputation in the area of machine learning, and he particularly liked the contributions from one regular poster. Even though the person said he wasn't interested in a new job when contacted, he agreed to fly out to Silicon Valley for an interview and ended up joining the company.

A decade ago, most people would have found the idea of openly sharing their hard-earned professional expertise online laughable. Your expertise is your paycheck, and giving it away for free reduced your earning potential in the job market. Now, by creating and sharing data that reveal your skills, you are able to build a reputation that extends far beyond your company and clients.

As people create and share these data that can be refined into a professional reputation, it will be possible for employers to devise compensation and bonus schemes that go beyond traditional performance metrics such as sales and profits. Your reputation as an expert among colleagues, the strength and speed of communication between your team and others, and even the efficiency of the meetings you run can now be quantified. For example, when an employee receives an internal call or chat request at one large Silicon Valley company, the communication track record of the person contacting her is displayed. If the person's calls average close to half an hour, the recipient can decide whether it makes sense to take the call or let it go to voicemail. Workers can better manage their time while managers get critical information about employee dynamics. As with sociometric badge data, the data make the time an employee spends helping colleagues more visible.

Yet, this system pales in comparison to the "radical transparency" established by Ray Dalio, the founder of Bridgewater Associates, the world's biggest hedge fund. Bridgewater collects and analyzes data about how the company makes its billion-dollar decisions. Nearly all meetings are recorded. Employees can register their reactions to colleagues, including frustration, and rate others' performance through an iPad app. Anyone can look up the ratings of their colleagues.[35] The company's software looks for behavioral patterns, such as what emotion is present in people's voices as they discuss a point, and identifies situations where very few doubts were raised about a decision. The goal is to encourage more skepticism and internal debate. Many of the videos and some of the analyses are shared with employees. Dalio believes that by making the implicit explicit, the company increases understanding, improves its decision-making processes, and gets better results.[36] I believe the results would be even better if everybody at Bridgewater had full access to the data and could amend and experiment.

As we saw with ride-sharing drivers, the right to port professional reputation and job review data may be most important to the one-third of Americans who get at least some of their income as independent contractors.[37] Some freelance project bidding and collaboration sites, like Freelancer.com and Upwork (formerly Elance-oDesk), give workers a platform for creating skill profiles and portfolios that are matched with companies looking to staff projects. Clients evaluate workers' communication, expertise, and quality of work, and potential clients can examine data on repeat hiring, on-budget and on-time performance, and completion rates. On Upwork, you can import your reputation from other platforms, including GitHub and Stack Overflow (for software developers) and Behance and Dribbble (for graphic designers). Like the mutually confirmed friendships on Facebook, the rating system is symmetrical, which verifies that employers and freelancers have in fact teamed up. When workers rate their clients, they indicate if the job description accurately reflected the full scope of work and time required, and whether they were paid promptly. In the past, only the company could see all the bids for a project, and the workers had to set their price in a vacuum. On Freelancer.com and Upwork, applicants can see each other's profiles, reviews, and bids. This transparency shifts the balance of power toward workers.

The Universal Declaration of Human Rights, which the United Nations General Assembly adopted in 1948, established that people have the right to work, engage in the employment of their choosing, and not be trapped in unsafe or unfair conditions. Seventy years later, we need to push beyond this, and ask for the right to port the records, ratings, and reviews earned for your work anywhere you choose. Social data can give us fairer, more transparent ways to match work with workers, match compensation to performance, and optimize the workforce—as long as workers can exercise their data rights.

Learning on the Playground

Nearly a century ago, American philosopher John Dewey argued that "education is not an affair of 'telling' and being told, but an active and constructive process."[38] Yet as Ken Robinson pointed out in his influential

TED Talk "Schools Kill Creativity," education is still mostly based on authority and lectures, a system designed to produce workers for industrial
factories, where breaking rules and taking risks was costly.[39]

Indeed, classroom arrangements haven't changed much in two thousand years. A teacher stands in front of a group of students, lectures to
them, then tests them to see how much they have retained. Too often,
the teacher learns very late, only after the final exams have been graded,
which students have grasped what material. Students have few opportunities to learn from their peers or connect their lessons to what they
are learning outside the classroom. Information is usually presented in a
one-directional, one-size-fits-all way.

Over the past century, we have increasingly focused on testing students' mastery of facts. It hasn't always been this way. When Socrates
entered into his dialogues with his student Plato, he framed every lesson
in the form of a series of questions. For Socrates, teaching his students
how to ask good questions was more important than providing them
with answers—a view that is even more applicable today when search
engines provide answers to pretty much anything we can think of asking (whether the answers are correct or not is another question). Or, as
Eric Mazur, a professor of physics at Harvard, put it: "You can forget
facts, but you cannot forget understanding."[40] After Mazur realized his
students learned more, and learned better, when they worked with each
other on a study topic than they did when listening to him pontificating,
he invented Learning Catalytics, a web-based educational system.

One of the first teachers to try the software was Jennifer Curtis, a
physics teacher at a high school in Maine. At the start of class, she would
tell her students to pull out their iPads. Rather than confiscating these
devices as distractions, she got them to launch the app and had them
spend the next hour learning from each other, guided by the software.
First, Curtis's students answered a few questions about reading or a video
they had been assigned as homework the night before. That quiz helped
Curtis match up her students based on their answers. From there, Curtis
told the pairs of students to persuade each other that their answers were
correct, and then enter their final answer through the app. Curtis could
then see who needed more help with the concepts. As they got familiar
with the process, the students learned how to solve problems through

dialectic questioning, deduction, and teamwork. Instead of learning to memorize answers, the method helped students grasp and explain concepts and the underlying structure of a problem and come up with a range of possible solutions.[41] Learning Catalytics raised the level of group discussion and the performance of Curtis's students.[42]

Every interaction with an education app leaves traces—and these traces can be used to increase a student's ability to learn. New educational programs are being set up where everything that can be recorded is recorded. Such data are central to the Minerva Schools at the Keck Graduate Institute (KGI), established by Ben Nelson, former CEO of the photo-sharing and -printing service Snapfish, and Stephen Kosslyn, a psychologist and former dean of Harvard's social sciences division. At the time of Minerva's launch in the fall of 2015, its students and faculty were based in seven cities and interacted mostly through computers. Their video feeds, chat messages, and quiz answers were analyzed in real time, helping the instructor moderate class discussion and successfully engage long-distance students.[43] Afterward, experts in emotional expression coded the videos to help identify areas where students became excited, bored, frustrated, confused, or any number of other emotions. The students get access to these data, as well as recommendations about what to read and what activities to pursue outside class to support their studies. A fully instrumented program could register when a student is losing focus—and suggest it's time to take a break.

Thoughtful experimentation with social data will reveal the full effects of context and conditions in learning. Some schools rotate class times each day of the week so that students who find it easier to concentrate in the morning (or the afternoon) get a chance to excel at every subject. A high school in New Jersey used an online platform called Schoology to experiment with a "work from home" school day.[44] As a scientist, I would systematically vary inputs that can be changed—for example, teaching style, the temperature of classrooms, the food served at lunch, or the distance between the desks of two friends in the same class—and analyze the effect on each student's learning and well-being. Both teachers and students will gain more insight into their progress than a grade on an occasional test provides them, and both students and parents must have access to the results, as well as the interpretations of them.

For a complete understanding and accurate evaluation of students' learning patterns, data will need to be kept throughout elementary school and high school, then during college and beyond, potentially including "lifelong learning" programs. Thus far, the debate over how much data to keep, and for how long, has been dominated by privacy concerns, with one of the most popular student behavior–tracking apps choosing to delete data at the end of the school year.[45] What a terrible loss! Instead of having these education data histories deleted, students, parents, teachers, and education policymakers ought to be able to continue to learn from them. Students themselves will also benefit from the ability to combine data from several education apps. Being able to port data from individual apps into a general education refinery—built by the department of education, a private foundation, or a for-profit company—would provide greater insight into the ways in which students learn. This would also ensure that parents, teachers, and school administrators can monitor the data safety, privacy efficiency, and return on data of the refinery.

I mention the possibility of porting data because I expect there will be a lot of interest in seeing how data from educational settings will predict a person's qualifications for a job or other position, much like scores on aptitude tests are one of the data points employers use to filter resumés. Unlike test scores, the data collected about students might reveal their suitability for certain types of work. That's because a child's responses to challenging situations can predict later life outcomes, including how well a person handles rejection.[46]

One of my favorite examples of an unanticipated, long-term prediction along these lines is psychologist Walter Mischel's "marshmallow test" experiment, conducted with four- to six-year-olds at the Bing Nursery School at Stanford, starting in the 1960s.[47] Mischel placed a treat of their choice—the kids often picked a marshmallow—on a table and told them that they could eat it right away, but if they waited fifteen minutes, they'd get a second marshmallow. He then left the children alone in the room. One-third held out; the others gave in. In general, the older children in the cohort were better at delaying their gratification. But things got more interesting when Mischel contacted his subjects after they had matured into teens and adults. The kids who had waited to get two marshmallows were judged to be much more competent than their peers and performed better on aptitude tests.[48] This correlation between the willpower exhibited by a preschooler and later success in life was unexpected, and has held up in subsequent studies.

Education is a series of marshmallow experiments. Children who learn in instrumented classrooms will benefit from more personalized feedback, but they will also graduate with data indicative of willpower and other personality traits. It seems highly likely that there will be interest in using these data for other parts of life. Employers are keen to assess the personality of potential employees; many companies ask applicants to take psychological tests during the interview process. In the future, you could port your educational data to demonstrate your willpower, or some other quality, to a potential employer alongside your resumé in a job application. But you may want to get a sense of what your data might have to say about you before you do so, by porting it to a data-based education or career counselor first.

Educational data should open doors, not close them, and the entire educational system will benefit from collecting and analyzing social data. Given finite resources, teachers are often forced to focus their attention on some of their students. Should they focus on the below-average students on the left tail of the distribution curve, the above-average students on the right tail, or the average students in the middle? My father was proudest when he got the underperformers in his high school science classes engaged enough that they didn't drop out. In my teaching at the college level, I get the most satisfaction from working with the best students, when I manage to inspire them to come up with ideas they would not have otherwise. Some teachers focus on improving the performance of the average students—the majority in the typical classroom.

Choosing which group to focus on is not an easy decision, and none of the data of and by students—about their response to teaching styles, learning conditions, challenges, and more—tells us which of these outcomes we should pursue as a society. There is no single correct answer. As a society, we must set the terms in our equation of learning, then measure the inputs and change the weights, experimenting again and again, looking for ways to continually improve, student by student and classroom by classroom.

Precisely What the Data Ordered

With medicine that is digitized and unplugged, we move from the flip
phone to flipping the entire health care model.[49]

DR. ERIC TOPOL

When the first X-ray was taken in 1895, it was quite scary. Indeed, the
woman whose hand was X-rayed—she was the wife of Wilhelm Röntgen,
who won the first Nobel Prize in physics for discovering the technology—reportedly responded to the sight of the image with the chilling
words, "I have seen my death."[50] Suddenly, doctors were able to see inside the body; the invisible had become visible. They could diagnose
diseases, suggest treatments, make incisions with their scalpels with far
more precision. Within six months, X-ray machines were used to detect
the location of bullets in the bodies of two Italian soldiers wounded in
the country's war with Ethiopia.

Over the past century, the practice of medicine has been transformed
through the invention of a series of technologies that let us see the body
in new ways. The X-ray led in the 1970s to computer axial tomography,
or CAT scans, whereby computers construct a three-dimensional view
of the body from multiple X-rays. Magnetic resonance imaging (MRI)
measures water and fat content in the body, allowing us to see not only
the bones but also soft tissues and blood flow. Then in 2004, the International Human Genome Sequencing Consortium published the full sequence of the human genome, which made possible the field of precision
medicine, whereby a person's whole genome is analyzed to identify the
best course of treatment.[51] Today, there are tens of millions of X-ray machines, hundreds of thousands of CT and MRI scanners, and thousands
of DNA sequencers around the globe.[52]

These tallies, however, pale in comparison to the medical technology
carried around by people every day in the form of 1 billion smartphones
and 100 million physical activity trackers manufactured by Fitbit,
Garmin, Jawbone, Pebble, and others. These devices collect data that
are becoming central to monitoring and managing a person's health and
well-being, by providing a continuous record of our vital signs, as well
as our exercise habits, sleep patterns, and mood. Activity trackers can
even reveal such private information as how often you have sex with

your partner (or someone else).[53] We have never before been able to get such a rich, detailed picture of the state of our bodies and ourselves. I believe ignoring the potential of these data is a form of malpractice. However, using them will require rethinking patient rights and data flows in medicine.

You typically see your general physician only when you are sick, or for an annual checkup. During the appointment, the doctor takes a handful of measurements—heart rate, blood pressure, and weight—which often don't capture your overall health. If there appears to be a serious problem, you may be sent to get more tests or to see a specialist. According to Dr. Eric Topol, the annual checkup is far from efficient: in a routine exam the doctor collects too little data to catch issues, yet the visits in aggregate take up a lot of time.[54] The lack of timely information can be a contributing factor in many health issues. For the most part, your medical record also sticks to sporadic measurements, clear facts, and diagnostic codes that are mostly chosen for billing purposes. Too much of the collection and use of health data is centered on the needs of institutions—doctors' offices, pharmacies, hospitals, and insurers. The focus of data collection and analysis must shift to the patient.

This will require more than a change in how billing systems are set up, since many patients are reluctant to share information about their health, even with their doctor. They may fear being judged for maintaining a diet or habit that is deemed to be bad for their health, or hope that by ignoring a problem, it will go away by itself. They may assume that doctors' offices and health insurance companies will perform no better than other corporations in protecting the data in their care.[55] Some people have also seen their health data used against them—their premium might have gone up as a result of a preexisting condition, or they might have been denied coverage in the past.[56] If we could stop worrying about how our medical records might be used against us, these data could greatly improve our health and well-being, both in the short and long term.

There is a separate but related problem. Only very recently has it become standard to give patients access to their full medical records, including test results,[57] despite the fact that these health data are essential to making some of the biggest decisions in a person's life. That's because doctors' notes have not been written with the patient's point of view in mind. As one prominent physician put it to me, a doctor keeps notes for three main reasons: (1) to submit an itemized bill for her services; (2) to greet a patient as though she remembers him; and (3) to maintain a record should something go wrong and she needed to defend herself against a lawsuit. There is very little on that list that would improve my health.

A program called OpenNotes, launched by Dr. Tom Delbanco of Harvard Medical School, has quickly made progress in making doctors' notes more accessible, growing from a pilot study with 19,000 patients in 2010 to 8 million enrollments in 2016. Patients in the pilot study received secure access to their official medical record, which lists test results, diagnoses, and prescriptions, as well as doctors' notes and recommendations for follow-up. Whenever a doctor added a note, the system notified the patient by email. Four out of five patients read the notes, and they said the transparency gave them a better understanding of their health and a better relationship with their doctor.[58] Further, patients in the pilot asked for the ability to make amendments, potentially to document side effects of prescriptions or to point out misunderstandings or errors— for instance, if during the consultation, the doctor noted that a person reported having five drinks of alcohol per night on average when she actually said five drinks per week. As the program has expanded, more patients have started to request corrections about volunteered information and to ask for translations of medical jargon.[59]

OpenNotes has also tackled the taboo of giving patients access to notes of the sessions with their therapists and other mental health professionals. Often, therapists have maintained that seeing notes on mental health would be detrimental to their patients' progress and well-being. This protective, paternalistic approach to mental health is not much different from the standard practice in the mid-twentieth century and earlier of withholding medical information from women—they were too fragile!— and instead consulting their husbands or fathers about what healthcare decisions should be made. Delbanco explained that he believes "patients have as equal a right to see what the doctor writes when their minds hurt as when their knees hurt."[60] Plus, giving patients more transparency and agency around healthcare decisions reduces feelings of isolation and anxiety, increases their trust in the therapist, engages them in changing behavior, and thus promises to improve long-term outcomes. Patients can also review session notes and remind themselves of coping mechanisms and other tools discussed with their therapist.

Amending medical records will improve patient care in other ways. Your doctor might advise you to have all your prescriptions filled at a single pharmacy, so that computers can do one of the things they're good at: remembering which prescriptions were picked up when and flagging possible adverse combinations and reactions for drugs prescribed by your various doctors. But such a vital service should not depend on your being able to fill all your prescriptions at a single place. Aggregating all doctors' notes and prescriptions into a single patient record is safer. You could also amend your health record by automatically uploading the data from your physical activity tracker, or by using an app like Im2Calories, developed by research scientist Kevin Murphy's group at Google, that turns your food photos into a food diary and calorie count.[61] Then, you could ask to get an alert if that glass of red wine you are about to enjoy with dinner is a bad idea given the medicine you are taking.

Healthcare providers are also trying to persuade patients to share new streams of data to improve long-term health outcomes. As part of a promotional program called Vitality, the South African insurance company Discovery Health has teamed up with supermarkets, sporting good retailers, and health supply stores[62] to offer shoppers financial incentives, including cash back on grocery bills and discounts on premiums, when their loyalty-card or credit-card purchases indicate that their shopping basket included healthy foods.[63] The success of the program suggests that patients might be willing to share other data on the condition of getting lower insurance premiums. You might agree to walk a specified distance a number of times each week, as verified by geolocation data from your mobile phone. Those data would need to be authenticated with a fingerprint, live video, or other unique identifier—similar to payment authentication systems—to prove to your insurer that it was in fact you who was carrying your phone, and had not handed it off to some paid phone-walker.

In 2012, I conducted a workshop at Stanford with the Social Data Lab and UnitedHealthcare to consider other ways in which sensor data might improve patient health outcomes. In one scenario, we considered how to ensure that someone who has chosen to stay in her home rather than move into an assisted-living community can have her care monitored without too many unnecessary visits by expensive nursing staff. Sensors on or under the carpet in the person's bedroom could observe that she has fallen while getting up; a sensor in a mobile phone could pick up the sound of a fall if she's in another room. Webcams could capture video for analysis by emotion recognition software, dispatching neighbors or health professionals to the home if the person's mood indicated a need. None of these technologies require the person to speak or push a button, which is how most medical alert systems currently work.

Personally, I would love to be able to keep an eye on my mother and her health. My mom is in her nineties and lives in an assisted-living home in Freiburg, Germany, so I do not get to check in on her as often as I would like. I mentioned the idea of having a webcam installed in her apartment, and she was very excited about it, without entirely understanding how the video would need to be analyzed to catch problems since I wasn't going to be able to watch the live feed 24/7. When I went to make arrangements, however, I was told that installing a camera would violate the privacy rights of the nurses, aides, and other workers at the home. I wondered, *Were they doing things they didn't want me to know about? Were they not doing things they were billing us for?* It would be much better if the owner offered video access as a service to family members, using blurring tools to obscure the identities of the workers entering my mom's room. This would address everyone's concerns—including, most of all, my desire to ensure my mom is in good care.

The right to port could also be used to improve other dimensions of health care. You could port data about your prescribed medications into a refinery to quickly see which health insurance plan and participating pharmacies offers the lowest total price to you. Or you could port data into a service like IFTTT ("If This, Then That"), which allows you to set up conditional rules under which data trigger an action. If the UV index rating for the day is high you can get a reminder to put on sunblock. You can also link electronic devices in your home to a personal goal—for instance, only after your activity tracker shows you've taken at least 10,000 steps that day can your TV be turned on.

The future of health care is in tailoring diets, medicines, and other treatments to each person, based on your unique DNA. Variations in your DNA indicate both how diseases develop in your body and how your body responds to viruses, bacteria, and chemicals. Your prescription will be formulated based on your DNA, because it affects how different components of medicines work on you. But a genetic test reveals more: since there is significant overlap between your DNA and your relatives' DNA, learning about your genetic makeup entails learning about the makeup of your parents, siblings, and children—and if you share your data, this might lead to inadvertent disclosures about your relatives. Samantha Clark, who was the second person to upload genetic data to open-source DNA research depository openSNP, had to grapple with this issue, discussing with her family her decision to share her data with the site, since her DNA would also reveal information about them.[64] In this area, high ratings for data safety and privacy efficiency are critical. You should never be penalized for things you are not responsible for or cannot change, like DNA, no matter what laws are in place, and that goes for your relatives, too. A complete access log of your genetic data will help you identify situations in which these data might have been used against you.

Personal data are underutilized in health care. Yet, as Nicholas Christakis and James Fowler note in their book *Connected,* our social graph and our social life also strongly influence our health.[65] They are not just referring to significant public issues like tracking the spread of the flu virus by means of Google Flu Trends,[66] or to the fact that having lots of friends decreases the chances that a person will become suicidal—except in the case where someone he knew had committed suicide. Christakis and Fowler discovered that some health conditions, such as obesity, which traditionally were considered to be caused by personal behavior or genetics, spread socially. If the people you are close to—emotionally as well as physically—are eating big servings, you tend to eat bigger servings, too. And if they do not judge you negatively for weight gain because they've gained weight themselves, you are more likely not to worry about a few extra pounds.[67]

As Christakis and Fowler's research amply demonstrates, it's not enough to have a sensor measure your weight or blood pressure; you also need to pay attention to your social graph. It would be eye-opening to experiment with your social network to detect risk factors and see the potential impact on your long-term health, perhaps even exploring how spending time with certain circles of friends might affect you based in part on changes in mean body mass detected through photo recognition and analyses.

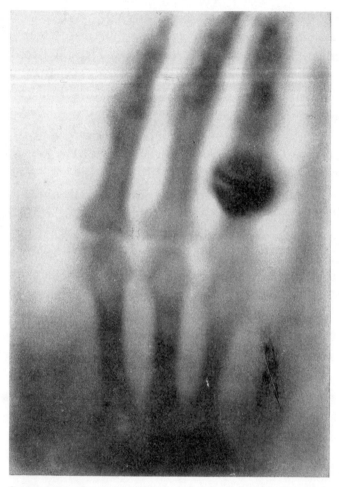

Seeing inside the body, 1895: The first X-ray, of Mrs. Röntgen's hand. Courtesy of the National Library of Medicine, US National Institutes of Health.

The US government has recognized the importance of precision medicine—which considers the combined effect of genetics, lifestyle, and environment on people's health—by funding an ambitious study, involving 1 million volunteers willing to share extensive data about themselves, that is investigating factors that lead to heart disease, diabetes, obesity, depression, and other conditions, as well as choices that can help keep a person healthy.[68] As more data refineries enter the sector, the nature of health care will inevitably evolve. We will move from measurement

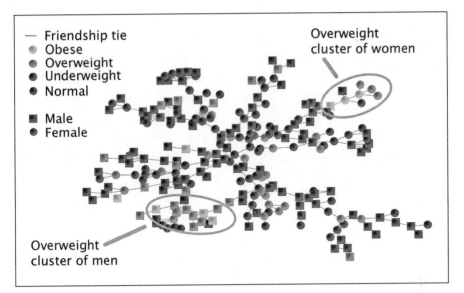

Seeing inside the body, 2015: Clusters of obese friends on Facebook. Courtesy of James Fowler and Nicholas Christakis, connectedthebook.com.

of behavior to modification of behavior, from reactive care to proactive care, and from descriptive medicine to predictive medicine. Patients will be better able to see how their actions today shape their health tomorrow. This is especially important for decisions regarding diet, exercise, and sleep, where feedback loops can extend over many years, and where various factors interact with each other. Doctors should walk patients through the process of exploring different scenarios, encouraging people to actively access, amend, experiment with, and port their health data to different refineries and become true co-managers and co-owners of their health records. As a result, patients will own something more important than their health data: they will own their health.

As we grow accustomed to being empowered agents for our health, many of us will view well-being as our own responsibility more so than the duty of the physician. Will we decide to reduce coverage for health issues that could have been prevented through a change in behavior? Instead of being denied insurance for preexisting conditions, people may have to consider the possibility of being denied—or charged more—for "chosen conditions." Occasionally, what the data orders will be tough medicine.

A Fair Deal?

Let's assume that the rights to data transparency and agency are granted. We are able to access all the data about ourselves, including data co-created and jointly owned with others. We can inspect and compare refineries in terms of data safety, privacy efficiency, and return-on-data investment. We can amend and blur our data, learning exactly what we get and what we risk by sharing more data. We can experiment with the refineries and port our data, to gain a better understanding of what they can do for us and choose the settings best for us.

Experimentation is relatively easy; we can vary the inputs and algorithms and see how this affects the outputs. Optimization is relatively easy as well, if we know what we want to optimize. But that doesn't mean there are no hard questions left to be addressed.

One of those hard questions is how we define fairness. When we had very little data to help us allocate scarce resources, we did the best we could: either we let people compete for those resources in a marketplace or, if the market wasn't an appropriate mechanism, we made up rules, such as "first come, first served," or relied on drawing random numbers, to avoid responsibility for each individual decision. But randomness is not our only option. When patients require an organ transplant, we do not flip a coin to decide who gets the next available liver, or send them to an auction where they can buy one. We turn to doctors to make the difficult decisions about who might get to live and who might die: they must assign an order of priority based on data about the patients' health. And unfortunately, some people will not get surgery soon enough. In 2002, Nobel Prize winner Alvin Roth created pioneering algorithms for optimally matching organ donors with patients.[69] Will we someday use social data to estimate the value of each patient's life, predicting with precision how much an additional year of life is worth to her family and society, and use it as an input for our algorithms? Will we venture beyond quantity of life to quality of life, which is both more complicated to define and more controversial? Even if everyone agreed on which variables to consider in a decision about priorities, we would still need to determine the weights on each of the terms in the equation of life.

This applies not only to deep philosophical questions like who gets life-saving surgery but also to more pedestrian problems such as how public parking spots get filled. Sensors can provide highly granular data about available parking spots. Bosch's Automatic Park Assist system uses cameras to gauge the position and size of a parking spot and guide the car into it. The cameras regularly capture images as the car travels, and these images can be joined with GPS data to identify the location of empty spots in real time. Many car makers now offer Bosch's auto-parking system, allowing for broad coverage, similar to how Vigilant's network of dashcams can collect license plate numbers across the whole country.

Drivers who share where they are going with a navigation app connected to the Bosch database can be alerted that the open parking spot they are about to pass is likely the closest one to their destination. In addition, the app might even suggest a route to the nearest available parking space rather than to the destination. The system is good for drivers and cities as a whole, as it reduces the level of traffic and emissions.

This approach is better than the existing just-drive-around-until-you-get-lucky system, but it is still mostly random. To reduce the level of chance, some developers have looked at ways to encourage people to share information about parking spaces that *could* become free, under the right conditions. One such app, MonkeyParking, let users set the price at which they would be willing to vacate a spot. The app increased transparency and agency, but it wasn't deemed to be fair. The city of San Francisco refused to let the app operate within the city limits, saying it was dangerous—drivers would text while driving—and against the law. Sunny Santa Monica was no more welcoming; the administrator in charge of the city parking said, "They do not have ownership of the space. That's unlawful. That's immoral. It's no different from a street bum that stands on a space, waves someone in, and asks for a tip."[70] So the parking app shifted direction, matching drivers to unused spaces in private driveways and garages that are available for rental at prices competitive with other parking spots.[71]

Many of the criticisms of MonkeyParking were focused on how the public resource of parking would quickly get priced out of the reach of many individuals. But think about how the market might work in practice: Imagine a person named Dot, who, while working behind the counter at Shutters on the Beach located on Santa Monica's Pico Boulevard, hears her smartphone buzzing. *Oh! Someone is willing to pay me forty bucks if I move my car right now.* Out on the street, a Malibu is circling the block, its driver desperate to find a spot close to the Santa Monica Courthouse in time for a court date. Dot accepts the bid, takes a break, and moves her car. If she cannot find another spot, she may receive a warning from her manager, or get docked on her pay. If she can find another spot before her break ends, she's made forty dollars for taking the time to look for parking on behalf of somebody else. It's not clear if the app will hurt or help those with more time than money, even when their time is not abundant.

A market for public parking spots could, however, be dominated and manipulated by a handful of players. A shrewd entrepreneur could buy a fleet of cheap cars and pay drivers to fill up many of the most coveted spots early each morning. This would make it harder for someone like Dot to find a spot for herself before her shift, let alone make money by setting a price on her time and flexibility. And it would become harder for people to grab a spot at the regular public price, whether it was free or metered. To make up for the decreased supply of spots, the city could assess a tax on buyers in marketplaces like MonkeyParking, using the funds raised to support more public transportation. Then the data would be for all the people, not just for some.

In these and a myriad of other ways, the social data revolution is making things measurable that have not been—or could not be—measured before. In the past, we could reasonably claim that we did not have the data or the tools to characterize and analyze the options available to us as a society. This is no longer the case. We can personalize and see the impact of our choices. But as I said, that doesn't mean *everything* is easy.

Transparency and agency will help us make progress toward specific goals, but they do not define the goals for us. In addition, there is no single combination of "right" settings for optimizing the use of data for everyone; even if we measure everything perfectly, not everyone will have the same terms with the same weights. In the future, we may well be able to predict with high accuracy the health and happiness of individuals by analyzing a range of data, from their search terms to their social graph, from their DNA to their facial expressions, and rank choices based on the analyses. If you knew you would be at higher risk of heart disease because of what you studied in college, and the career paths that typically follow, what would you do differently? Would you change your job, your health insurance, or the city you call home? As you access, inspect, amend, blur, experiment with, and port personal data, you will better understand your goals, and how you value and weigh the various terms in your personal fitness function. By experiencing how you feel when you consider various scenarios, you will be able to home in on what your values are and, when necessary, adjust your equation.

We now have the capacity to quantify the trade-offs of hard decisions, make our values explicit, and measure the outcomes, forcing us to choose what is fair and what is not. Ignorance is no longer an option, and we no longer have to resort to randomness. And as we gain the ability to refine everything under the sun, exercising our transparency and agency rights as we do so, data of the people and by the people will become data for the people.

EPILOGUE

Into the Sunlight

How could they see anything but the shadows if they were never allowed to move their heads?[1]

PLATO

DURING THE Peloponnesian wars Socrates sat down with Glaucon, his student and Plato's older brother, to show him how knowledge comes from casting light on reality and making the truth visible. Socrates did this through the "Allegory of the Cave," in which a group of people have been forced to live their whole lives in a cave, facing into the darkness. Their necks are chained, so they cannot turn their heads. Behind them, a wall has been built, and behind the wall, a fire has been stoked, and representations of people and things are carried back and forth above the wall. The light of the fire is strong enough that the people, imprisoned since childhood, can see the shadows of the puppets thrown up against the wall—moving to and fro, interacting, exchanging objects. Occasionally, the shimmering figures lurch from one position to another, but there is some continuity, some orderliness. The people in the cave watch the figures day after day, associating voices and sounds from outside with them. Their entire understanding of the world is based on what they can see.

Then, Socrates posits, one of the people in the cave is given the opportunity to turn his head. Having sat peering into the darkness for so long, his eyes have adjusted to being able to see the faintest shimmer of a shadow. When he looks toward the fire, the light is blinding. He struggles to see anything. Confused and frustrated, he turns back to the darkness of the cave, where he can see once again. Relieved, he might even report to the others that there is nothing to see beyond the figures on the wall.

Later, the man is granted his freedom. The light of the fire blinds him again, but this time he gives his eyes time to adjust. He's free, after

233

all! After a while, he can make out the puppets being moved to and fro, and see how their shadows are thrown onto the cave's walls. He gradually comes to understand the relationship between the puppets and their shadows.

Eventually, the man leaves the cave, and the light of the sun overpowers him. He has now learned that he needs to give himself time to adjust to the light, and he is patient. He watches the shadows, but he recognizes that they are shadows, not reality.

Should the man return to the cave and try to persuade the others to come out into the sun, he might meet resistance. Back in darkness, he would once again be temporarily blinded; he wouldn't be able to distinguish the puppets' shadows from the background. Since he is no longer able to see anything, the remaining cave dwellers might believe he has been harmed by the light. And who can blame them? No one likes to have their universe ripped out from under them.

Plato shared the story of Socrates' dialogue more than two thousand years ago. Today, we are in a strikingly similar situation. Data refineries like Facebook and Google project shadows on their walls and pages for us to interpret. As with the shadows in the allegorical cave, the digital traces of our lives are the result of real things: Google doesn't make up webpages to answer search queries, and Facebook doesn't make up friends' posts to populate your News Feed. At the same time, we depend on the refineries to shed light on and help us make sense of the vast amount of data being created—so many interactions and movements that Plato could not have imagined them, so many that we could not possibly observe them all on our own without being overwhelmed.

Yet, too much happens in the dark. We are at risk of accepting whatever the algorithms project on the wall as our entire reality. It will take time for us to adjust to these new data sources, and learn how to take advantage of tools to help us see and use—even bask—in them. The transparency rights will let us see the shape of the light and make sense of how the shadows are created without being blinded; the agency rights will let us vary and move the light source, allowing us to direct it as we need.

Sitting in the dark is no longer an option. Our heads, unlike those of the cave's prisoners, are not chained. We must be free to see and we must be free to act, even if it requires work.

And even if at first we find the glare of the light overwhelming.

ACKNOWLEDGMENTS

I would like to deeply thank Robin Dennis, my writer in London, for turning a hundred speeches and a thousand hours on Skype into this book. I am very grateful to Jim Levine, my literary agent, and TJ Kelleher, my editor at Basic Books, for making it all happen.

But there are many more. In the spirit of the book, I invite you to exercise your right to amend the data I created on weigend.com/thanks, the list of people who helped with this book—my friends, assistants, collaborators, and students.

I am also curious about your experiences with the data rights and the ideas discussed in this book—for example, what you might learn from porting your data to refineries. You can find out more about the book on ourdata.com, join others in a discussion of the book on its facebook page, fb.com/ourdata, or learn more about my work on weigend.com. My email is andreas@weigend.com.

August 2016
Shanghai and San Francisco

NOTES

Prologue

1. McLuhan, Marshall, with Wilfred Watson, *From Cliché to Archetype* (Berkeley: Gingko Press, 2011), p. 13. The book was originally published in 1970.

2. Pidd, Helen, "Germans Piece Together Millions of Lives Spied on by Stasi," *Guardian*, March 13, 2011, http://www.theguardian.com/world/2011/mar/13/east-germany-stasi-files-zirndorf.

3. Koehler, John O., *Stasi: The Untold Story of the East German Secret Police* (Boulder, CO: Westview Press, 1999), p. 8.

4. Federal Commissioner for the Records of the State Security Service of the former German Democratic Republic, "What Was the Stasi?," Bundesregierung, http://www.bstu.bund.de/EN/PublicEducation/SchoolEducation/WhatWasTheStasi/_node.html.

5. Crocker, Andrew, "EFF Case Analysis: Appeals Court Rules NSA Phone Records Dragnet Is Illegal," Electronic Frontier Foundation, May 9, 2015, https://www.eff.org/deeplinks/2015/05/eff-case-analysis-appeals-court-rules-nsa-phone-records-dragnet-illegal.

6. Kravets, David, "Worker Fired for Disabling GPS App That Tracked Her 24 Hours a Day," *ArsTechnica*, May 11, 2015, http://arstechnica.com/tech-policy/2015/05/worker-fired-for-disabling-gps-app-that-tracked-her-24-hours-a-day.

7. I'll spend more time discussing social network experiments in Chapter 3. See McNeal, Gregory S., "Facebook Manipulated User News Feeds to Create Emotional Responses," *Forbes*, June 28, 2014, http://www.forbes.com/sites/gregorymcneal/2014/06/28/facebook-manipulated-user-news-feeds-to-create-emotional-contagion; and Booth, Robert, "Facebook Reveals News Feed Experiment to Control Emotions," *Guardian*, June 29, 2014, https://www.theguardian.com/technology/2014/jun/29/facebook-users-emotions-news-feeds.

8. Sesame Credit is one of eight pilot projects to expand credit in the country by 2020. See Shu, Catherine, "Data from Alibaba's E-Commerce Sites Is Now Powering a Credit-Scoring Service," *TechCrunch*, January 27, 2015, http://techcrunch.com/2015/01/27/data-from-alibabas-e-commerce-sites-is-now-powering-a-credit-scoring-service.

9. Hatton, Celia, "China 'Social Credit': Beijing Sets Up Huge System," *BBC News*, October 26, 2015, http://www.bbc.com/news/world-asia-china-34592186.

10. You can view my activities at http://weigend.com/past (for past events) and http://weigend.com/future (for current and future events).

Introduction

1. Emerson, Ralph Waldo, *The Prose Works of Ralph Waldo Emerson,* vol. 1, rev. ed. (Boston: James R. Osgood, 1875), p. 220.

2. I have been teaching the course entitled "The Social Data Revolution" at Stanford University since 2008 and at the University of California–Berkeley since 2011, but I've been developing the concept of "social data" for longer than that. In the earliest stages, social data were merely data that people socialized, including reviews on Amazon and posts on social media platforms.

3. For those interested in a fuller discussion of sketchy data, I'd recommend the video of a panel at which I spoke at the UC–Berkeley School of Information's 2013 DataEdge conference, available at http://www.youtube.com/watch?v=BaWmQnkKrUg.

4. The big difference in data protection policies between the United States and Europe involves how rules are enforced. In the United States, business sectors have been left to create their own regulatory bodies to protect individuals from the risks of privacy breaches; in Europe, the rules are uniform across industries. See Executive Office of the President, *Big Data: Seizing Opportunities, Preserving Values,* Report of the Big Data and Privacy Working Group and the Council of Advisors on Science and Technology, May 2014, pp. 17–18, https://www.whitehouse.gov/sites/default/files/docs/big_data_privacy _report_may_1_2014.pdf.

5. Understanding an algorithm usually involves seeing how it works on real data, ideally your own data in combination with the data of others (which provides greater scope for comparison). Under current laws, most data companies cannot release others' data to you without their consent. This limits the possible avenues for helping you decipher the algorithms in your life.

6. See, for instance, the "Consumer Privacy Bill of Rights" proposed by the White House in February 2012, discussed on pp. 19–20 of Executive Office of the President, *Big Data: Seizing Opportunities, Preserving Values.*

7. I am grateful to Esther Dyson for suggesting this metaphor of the one-way mirror versus the window.

8. In case you missed the media coverage, you can hear the excruciating recording of the call on SoundCloud: Block, Ryan, "Comcastic Service Disconnection (Recording Starts 10 Mins into Call)," SoundCloud, July 14, 2014, https://soundcloud.com/ryan-block-10 /comcastic-service.

9. My friend Doc Searls, a co-author of *The Cluetrain Manifesto* and author of *The Intention Economy,* has long been an advocate for agency in the interactions between customers and companies, and I thank him for suggesting this term as a way to gather together the aspects of individual power in decision-making represented in these rights.

Chapter 1: Becoming Data Literate

1. Miller, George A., "The Challenge of Universal Literacy," *Science* 241 (September 9, 1988), p. 1293, http://science.sciencemag.org/content/241/4871/1293.

2. I have been using this metaphor for many years in my teaching, and described data refineries at two talks in 2011, one at the United Nations and the other at the O'Reilly Strata Summit, but I am not alone in making the comparison. Among those who refer to data as

the new oil is Clive Humby, who helped create the British supermarket Tesco's Clubcard, one of the earliest loyalty cards to track all of the items in your grocery cart. My talk at the United Nations was part of the Secretary-General's Global Pulse initiative for big data innovation; the video is available at http://www.youtube.com/watch?v=lbmsDH8RJA4.

3. "Planet of the Phones," *The Economist,* February 28, 2015, http://www.economist .com/news/leaders/21645180-smartphone-ubiquitous-addictive-and-transformative -planet-phones; Rogowsky, Mark, "More Than Half of Us Have Smartphones, Giving Apple and Google Much to Smile About," *Forbes,* June 6, 2013, http://www.forbes .com/sites/markrogowsky/2013/06/06/more-than-half-of-us-have-smartphones-giving -apple-and-google-much-to-smile-about.

4. Lunden, Ingrid, "80% of All Online Adults Now Own a Smartphone, Less Than 10% Use Wearables," *TechCrunch,* January 12, 2015, http://techcrunch.com/2015/01/12/80-of -all-online-adults-now-own-a-smartphone-less-than-10-use-wearables.

5. Tecmark, "Tecmark Survey Finds Average User Picks Up Their Smartphone 221 Times a Day," October 8, 2014, http://www.tecmark.co.uk/smartphone-usage-data-uk-2014.

6. Miller, "The Challenge of Universal Literacy," p. 1293.

7. Madison, James H., "Changing Patterns of Urban Retailing: The 1920s," paper presented at the 22nd Annual Meeting of the Business History Conference, *Business and Economic History,* vol. 5 (1976), p. 104, http://www.thebhc.org/sites/default/files/beh/BEHprint /v005/p0102-p0111.pdf.

8. Clark, Anna, "The Tyranny of the ZIP Code," *New Republic,* March 8, 2013, https:// newrepublic.com/article/112558/zip-code-history-how-they-define-us.

9. "Apple Pie Families" is one of Acxiom's segments. See Hicken, Melanie, "What Type of Consumer Are You?," *CNNMoney,* April 19, 2013, http://money.cnn.com/2013/04/18 /pf/consumer-type. "Blue Blood Estates" and "Shotguns and Pickups" are two categories in the Potential Rating Index by Zip Markets (PRIZM) program developed by the marketing firm Claritas, which was founded in the 1990s. Claritas is now a unit of the Nielsen Company— the people who provide point-of-purchase sales data to manufacturers and who measure TV audiences using set meters. See Kotler, Philip, and Kevin Lane Keller, *Marketing Management 14* (Upper Saddle River, NJ: Prentice-Hall, 2012), p. 215. "Suburban Soccer Moms" is a classification in the retailer Best Buy's database of 75 million customer households, one of the more aggressive efforts by a big-box chain to use data for personalizing offers. See Kotler and Keller, *Marketing Management 14,* p. 71; and Zmuda, Natalie, "Best Buy Touts Data Project as Key to Turnaround," *Advertising Age,* February 27, 2014, http://adage.com/article /datadriven-marketing/buy-touts-data-project-key-turnaround/291897.

10. Tynan, Dan, "Acxiom Exposed: A Peek Inside One of the World's Largest Data Brokers," *IT World,* May 15, 2013, http://www.itworld.com/article/2710610/it-management /acxiom-exposed—a-peek-inside-one-of-the-world-s-largest-data-brokers.html.

11. *Acxiom Corporation Annual Report 2000,* June 26, 2000, p. 3, http://www.getfilings .com/o0000733269–00–000012.html.

12. This was less than a decade after Don Peppers and Martha Rogers suggested a radical new approach to marketing in *The One to One Future.* See Peppers, Don, and Martha Rogers, *The One to One Future: Building Relationships One Customer at a Time* (New York: Doubleday, 1993).

13. The title of *Bloomberg Businessweek* reporter Brad Stone's history of Amazon has become common shorthand for Jeff Bezos's entrepreneurial idea. See Stone, Brad, *The Everything Store* (New York: Little, Brown, 2013), p. 13. However, Amazonians think of Amazon first and foremost as a data company—and indeed, Jeff came up with the idea while he was at D. E. Shaw & Company, the hedge fund that revolutionized speculative trading by relentlessly focusing on new data sources.

14. This way of talking about personalization based on situational context as a segmentation size of one-tenth was first developed in a conversation with my frequent social data co-conspirator Gam Dias, CEO and founder of MoData.

15. Duhigg, Charles, "How Companies Learn Your Secrets," *New York Times Magazine,* February 16, 2012, http://www.nytimes.com/2012/02/19/magazine/shopping-habits.html.

16. The percentage of retail searches done at Amazon has increased from around 30 percent in 2012 to around 50 percent in 2015. See Ludwig, Sean, "Forrester: 30% of Online Shoppers Research Amazon Before Buying," *VentureBeat,* July 26, 2012, http://venture beat.com/2012/07/26/amazon-online-shoppers-research; Mulpuru, Sucharita, and Brian K. Walker, "Why Amazon Matters Now More Than Ever," *Forrester Research,* July 26, 2012, https://www.forrester.com/Amazon/fulltext/-/E-RES76262; and Cassidy, Mike, "Survey: Amazon Is Burying the Competition in Search," *BloomReach,* October 6, 2015, http:// bloomreach.com/2015/10/survey-amazon-is-burying-the-competiton-in-search.

17. For 2015, Facebook reported having 1.59 billion visitors each month, with 1.04 billion visitors each day on average. See Isaac, Mike, "Facebook Reports Soaring Revenue, Buoyed by Mobile Ads," *New York Times,* January 27, 2016, http://www.nytimes .com/2016/01/28/technology/facebook-earnings-zuckerberg.html.

18. Google does not regularly report the number of searches conducted through its services. However, the 2012 Google "Zeitgeist" report said that 3.3 billion searches were conducted each day. See https://www.google.com/zeitgeist/2012/#the-world.

19. Lanier, Jaron, *Who Owns the Future?* (New York: Simon & Schuster, 2013), pp. 273–274.

20. *Facebook Annual Report 2015,* January 28, 2016, https://investor.fb.com/financials /default.aspx.

21. Gittins, J. C., "Bandit Processes and Dynamic Allocation Indices," *Journal of the Royal Statistical Society B (Methodological)* 41, no. 2 (1979), pp. 148–177, http://www.jstor.org /stable/2985029.

22. I am grateful to Jan O. Pedersen, now a distinguished engineer at Microsoft, for sharing with me how Yahoo! (where he was previously chief scientist for search) addressed the exploration-exploitation problem, using this example of the search query "jaguar."

23. Gardner tackled what was then called the secretary problem in the February/March 1960 issue of *Scientific American.* See Gardner, Martin, *Martin Gardner's New Mathematical Diversions* (New York: Simon & Schuster, 1966), p. 35.

24. Founded in 1998 by myself, Christian Pirkner, Elion Chin, and Tom Sulzer, MoodLogic was one of the first online music recommendation systems. At its height, the site had ratings from about 50,000 users on more than 1 million songs. The company's software and data were acquired by All Media Guide, a subsidiary of Rovi, in 2006.

25. Glassdoor was founded in 2008 by Rich Barton, Tim Besse, and Robert Hohman, who worked together at travel search and booking platform Expedia. Barton was also a founder of Zillow, the data refinery for real estate properties.

26. The National Longitudinal Survey of Youth 1979, which regularly interviews Americans born between 1957 and 1964, started with a nonmilitary sample size of 11,000; the National Longitudinal Survey of Youth 1997, which interviews Americans born between 1980 and 1984, started with a sample size of 8,000. See https://www.nlsinfo.org for more details.

27. This is one of Sherlock Holmes's most frequently quoted lines of dialogue. See Doyle, Sir Arthur Conan, "The Adventure of the Copper Beeches," *Strand Magazine* (June 1892).

28. Inrix is just one of many commercial enterprises that analyze mobile phone location data to study traffic; data from Garmin and other dedicated GPS devices for route-planning and traffic reporting are also used to analyze trends.

29. My friend John Squire, CEO of DynamicAction and former chief strategy officer of IBM Smarter Commerce, emphasizes the importance of combining data from different sources in analysis with the saying "The value is in the join."

30. Author interview with Claudia Perlich, chief scientist, Dstillery, January 25, 2015. Claudia is a good friend and former student of mine at the University of Colorado–Boulder and New York University.

31. Finley, Klint, "Christmas Delivery Fiasco Shows Why Amazon Wants Its Own UPS," *Wired*, December 30, 2013, http://www.wired.com/2013/12/amazon_ups.

32. Kastrenakes, Jacob, "Amazon Guarantees Packages Ordered Through Friday Will Arrive Before Christmas," *The Verge*, December 16, 2014, http://www.theverge .com/2014/12/16/7401299/amazon-sets-dec-19th-cutoff-for-christmas-free-shipping.

33. Snyder, Brett, "Sabre Makes the Wrong Choice by Removing American Airlines," *CBS News Moneywatch*, January 7, 2011, http://www.cbsnews.com/news/sabre-makes-the -wrong-choice-by-removing-american-airlines.

34. American Airlines, "November Line of Sale Analysis," memo to R. E. Murray from S. D. Nason, December 3, 1981.

35. Tefft, Sheila, "Reservation Systems' Bias a Sore Spot for Smaller Airlines," *Chicago Tribune*, February 11, 1983, http://archives.chicagotribune.com/1983/02/11/page/87/article /new-technology.

36. Whiteley, David, *An Introduction to Information Systems* (New York: Palgrave Macmillan, 2013), p. 109.

37. After the Airline Deregulation Act of 1978, the Civil Aeronautics Board adopted anti-bias regulations. See Pearlstein, Debra J., and Robert E. Iloch et al., eds., *Antitrust Law Developments*, vol. 1 (Chicago: American Bar Association, 2002), p. 1428.

38. I was an adviser to Agoda from 2004 to 2007. The company was acquired by Priceline in November 2007.

39. In engineering, prescriptive analytics is called "control theory."

40. Hern, Alex, "Why Google Has 200M Reasons to Put Engineers over Designers," *Guardian*, February 5, 2014, http://www.theguardian.com/technology/2014/feb/05 /why-google-engineers-designers.

41. Kohavi, Ron, Roger Longbotham, and Toby Walker, "Online Experiments: Practical Lessons," *IEEE Computer* 43, no. 9 (September 2010), pp. 82–85, http://www.computer .org/csdl/mags/co/2010/09/mco2010090082-abs.html.

42. Döpfner, Mathias, "An Open Letter to Eric Schmidt: Why We Fear Google," *Frankfurter Allgemeine Zeitung*, April 17, 2014, http://www.faz.net/aktuell/feuilleton/debatten /mathias-doepfner-s-open-letter-to-eric-schmidt-12900860.html.

Chapter 2: Character and Characteristics

1. As quoted in Hochschild, Jennifer L., "How Ideas Affect Actions," in Robert Goodin and Charles Tilly, eds., *Oxford Handbook of Contextual Political Analysis* (Oxford: Oxford University Press, 2006), pp. 284–296.

2. The German title of Musil's book, *Der Mann ohne Eigenschaften,* translates literally as "The Man Without Properties." I suspect the English publisher was worried that readers might imagine the protagonist didn't own anything.

3. Credit for introducing me to the idea of the chimney as a privacy-enabling technology goes to the remarkable John Taysom, founder of BlinkBox Music and Reuters Venture Capital. The ability to maintain some privacy while also gaining access to the personalized services of the data refineries has been a key project for John. See Taysom, John, "How Much Privacy Do We *Need?,*" presentation at the Alan Turing Institute Financial Summit, British Library, London, October 14, 2015.

4. This was particularly true in Britain, where land was shifted from the commons to private ownership as part of the enclosure movement. Other contemporaneous agricultural innovations spurred the change, including crop rotation, selective breeding of livestock, more efficient metal plows, more efficient land draining, and an extensive network of canals. See Overton, Mark, *Agricultural Revolution in England: The Transformation of the Agrarian Economy 1500–1850* (Cambridge: Cambridge University Press, 1996).

5. Benjamin Franklin's Pennsylvanian Fire Place was actually a stove, not a bricked part of the house, but his chimney was unquestionably revolutionary. See Butler, Orville R., "Smoke Gets in Your Eye: The Development of the House Chimney," n.d., http://www .ultimatehistoryproject.com/chimneys.html.

6. This history of the secret ballot is greatly indebted to Lepore's fascinating account in *The New Yorker:* Lepore, Jill, "Rock, Paper, Scissors: How We Used to Vote," *The New Yorker,* October 13, 2008, http://www.newyorker.com/reporting/2008/10/13/081013fa_fact_lepore.

7. Mill had taken up the opposing view by at least 1853, according to a review of his surviving letters. See Buchstein, Hubertus, "Public Voting and Political Modernization," in John Elster, ed., *Secrecy and Publicity in Votes and Debates* (Cambridge: Cambridge University Press, 2015), pp. 29, 30.

8. Mill, John Stuart, "Thoughts on Parliamentary Reform," in *Dissertations and Discussions: Political, Philosophical, and Historical,* vol. 4 (New York: Henry Holt, 1873), pp. 36–37.

9. Buchstein, "Public Voting and Political Modernization," p. 31.

10. To my amazement, when Thomas Edison applied for a patent in 1869 for a mechanical voting machine that used toggle levers, he found there was no market for it. Politicians wanted to hear from their public—and, in what we might imagine were quite a few cases, influence them. It wasn't until the late 1950s that Edison's lever-voting machine gained backers; see Stephey, M. J., "A Brief History of Ballots in America," *Time,* November 3, 2008, http://content.time.com/time/politics/article/0,8599,1855857,00.html.

11. Of course, for decades some Americans were barred from voting, through the widespread use of "poll tests"—literacy tests specifically targeted at those individuals, mostly black men in the South, whom local election officials preferred to send home.

12. Warren, Samuel D., and Louis D. Brandeis, "The Right to Privacy," *Harvard Law Review* 4, no. 5 (December 15, 1890), http://groups.csail.mit.edu/mac/classes/6.805/articles /privacy/Privacy_brand_warr2.html.

13. Glancy, Dorothy J., "The Invention of the Right to Privacy," *Arizona Law Review* 21, no. 1 (Spring 1979), pp. 9–10, http://digitalcommons.law.scu.edu/facpubs/317.

14. This decision meant that the teacher was allowed to teach German, but the precedent has been used as the foundation to a "right to privacy" in many other areas of life, from a married couple's decision to use birth control (*Griswold v. Connecticut*, 1965) to a gay couple's decision to have consensual sex (*Lawrence v. Texas*, 2003). See *Meyer v. Nebraska*, 262 US Supreme Court 390 (1923), p. 399, https://supreme.justia.com/cases/federal/us/262/390/case.html.

15. Google, "Google's Targeted Keyword Ad Program Shows Strong Momentum with Advertisers," press release, August 16, 2000, http://googlepress.blogspot.co.uk/2000/08/googles-targeted-keyword-ad-program.html.

16. Miller, Ross, "Gmail Now Has 1 Billion Monthly Active Users," *The Verge*, February 1, 2016, http://www.theverge.com/2016/2/1/10889492/gmail-1-billion-google-alphabet.

17. This wasn't a novel idea: comparing people's photos was first popular on University of California–Berkeley grads James Hong and Jim Young's "Hot or Not" rating site, which went online in October 2000.

18. The extent of Facebook use is limited in part by blocks in several countries, including the People's Republic of China, which has mostly blocked it since at least 2009. See Chen, George, "China to Lift Ban on Facebook—But Only Within Shanghai Free-Trade Zone," *South China Morning Post*, September 24, 2013, http://www.scmp.com/news/china/article/1316598/exclusive-china-lift-ban-facebook-only-within-shanghai-free-trade-zone.

19. These figures are as reported by Facebook in August 2016 at http://newsroom.fb.com/company-info.

20. I was visiting a former student who had taken a job as one of the first data scientists at the company.

21. The specific identity documents vary from country to country. In the United States today, about half of eighteen-year-olds have a driver's license; this is a drop from a generation ago, when two-thirds of the eighteen-year-olds had one. See Halsey, Ashley III, "Fewer Teens Get Driver's Licenses," *Washington Post*, July 31, 2013, https://www.washingtonpost.com/local/trafficandcommuting/fewer-teens-get-drivers-licenses/2013/07/31/60a32aae-f9c7-11e2-a369-d1954abcb7e3_story.html. As of 2012, one-third of US citizens have a passport; in 1989, a measly 3 percent had one. See Bender, Andrew, "Record Number of Americans Now Hold Passports," *Forbes*, January 30, 2012, http://www.forbes.com/sites/andrewbender/2012/01/30/record-number-of-americans-now-hold-passports.

22. One reason Facebook may have chosen the age of thirteen is to more easily comply with the Children's Online Privacy Protection Act (COPPA) of 1998, which requires that commercial websites aimed at those younger than thirteen get a parent or guardian's consent for online data collection. See https://www.ftc.gov/enforcement/rules/rulemaking-regulatory-reform-proceedings/childrens-online-privacy-protection-rule.

23. The cartoon, published in the July 5, 1993, edition—two and a half years after the world's first website went live—has been reproduced more than any other in the magazine's history, according to the *New York Times*. See Fleishman, Glenn, "Cartoon Captures Spirit of the Internet," *New York Times*, December 14, 2000, http://www.nytimes.com/2000/12/14/technology/cartoon-captures-spirit-of-the-internet.html.

24. At the time of the study, Sweeney was a graduate student at MIT. She is now a professor of government and technology at Harvard University and the director of the Data Privacy Lab at Harvard.

25. Ohm, Paul, "Broken Promises of Privacy: Responding to the Surprising Failure of Anonymization," *UCLA Law Review* 57, no. 6 (August 2010), p. 1720, http://www.uclalawreview.org/broken-promises-of-privacy-responding-to-the-surprising-failure-of-anonymization-2.

26. Sweeney, Latanya, *Uniqueness of Simple Demographics in the U.S. Population,* Laboratory for International Data Privacy working paper LIDAP-WP4–2000, http://dataprivacylab.org/projects/identifiability/index.html.

27. Golle, Philippe, "Revisiting the Uniqueness of Simple Demographics in the U.S. Population," *Proceedings of the 5th ACM Workshop on Privacy in the Electronic Society* (New York: Association for Computing Machinery, 2006), pp. 77–80, http://dl.acm.org/citation.cfm?id=1179615.

28. US Post Office FAQ, http://faq.usps.com. If all 90,000 possible numbers (10000–99999) were allocated, the percentage of people who are uniquely identifiable would be higher. Another reason the identification rate isn't higher is that the US population isn't uniformly distributed across ZIP codes.

29. Barbaro, Michael, and Tom Zeller, Jr., "A Face Is Exposed for AOL Searcher No. 4417749," *New York Times,* August 9, 2006, http://www.nytimes.com/2006/08/09/technology/09aol.html.

30. Singel, Ryan, "Netflix Spilled Your *Brokeback Mountain* Secret, Lawsuit Claims," *Wired,* December 17, 2009, http://www.wired.com/2009/12/netflix-privacy-lawsuit.

31. Narayan, Arvind, and Vitaly Shmatikov, "Robust De-Anonymization of Large Sparse Datasets," paper presented at the 2008 IEEE Symposium on Security and Privacy, Oakland, CA, May 18–21, 2008, pp. 111–125, http://dl.acm.org/citation.cfm?id=1398064.

32. On the topic of suicide, a meta-analysis conducted by researchers at Oxford University found that "well over half (59 percent) of young people interviewed said they had researched suicide online." See Daine, Kate, Keith Hawton, Vinod Singaravelu, Anne Stewart, Sue Simkin, and Paul Montgomery, "The Power of the Web: A Systematic Review of Studies of the Influence of the Internet on Self-Harm and Suicide in Young People," *PLoS One* 8, no. 10 (October 30, 2013), http://journals.plos.org/plosone/article?id=10.1371/journal.pone.0077555.

33. This figure comes from former California Highway Patrol sergeant Kevin Briggs's TED Talk about patrolling the Golden Gate Bridge. See Briggs, Kevin, "The Bridge Between Suicide and Life," TED Talk, March 21, 2014, https://www.ted.com/talks/kevin_briggs_the_bridge_between_suicide_and_life.

34. Based on Google Trends, "big data" wasn't on the public's mind until 2011.

35. You can do this on your "My Amazon" page: https://www.amazon.com/gp/yourstore/iyr.

36. Facebook refers to this as "deleting" activity, but these data are not permanently deleted. That's because it is more costly to find and purge all appearances of the data from the servers than to keep them but modify how they are used. In addition, as we'll see in Chapter 3, Facebook constantly runs experiments to improve user experience and increase user activity. One investigation looked into "self-censorship": occasions when people started to write status updates and comments but decided not to post them in the end. Aborted updates and comments can't be deleted from your Activity Log because they were never actually shared, yet Facebook is studying the context—the "how and where." See Das, Sauvik, and Adam Kramer, "Self-Censorship on Facebook," Proceedings of the 7th International AAAI Conference on Weblogs and Social Media, Cambridge, MA, July 8–11, 2013 (Palo

Alto: AAAI Press, 2013), https://www.aaai.org/ocs/index.php/ICWSM/ICWSM13/paper/viewFile/6093/6350.

37. Bachrach, Yoram, Michal Kosinski, Thore Graepel, Pushmeet Kohli, and David Stillwell, "Personality and Patterns of Facebook Usage," *Proceedings of the 4th Annual ACM Conference on Web Sciences,* Evanston, IL, June 22–24, 2012 (New York: Association for Computing Machinery, 2012), pp. 24–32, http://dl.acm.org/citation.cfm?id=2380722.

38. Kosinski, Michal, David J. Stillwell, and Thore Graepel, "Private Traits and Attributes Are Predictable from Digital Records of Human Behavior," *Proceedings of the National Academy of Sciences USA* 110, no. 15 (April 9, 2013), p. 5802, http://www.pnas.org/content/early/2013/03/06/1218772110. One difficulty of assessing the validity of studies like this one arises from the statistics of expressed identity. For instance, if the model predicted that 100 percent of the men it analyzed were straight, it would still be correct around 90 percent of the time, since around 10 percent of male users identify themselves as "interested in men." However, the findings of the YouAreWhatYouLike app study are still interesting, especially when personality traits, such as intelligence, are identified by other methods.

39. Kosinski, Stillwell, and Graepel, "Private Traits and Attributes Are Predictable from Digital Records of Human Behavior," p. 5804.

40. The researchers accessed Facebook likes using an application programming interface (API); people who use privacy settings to limit the audience of their likes would not be as identifiable, even if they signed up to have their personality assessed with the app. See http://applymagicsauce.com. In interviews, Kosinski has said, "HR recruitment might benefit from this a lot"; Adams, Stephen, "'Like' Curly Fries on Facebook? Then You're Clever," *Telegraph,* March 12, 2013, http://www.telegraph.co.uk/technology/news/9923070/Like-curly-fries-on-Facebook-Then-youre-clever.html.

41. Simonite, Tom, "Facebook Creates Software That Matches Faces Almost as Well as You Do," *MIT Technology Review,* March 17, 2014, http://www.technologyreview.com/news/525586/facebook-creates-software-that-matches-faces-almost-as-well-as-you-do; Taigman, Yaniv, Ming Yang, Marc'Aurelio Ranzato, and Lior Wolf, "DeepFace: Closing the Gap to Human-Level Performance in Face Verification," paper presented at the IEEE Conference on Computer Vision and Pattern Recognition, Columbus, OH, June 24–27, 2014, pp. 1701–1708, https://www.cs.toronto.edu/~ranzato/publications/taigman_cvpr14.pdf.

42. Cynthia uses this example in her lecture titled "I'm in the Database (But Nobody Knows), Dean's Lecture, University of California–Berkeley School of Information, February 4, 2015, http://www.ischool.berkeley.edu/events/deanslectures/20150204/audio.

43. The format of national passports was not standardized until shortly after World War I, but the concept of a government-issued document that confirmed the identity of a traveler is much older; the term "passport" had been coined in the English language by 1540. See Benedictus, Leo, "A Brief History of the Passport: From a Royal Letter to a Microchip," *Guardian,* November 17, 2006, http://www.theguardian.com/travel/2006/nov/17/travelnews.

44. Checks required authentication—in the early days, by comparing the check's signature against a signature kept on file at the bank. See Quinn, Stephen, and William Roberds, "The Evolution of the Check as a Means of Payment: A Historical Survey," *Economic Review* 93, no. 4 (December 2008), https://www.frbatlanta.org/-/media/Documents/research/publications/economic-review/2008/vol93no4_quinn_roberds.pdf.

45. Quoted in Leber, Jessica, "Forget Passwords: This Startup Wants to Authenticate Your Mind," *Fast Company Exist,* July 24, 2014, http://www.fastcoexist.com/3033383/forget-passwords-this-startup-wants-to-authenticate-your-mind.

46. O'Hear, Steve, "Pre-Crime Startup BioCatch Authenticates Users via Touch and Your Phone's Accelerometer," *TechCrunch,* July 7, 2015, http://techcrunch.com/2015/07/07/pre-crime-startup-biocatch-authenticates-users-via-touch-and-your-phones-accelerometer.

47. Around the age of thirteen, a child's motor skills plateau (author interview with Lane Merrifield, CEO of FreshGrade and co-founder of Club Penguin, January 21, 2016). After Disney acquired Club Penguin in 2007, Lane became executive vice president of the media company's internet group; he is now working on FreshGrade, an educational technology start-up.

48. For an early computer-based analysis of word patterns in the Federalist Papers, see Mosteller, Frederick, and David Wallace, *Inference and Disputed Authorship: The Federalist* (Reading, MA: Addison-Wesley, 1964).

49. Anonymous, "Silly Novels by Lady Novelists," *Westminster Review,* new series, vol. 10 (October 1856), p. 442.

50. Wilkes, Geoff, "Afterword," in *Alone in Berlin* [English title of *Jeder stirbt für sich allein* ("Every man dies alone")] (London: Penguin, 2009), pp. 578–579.

51. Fallada had not only tried to kill himself, which in and of itself was considered shameful; he had entered into a suicide pact with another man, who Fallada succeeded in killing. See Oltermann, Philip, "The Cow, the Shoe, Then You," *London Review of Books* 34, no. 5 (March 8, 2012), p. 27, http://www.lrb.co.uk/v34/n05/philip-oltermann/the-cow-the-shoe-then-you.

52. The seminal paper outlining this concept is Friedman, Eric J., and Paul Resnick, "The Social Cost of Cheap Pseudonyms," *Journal of Economics and Management Strategy* 10, no. 2 (Summer 2001), pp. 173–199, http://onlinelibrary.wiley.com/doi/10.1111/j.1430–9134.2001.00173.x/abstract.

53. There were three levels under discussion at Amazon: pragmatically anonymous reviews, where it is extremely simple to create a new username; traceable pseudonymous reviews, where reviewers can pick any username, but the name has to be coupled to an Amazon account set up with an authenticated credit card; or real-name reviews, where the username is generated by the authenticated credit card but the reviewers have the choice of using initials rather than a first name if they do not want to reveal their gender.

54. Rubin, Ben Fox, "Amazon Looks to Improve Customer-Reviews System with Machine Learning," *CNET,* June 19, 2015, http://www.cnet.com/news/amazon-updates-customer-reviews-with-new-machine-learning-platform.

55. Rubin, Ben Fox, "Amazon Sues Alleged Reviews-for-Pay Sites," *CNET,* April 9, 2015, http://www.cnet.com/news/amazon-sues-alleged-reviews-for-pay-sites. In some cases, it appears a company shipped an empty box or envelope by tracked mail to attain "Verified Purchase" status.

56. Rudder, Christian, "How Your Race Affects the Messages You Get," OkTrends blog, October 5, 2009, http://blog.okcupid.com/index.php/your-race-affects-whether-people-write-you-back; and "Race and Attraction, 2009–2014," OkTrends blog, September 10, 2014, http://blog.okcupid.com/index.php/race-attraction-2009–2014. For those who date by the numbers, there are far more details in Rudder's *Dataclysm: Who We Are (When We Think No One's Looking)* (New York: Crown, 2014).

57. At the music recommendation start-up MoodLogic, I often said that a "skip" was a terrible thing to waste: the negative feedback of a person skipping over a music track was incredibly helpful in refining the recommendation algorithms. Like a long click, listening to the full length of the song indicated interest, though the level of interest had to be interpreted over the long term, based on repeated listening and ratings.

58. *Nisbett*, Richard E., and Timothy D. Wilson, "Telling More Than We Can Know: Verbal Reports on Mental Processes," *Psychological Review* 84, no. 3 (March 1977), pp. 231–259, http://psycnet.apa.org/psycinfo/1978-00295-001.

59. The first time I noticed this surprising age histogram, with a peak at age twenty-nine and a trough at age thirty, I was working with Gay.com. (Age twenty-eight showed significantly fewer people than age twenty-nine but more than age thirty.) I have since seen it on several other sites, including Baihe, a Chinese dating site that in 2015 had a valuation of $250 million. The dating scene in China is incredibly age sensitive, and hard limits had to be taken into account when writing matching algorithms for the site's users. See Hufford, Austen, "Chinese Dating Site Jiayuan Agrees to Be Bought by Baihe," *Wall Street Journal*, December 7, 2015, http://www .wsj.com/articles/chinese-dating-site-jiayuan-agrees-to-be-bought-by-baihe-1449501088.

60. I served on Skout's board of directors from 2007 to 2012. The company was acquired by MeetMe in June 2016. See Yeung, Ken, "MeetMe Acquires Mobile Flirting App Skout for $55 Million in Cash and Stock," *VentureBeat*, June 27, 2016, http://venturebeat .com/2016/06/27/meetme-acquires-mobile-flirting-app-skout-for-55-million-in-cash-and- stock.

61. Brin, David, "Questions I Am Frequently Asked About (Part V): Transparency, Privacy and the Information Age," Contrary Brin, April 10, 2013, http://davidbrin.blogspot. co.uk/2013/04/questions-i-am-frequently-asked-about.html. Reprinted with permission of the author.

62. "The Man Who Sued Google to Be Forgotten," Reuters, May 30, 2014, http://www .newsweek.com/man-who-sued-google-be-forgotten-252854.

63. Google had received 520,000 removal requests, corresponding to 1.6 million URLs, as of August 2016. See Google, "Transparency Report: European Privacy in Search," accessed August 8, 2016, https://www.google.com/transparencyreport/removals/europeprivacy.

64. These are among twenty-three examples highlighted by Google—all of them cases with obvious cause to approve or deny the request. See Google, "Transparency Report: European Privacy in Search," accessed August 1, 2016, http://www.google.com/transparencyreport /removals/europeprivacy.

65. Although Immanuel Kant was the leading philosophical voice at the time, it was Friedrich Karl von Savigny (inspired by Kant) who fully developed the idea of "freedom based upon human autonomy, human will, and human personality" in German law. See Eberle, Edward J., "The German Idea of Freedom," *Oregon Review of International Law* 10, no. 1 (2008), p. 16, http://docs.rwu.edu/law_fac_fs/56.

66. Bloustein, Edward J., "Privacy as an Aspect of Human Dignity: An Answer to Dean Prosser," *New York University Law Review* 39, no. 962 (December 1964), p. 962–1007, http://heinonline.org/HOL/LandingPage?collection=journals&handle=hein.journals /nylr39&div=71.

67. Schwartz, Paul M., and Karl-Nikolaus Peifer, "Prosser's Privacy and the German Right of Personality: Are Four Privacy Torts Better than One Unitary Concept?," *California*

Law Review 98, no. 6 (December 2010), pp. 1925–1986, http://papers.ssrn.com/sol3
/papers.cfm?abstract_id=1816885.

68. Ibid., p. 1931.

69. Ibid., p. 1934.

Chapter 3: Connections and Conversations

1. Attributed to Darwin in Ritchie, Anne, *Records of Tennyson, Ruskin, Browning* (New York: Harper & Brothers, 1893), p. 170.

2. Creating a profile for a fake person or posting fake information about yourself contravenes Facebook's terms of service, according to Facebook's "Statement of Rights and Responsibilities" as of August 1, 2015 (https://www.facebook.com/legal/terms).

3. To respect the terms under which my friend shared Rebecca's story with me, this is a paraphrasing of the actual message.

4. Attributed to Darwin in Ritchie, *Records of Tennyson, Ruskin, Browning*, p. 170.

5. Dunbar, Robin, *Grooming, Gossip, and the Evolution of Language* (Cambridge, MA: Harvard University Press, 1996).

6. As Kafka eloquently captured in his 1909 story "Gemeinschaft," "fellowship" or "belongingness" is often defined not by what a group of people share but by who they don't let into their group. An English translation of the story can be found at http://www.ethnography.com/2014/12/fellowship-gemeinschaft-by-franz-kafka-1909.

7. Dunbar, Robin I.M., "Neocortex Size as a Constraint on Group Size in Primates," *Journal of Human Evolution* 22, no. 6 (June 1992), pp. 469–493, http://www.sciencedirect.com/science/article/pii/004724849290081J.

8. Farber, Dan, "Facebook's Zuckerberg Uncorks the Social Graph," *ZDNet*, May 24, 2007, http://www.zdnet.com/article/facebooks-zuckerberg-uncorks-the-social-graph.

9. This distinction between "social graph" and "social network" is not entirely standardized, but I've decided to use it in order to emphasize the basic point that it will soon be possible to map the interactions and relationships of everyone on the planet.

10. Moreno, Jacob Levy, *Who Shall Survive? A New Approach to the Problem of Human Interrelations* (Washington, DC: Nervous and Mental Disease Publishing Co., 1934).

11. Borgatti, Stephen P., Ajay Mehra, Daniel J. Brass, and Giuseppe Labianca, "Network Analysis in the Social Sciences," *Science* 323, no. 892 (2009), http://www.sciencemag.org/cgi/content/full/323/5916/892; Moreno, Jonathan D., "Social Networking Didn't Start at Harvard," *Slate*, October 21, 2014, http://www.slate.com/articles/technology/future_tense/2014/10/j_l_moreno_a_psychologist_s_30s_experiments_invented_social_networking.html. For those interested in more details about Jacob Moreno's research, I recommend Jonathan Moreno's biography of his father, *Impromptu Man: J. L. Moreno and the Origins of Psychodrama, Encounter Culture, and the Social Network* (New York: Bellevue Literary Press, 2014).

12. "Values" may seem a strange word to associate with runaways from a school for delinquent youth. But consider this: the girls valued freedom more than they valued getting testimony from the schoolmistress that they had been "reformed."

13. McAdam, Doug, "Recruitment to High-Risk Activism: The Case of Freedom Summer," *American Journal of Sociology* 92, no. 1 (July 1986), p. 71, http://www.jstor.org/stable/2779717. I'm thankful to J. Nathan Matias for reminding me of McAdam's work; see

Matias, J. Nathan, "Were All Those Rainbow Profile Photos Another Facebook Study?," *Atlantic,* June 28, 2015, http://www.theatlantic.com/technology/archive/2015/06/were-all -those-rainbow-profile-photos-another-facebook-experiment/397088.

14. McAdam, "Recruitment to High-Risk Activism," p. 72.

15. Ibid., p. 86.

16. Ackerman, Mark S., Volkmar Pipek, and Volker Wolf, *Sharing Expertise: Beyond Knowledge Management* (Cambridge, MA: MIT Press, 2003), p. 371.

17. Cross, Rob, Andrew Parker, and Stephen P. Borgatti, "A Bird's-Eye View: Using Social Network Analysis to Improve Knowledge Creation and Sharing," IBM Institute for Business Value executive strategy report no. G510–1669–00, 2002, https://www-07.ibm.com /services/hk/strategy/e_strategy/social_network.html.

18. Heath, Chip, and David Hoyt, "AT&T/MCI: The Long-Distance Phone Wars (A): MCI Introduces 'Friends and Family,'" Stanford Graduate School of Business case no. M298A, February 27, 2002, http://www.gsb.stanford.edu/faculty-research/case-studies /attmci-long-distance-phone-wars-mci-introduces-friends-family.

19. Arabie, Phipps, and Yoram Wind, "Marketing and Social Networks," in S. Wasserman and J. Galaskiewicz, eds., *Advances in Social Networks Analysis* (London: Sage Publications, 1994), p. 255; Givens, Jennifer L., and James Kyle Lynch, "MCI Communications Corporation: Friends and Family," in Robert J. Thomas, ed., *New Product Success Stories: Lessons from Leading Innovators* (New York: John Wiley & Sons, 1995), pp. 196–207.

20. I remember vividly when Mike Schwartz alerted all of us affiliated with the University of Colorado–Boulder Department of Computer Science about the existence of the new internet-discovery architecture, the World Wide Web. He was always at the cutting edge of information systems. He's now at Google.

21. Schwartz, Michael F., and John S. Quarterman, "Discovering Shared Interests Using Graph Analysis," *Communications of the ACM* 36, no. 8 (August 1993), pp. 78–89, http:// dl.acm.org/citation.cfm?id=163402.

22. Truong, Alice, "Everything Facebook Announced on the First Day of Its F8 Developer Conference," *Quartz,* April 12, 2016, http://qz.com/660691/everything-facebook -announced-on-the-first-day-of-its-f8-developer-conference.

23. Lazarsfeld, Paul F., and Robert K. Merton, "Friendship as a Social Process: A Substantive and Methodological Analysis" in M. Berger, ed., *Freedom and Control in Modern Society* (New York: Van Nostrand, 1954), pp. 18–66.

24. Maccoby, Eleanor E., "The Uniqueness of the Parent-Child Relationship," in W. Andrew Collins and Brett Laursen, eds., *Relationships as Developmental Contexts: The Minnesota Symposia on Child Psychology,* vol. 30 (Mahwah, NJ: Psychology Press/Lawrence Erlbaum Associates Publishers, 1999), p. 159.

25. Granovetter, Mark, "The Strength of Weak Ties," *American Journal of Sociology* 78, no. 6 (May 1973), p. 1361, http://www.jstor.org/stable/2776392.

26. Tichy, Noel M., Michael L. Tushman, and Charles Fombrun, "Social Network Analysis for Organizations," *Academy of Management Review* 4, no. 4 (October 1979), p. 509, http:/www.jstor.org/stable/257851.

27. The phrase "selective revelation of information" is associated with Michael Ginn, who patented several innovations in information sharing and privacy in the 1990s that today serve as the basis for social networking platforms like Facebook. In talking about

Michael's work over the years, my great friend and information guru Barney Pell—who knew Michael well—threw out the idea of "sequential revelation." For me, sequential sharing is more interesting than selective sharing, since it operates to create trust rather than barriers to trust.

28. Selman, Robert L., "The Child as a Friendship Philosopher," in Steven R. Asher and John M. Gottman, eds., *The Development of Children's Friendships* (Cambridge: Cambridge University Press, 1981), p. 250.

29. Aron, Arthur, Edward Mellinat, Elaine N. Aron, Robert Darrin Vallone, and Renee J. Bator, "The Experimental Generation of Interpersonal Closeness: A Procedure and Some Preliminary Findings," *Personality and Social Psychology Bulletin* 23, no. 4 (April 1997, pp. 363–377, http://psp.sagepub.com/content/23/4/363.abstract.

30. Simmel, Georg (trans. by Albion Woodbury Small), "The Sociology of Secrecy and of Secret Societies," *American Journal of Sociology* 11, no. 4 (January 1906), p. 443, http://www.jstor.org/stable/2762562.

31. One of the typical examples of dishonest TV ad "endorsements" involves an actor wearing a white lab coat with a stethoscope hung around his neck, not much different from that Florida teen who got busted in Chapter 2. Truth-in-advertising laws prohibit advertisers from passing nondoctors off as doctors, however.

32. Stone, Linda, "Q&A: Continuous Partial Attention," n.d. (accessed September 30, 2016), http://lindastone.net/qa/continuous-partial-attention.

33. At the time of this book's publication, Ding was at a new start-up, DoorDash.

34. The researchers who published an account of the test were not able to specify the product, but reading between the lines we can deduce that it was probably a new device—possibly a handset or PDA—aimed at "early teach adopters" who tended to respond to "buzz" about a product debut.

35. Hill, Shawndra, Foster Provost, and Chris Volinsky, "Network-Based Marketing: Identifying Likely Adopters via Consumer Networks," *Statistical Science* 21, no. 2 (2006), pp. 256–276, https://arxiv.org/pdf/math/0606278.

36. Granovetter, Mark, *Getting a Job: A Study of Contacts and Careers* (Cambridge, MA: Harvard University Press, 1974).

37. It's not precisely true that there was no email: computer scientist Ray Tomlinson was experimenting with email sent over the Arpanet (Advanced Research Projects Agency Network) system in 1971. See Tomlinson, Ray, "The First Network Email," n.d. (accessed September 30, 2016), http://openmap.bbn.com/~tomlinso/ray/firstemailframe.html.

38. Masnick, Mike, "Social Networking Services in the Enterprise Bringing Out Critics," *TechDirt,* December 15, 2003, https://www.techdirt.com/articles/20031215/132222_F.shtml.

39. Ellen and I briefly shared a mentor at Stanford, David E. Rumelhart, one of the people who deserves credit for inventing neural networks. I originally arrived from Germany in 1986 to pursue a PhD in physics, but after reading Chapter 8 in *Parallel-Distributed Processing: Explorations in the Microstructure of Cognition* (Cambridge: MIT Press, 1986), of which Dave was a co-author, I got very interested in the possibilities of computers learning from data. In my second year at Stanford, I asked Dave to become my adviser. Always open to new ideas, he agreed. Dave was known to accept people from many different backgrounds and disciplines, yet we hardly ever talked about the "interdisciplinary" nature of the work.

Unfortunately, Dave was ill by the time Ellen arrived in the psychology department, so she studied memory, perception, and information science under Roger Shepard.

40. Bluestein, Adam, "The Most Connected Woman in Silicon Valley?," *Fast Company*, June 29, 2012, http://www.fastcompany.com/1841490/most-connected-woman-silicon-valley.

41. Ponting, Clive, *A New Green History of the World: The Environment and the Collapse of Great Civilizations* (New York: Random House, 2011), p. 147.

42. Lorenz, Edward N., "Predictability: Does the Flap of a Butterfly's Wings in Brazil Set Off a Tornado in Texas?," presentation at the 139th meeting of the American Association for the Advancement of Science, Massachusetts Institute of Technology, Cambridge, MA, December 29, 1972, http://eaps4.mit.edu/research/Lorenz/Butterfly_1972.pdf.

43. The lack of a dislike button for Facebook content is a classic example of a design decision having a significant impact on a social data ecosystem. According to Mark Zuckerberg, Facebook hadn't adopted a dislike button because the site didn't want to encourage negativity. As Facebook watches users interact with a range of emotional-reaction emojis alongside the like button, it will closely observe how the emojis affect the frequency and pattern of user interaction.

For a sense of how Facebook's approach to a dislike button has evolved over the years, see Oremus, Will, "You Can't Dislike This Article," *Slate*, December 15, 2014, http://www.slate.com/articles/technology/future_tense/2014/12/facebook_dislike_button_why_mark_zuckerberg_won_t_allow_it.html; Bosker, Bianca, "Facebookers Like the Idea of a 'Sympathize' Button (Keep Waiting for 'Dislike')," *Huffington Post*, December 5, 2013, http://www.huffingtonpost.com/2013/12/05/facebook-sympathize-button_n_4394451.html; King, Hope, "Mark Zuckerberg: Facebook Working on a 'Dislike' Button," *CNNMoney*, September 15, 2015, http://money.cnn.com/2015/09/15/technology/facebook-dislike-button/index.html; Lunden, Ingrid, "With Reactions, Facebook Supercharges the Like Button with 6 Empathetic Emoji," *TechCrunch*, October 8, 2015, http://techcrunch.com/2015/10/08/with-reactions-facebook-supercharges-the-like-button-with-6-empathetic-emoji; and Barrett, Brian, "Facebook Messenger Finally Bridges the Great Emoji Divide," *Wired*, June 6, 2016, http://www.wired.com/2016/06/facebook-messenger-emoji.

44. Millward, Steven, "WeChat Now Has 500 Million Monthly Active Users," *Tech in Asia*, March 18, 2015, https://www.techinasia.com/wechat-500-million-active-users-q4-2014; Sedghi, Ami, "Facebook: 10 Years of Social Networking, in Numbers," *Guardian*, February 4, 2014, http://www.theguardian.com/news/datablog/2014/feb/04/facebook-in-numbers-statistics.

45. Before WeChat, Tencent offered another messaging and video communication platform, QQ, which didn't have a social graph component. However, like WeChat, QQ was about fleeting communication; once the "game"—that is, the chat—was over, it was over. And it wasn't just the communication that was fleeting. The accounts were fleeting, too, and QQ gained a reputation as the communication platform of choice for sketchy characters. Adding the social graph helped Tencent rein in these less savory aspects of its more ephemeral messaging service.

46. WeChat offers some options for discovering people randomly, including "Shake," where users who happen to simultaneously shake their phones see each other's profile, and "Look Around," which lets users see the profiles of nearby WeChat users.

47. An earlier iteration asked you only to confirm two people who are your friends from a set of WeChat user names.

48. Bursztein, Elie, "New Research: Some Tough Questions for 'Security Questions,'" Google Online Security, May 21, 2015, https://googleonlinesecurity.blogspot.co.uk/2015 /05/new-research-some-tough-questions-for.html. There are other dynamic approaches to password security that do not depend on social graph data. For example, you might be asked to provide only specific digits or characters from a longer string, or use a random-number generator.

49. Skydeck was developed by Jason Devitt, the CEO and founder of the call-blocking app Mr. Number, which in 2013 was acquired by Whitepages, since renamed Hiya, discussed in Chapter 2.

50. Diuk, Carlos, "The Formation of Love," Facebook Data Science, February 14, 2014, https://www.facebook.com/notes/facebook-data-science/the-formation-of-love/10152064 609253859.

51. Backstrom, Lars, and Jon Kleinberg, "Romantic Partnerships and Dispersion of Social Ties: A Network Analysis of Relationship Status on Facebook," paper presented at the 17th ACM Conference on Computer-Supported Cooperative Work and Social Computing (CSCW 2014), Baltimore, MD, February 15–19, 2014, http://arxiv.org/abs/1310.6753v1.

52. Eslami, Motahhare, Aimee Rickman, Kristen Vaccaro, Amirhossein Aleyasen, Andy Vuong, Karrie Karahalios, Kevin Hamilton, and Christian Sandvig, "'I Always Assumed That I Wasn't Really That Close to [Her]': Reasoning about Invisible Algorithms in the News Feed," *Proceedings of the 33rd Annual ACM Conference on Human Factors in Computing Systems,* Seoul, Korea, April 2015 (New York: Association for Computing Machinery, 2015), p. 154 [pp. 153–162], http://social.cs.uiuc.edu/papers/pdfs/Eslami_Algorithms_CHI15.pdf.

53. Eslami, Motahhare, Amirhossein Aleyasen, Karrie Karahalios, Kevin Hamilton, and Christian Sandvig, "FeedVis: A Path for Exploring News Feed Curation Algorithms," paper presented at the 18th ACM Conference on Computer-Supported Cooperative Work and Social Computing (CSCW 2015), Vancouver, British Columbia, Canada, March 14–18, 2015, p. 3, http://social.cs.uiuc.edu/papers/pdfs/Eslami-CSCW-demo-2015.pdf.

54. Kramer, Adam D. I., Jamie E. Guillory, and Jeffrey T. Hancock, "Experimental Evidence of Massive-Scale Emotional Contagion Through Social Networks," *Proceedings of the National Academy of Sciences USA* 111, no. 24 (June 2, 2014), pp. 8788–8790, http://www .pnas.org/content/111/24/8788.full.

55. In describing the experiment, the authors wrote: "The experiment manipulated the extent to which people (N = 689,003) were exposed to emotional expressions in their News Feed. This tested whether exposure to emotions led people to change their own posting behaviors" (p. 8788). As a result, media coverage frequently invoked the term "manipulation" to describe the study, when the term is standard language among researchers for changing a single variable to see how it affects an experiment's subjects. For examples, see McNeal, Gregory S., "Facebook Manipulated User News Feeds to Create Emotional Responses," *Forbes,* June 28, 2014, http://www.forbes.com/sites/gregorymcneal/2014/06/28 /facebook-manipulated-user-news-feeds-to-create-emotional-contagion; Meyer, Robinson, "Everything We Know About Facebook's Secret Mood Manipulation Experiment," *Atlantic,* June 28, 2014, http://www.theatlantic.com/technology/archive/2014/06/everything -we-know-about-facebooks-secret-mood-manipulation-experiment/373648; and Dewey, Caitlin, "9 Answers About Facebook's Creepy Emotional-Manipulation Experiment,"

Washington Post, July 1, 2014, https://www.washingtonpost.com/news/the-intersect/wp/2014/07/01/9-answers-about-facebooks-creepy-emotional-manipulation-experiment.

56. The study reviewed emotional expression in status updates made by English-speaking Facebook users in the 100 most-populated American cities for 1,180 days between January 2009 and March 2012, categorizing days as rainy or nonrainy based on the level of the city. See Coviello, Lorenzo, Yunkyu Sohn, Adam D. I. Kramer, Cameron Marlow, Massimo Franceschetti, Nicholas A. Christakis, and James H. Fowler, "Detecting Emotional Contagion in Massive Social Networks," *PLoS One* 9, no. 3 (March 2014), http://journals.plos.org/plosone/article?id=10.1371/journal.pone.0090315.

57. Facebook and other social data platforms couldn't guarantee that users get to participate in every study that interests them, or *only* in studies that interest them, as doing so would bias the results. But these data would help users judge whether the experiments being conducted are aligned with their interests, individually and/or for the ecosystem at large.

58. Duffy, Nick, "Facebook's Rainbow Filter Was 'Dreamed Up by Interns,'" *Pink-News,* July 5, 2015, http://www.pinknews.co.uk/2015/07/05/facebooks-rainbow-filter-was-dreamed-up-by-interns.

59. The number of rainbow filters applied—about 30 million—was widely publicized by Facebook, leading to a great deal of speculation about the extent to which the filters were introduced for experimental purposes rather than for expressive ones. See, for instance, Matias, J. Nathan, "Were All Those Rainbow Profile Photos Another Facebook Study?," Atlantic, June 28, 2015, http://www.theatlantic.com/technology/archive/2015/06/were-all-those-rainbow-profile-photos-another-facebook-experiment/397088; and McDonald, James, "26 Million People Change Profile Picture with Facebook's Rainbow Pride Filter," Out, June 29, 2015, http://www.out.com/popnography/2015/6/29/26-million-people-change-profile-pictures-facebooks-rainbow-pride-filter.

60. A much smaller number of users, about 3 million, adopted the "equals sign" as a profile image in March 2013. See State, Bogdan, and Lada Adamic, "The Diffusion of Support in an Online Social Movement: Evidence from the Adoption of Equal-Sign Profile Pictures," *Proceedings of the 18th ACM Conference on Computer-Supported Cooperative Work and Social Computing* (New York: ACM, 2015), pp. 1741–1750, http://dl.acm.org/citation.cfm?id=2675290%22.

61. Bond, Robert M., Christopher J. Fariss, Jason J. Jones, Adam D. I. Kramer, Cameron Marlow, Jaime E. Settle, and James H. Fowler, "A 61-Million-Person Experiment in Social Influence and Political Mobilization," *Nature* 489 (September 13, 2012), pp. 295–298, http://www.nature.com/nature/journal/v489/n7415/full/nature11421.html. In a supplement to their letter to *Nature,* the authors admitted that the experiment wasn't conducted using an ideal A/B design. One "treatment"—the "social" get-out-the-vote message—was applied to the vast majority of participants, 98 percent. The control group, which was shown no message about voting day, comprised 1 percent of the study population; the other treatment—the "informational" message—was shown to the remaining 1 percent. The authors wrote: "Ideally, we would have designed the experiment with equal sized treatment and control groups to maximize power. However, Facebook wanted to encourage all users to participate in the 2010 US Congressional Election, and they therefore asked us to limit the size of the groups that did not receive the standard 'get out the vote' (GOTV) message." See

Bond et al., "Supplementary Information for 'A 61-Million-Person Experiment in Social Influence and Political Mobilization,'" p. 2.

62. Zittrain, Jonathan, "Facebook Could Decide an Election Without Anyone Ever Finding Out," *New Republic,* June 1, 2014, http://www.newrepublic.com/article/117878 /information-fiduciary-solution-facebook-digital-gerrymandering.

63. Holmes, Oliver Wendell, *The Autocrat of the Breakfast-Table: Or, Every Man His Own Boswell* (Boston: Phillips, Sampson, 1859), p. 54.

64. Weirzbicki, Adam, *Trust and Fairness in Open, Distributed Systems* (Berlin: Springer Verlag, 2010), pp. 3, 120.

65. Airbnb has used four main categories of data to verify and vet hosts and guests: internal data (profiles, searches, reviews, interaction history); social graph data (which social networks a user participates in, contacts, and interaction patterns); public data (what information can be discovered through a web search—for example, LinkedIn profile or blog posts); and proprietary data (government and pay-for-use records—for example, databases that can be used to confirm IDs and check for criminal history). These data categories were discussed in a presentation by Alok Gupta, data science manager, Airbnb, in my class, "Social Data Revolution," University of California–Berkeley, October 13, 2015, https:// www.youtube.com/watch?v=Sml06XHN6_0.

66. Yelp also checks the IP address from which a review is posted. If it's the same as the IP address used to post the business's listing on Yelp, the review gets filtered out of searches.

67. Roberts, Daniel, "Yelp's Fake Review Problem," *Fortune,* September 26, 2013, http:// fortune.com/2013/09/26/yelps-fake-review-problem.

68. Broadcasting the exact formulae Yelp uses to decide which reviews are removed from the site would probably make it easier for reputation firms to devise fake reviews that avoid detection, which may be why the company hasn't published that information. See "Five-Star Fakes," *The Economist,* October 24, 2015, http://www.economist.com/news/business/21676835 -evolving-fight-against-sham-reviews-five-star-fakes; and Luca, Michael, "Reviews, Reputation, and Revenue: The Case of Yelp.com," Harvard Business School working paper no. 12–016, September 2011, http://people.hbs.edu/mluca/Yelp.pdf.

69. Meituan-Dianping was formed through a merger of Alibaba-sponsored Meituan with Tencent-sponsored Dianping in October 2015. See Chen, Lulu Yilun, "China's Big Web Deal: Five Key Numbers for Meituan, Dianping," *BloombergBusiness,* October 8, 2015, http://www.bloomberg.com/news/articles/2015-10-08/china-s-big-web-deal -five-key-numbers-for-meituan-dianping.

70. As of 2015, Tencent held a 20 percent stake in Dianping. See Carew, Rick, and Juro Osawa, "China's Dianping Valued at $4 Billion," *Wall Street Journal,* April 2, 2015, http:// www.wsj.com/articles/chinas-dianping-valued-at-4-billion-1427962959.

71. Booker, Elias, "Travel Stress Quantified Using Big Data," *Information Week,* May 6, 2013, http://www.informationweek.com/big-data/big-data-analytics/travel-stress -quantified-using-big-data/d/d-id/1109824.

72. Facebook admonished the company for buying data from app developers, and Rap-Leaf agreed to stop collecting social graph data from the site. In 2013, RapLeaf was acquired by email services company TowerData. See Steel, Emily, "Online Tracking Company

RapLeaf Profiles Users by Name," *Wall Street Journal,* October 25, 2010, http://www.wsj.com /articles/SB10001424052702304410504575560243259416072.

73. Sullivan, Mark, "Facebook Patents Technology to Help Lenders Discriminate Against Borrowers Based on Social Connections," *VentureBeat,* August 4, 2015, http://venture beat.com/2015/08/04/facebook-patents-technology-to-help-lenders-discriminate-against -borrowers-based-on-social-connections.

74. Lunt, Christopher, "Authorization and Authentication Based on an Individual's Social Network," US Patent no. 9,100,400, August 4, 2015, http://www.google.com/patents /US9100400.

75. These coefficients can only be positive for the ecosystem to work. If a person assigned a negative coefficient to someone, it would be the equivalent of him "shorting" her—that is, of him betting on the fact that her reputation is going to go down, which would be bad for her as well as for the ecosystem.

76. I have had many discussions since September 2013 with Friendsurance's founder Tim Kunde about the evolution of the company's services.

77. Felix, Samantha, "This Is How Facebook Is Tracking Your Internet Activity," *Business Insider,* September 9, 2012, http://www.businessinsider.com/this-is-how-facebook-is-tracking -your-internet-activity-2012-9. In some cases, the tracking tool even collected data about people who weren't Facebook users; see Alba, Alejandro, "Facebook Admits Tracking People Who Don't Use the Site, Blames Bug," *New York Daily News,* April 13, 2015, http://www.nydailynews.com /news/world/facebook-admits-tracking-non-users-blames-unintended-bug-article-1.2183409.

78. This is part of Facebook's development of cross-device reporting for advertisers. See Facebook for Business, "Measuring Conversions on Facebook, Across Devices and in Mobile Apps," August 14, 2014, https://www.facebook.com/business/news/cross-device-measurement.

Chapter 4: Context and Conditions

1. Ansel Adams attributed this quote to Stieglitz when he had it stenciled on the wall of an exhibition of his work, *Recent Photography of Ansel Adams,* at the San Francisco Museum of Modern Art in 1939, as recounted in Alinder, Mary Street, *Ansel Adams: A Biography* (New York: Bloomsbury Publishing USA, 2014), p. 134.

2. The descriptions and dialogue reproduced in this chapter are taken from the video posted at the Photography Is Not a Crime website. The first video was recorded by the photograph-taker himself; the dashcam video and audio were obtained by Felipe Hemming, an investigative researcher for the website, via a Freedom of Information request. See Sanders, Brett, "Dashcam Video Reveals Suspicious Dialogue Between Orlando Cops Who Arrested PINAC Reporter," Photography Is Not a Crime, June 23, 2015, http://photographyisnotacrime .com/2015/06/orlando-police-jeff-gray.

3. Turnbell, Michael, "License Plate Frames Can't Obstruct Any Information on Plate," *Sun Sentinel,* January 24, 2010, http://articles.sun-sentinel.com/2010-01-24/news/10012 30055_1_tolls-turnpike-s-work-program-turnpike-in-south-florida.

4. Miller, Carlos, "PINAC Reporter Arrested by Clueless Cop, Leading to Facebook Damage Control by Police," Photography Is Not a Crime, January 29, 2015, http:// photographyisnotacrime.com/2015/01/pinac-reporter-arrested-clueless-cop-leading -facebook-damage-control-police.

5. Sanders, Brett, "Dashcam Video Reveals Suspicious Dialogue Between Orlando Cops who Arrested PINAC Reporter," Photography Is Not a Crime, June 23, 2015, http://photographyisnotacrime.com/2015/06/orlando-police-jeff-gray.

6. Burt, Frank, Richard J. Ovelen, and Jason Patrick Karialla, "Florida Open Government Guide: Foreword," Reporters Committee for Freedom of the Press, n.d. (accessed September 30, 2016), http://www.rcfp.org/florida-open-government-guide/foreword.

7. In March 2015, all of the charges against Gray were dismissed by the courts. See Miller, Carlos, "Charges Dismissed Against PINAC's Jeff Gray in Manipulated Probable Cause Arrest," Photography Is Not a Crime, April 3, 2015, http://photographyisnotacrime.com/2015/04/charges-dismissed-against-pinacs-jeff-gray-in-manipulated-probable-cause-arrest.

8. Argyle, Rachel, "The End of the CCTV Era?," *BBC News Magazine,* January 15, 2015, http://www.bbc.co.uk/news/magazine-30793614.

9. The estimate—1.85 million—was actually lower than a previously reported figure of 4 million put forward by the British government in 2002 after a survey of one London neighborhood. See Lewis, Paul, "You're Being Watched: There's One CCTV Camera for Every 32 People in UK," *Guardian,* March 2, 2011, http://www.theguardian.com/uk/2011/mar/02/cctv-cameras-watching-surveillance; and Gerrard, Graeme, and Richard Thompson, "Two Million Cameras in UK," *CCTVImage,* no. 42 (Winter 2011), pp. 10–12, http://2x9l6r2ys89s2leu9z30a8t1.wpengine.netdna-cdn.com/wp-content/uploads/2011/03/CCTV-Image-42-How-many-cameras-are-there-in-the-UK.pdf.

10. The number of smartphone users hit 1 billion several years ago, and with more than 1 billion smartphones now shipped to market each year, the user base has most likely expanded; see Reisinger, Don, "Worldwide Smartphone User Base Hits 1 Billion," *CNET,* October 17, 2012, http://www.cnet.com/news/worldwide-smartphone-user-base-hits-1-billion.

11. Merchant, Brian, "With a Trillion Sensors, the Internet of Things Would Be the 'Biggest Business in the History of Electronics,'" *Motherboard,* October 29, 2013, http://motherboard.vice.com/blog/the-internet-of-things-could-be-the-biggest-business-in-the-history-of-electronics.

12. Photos and videos (without an audio track) of a police officer in a public place have, since 2012, been classified as free speech by the US Department of Justice. See Smith, Jonathan M., Letter to Mark H. Grimes, Baltimore Police Department, and Mary E. Borja, Wiley Rein LLP, Re: *Christopher Sharp v. Baltimore City Police Department et al.,* May 14, 2012, http://www.wired.com/images_blogs/threatlevel/2012/05/united_states_letter_re_photography_5_14_2012_0.pdf, cited in Zetter, Kim, "Justice Dept. Defends Public's Constitutional 'Right to Record' Cops," *Wired,* May 16, 2012, http://www.wired.com/2012/05/doj-supports-right-to-record.

13. Not all of the department's dashcams work. In early 2015, the *Orlando Sentinel* reported that fourteen of the force's forty-eight in-car cameras "needed maintenance." See Cherney, Elyssa, "After DUI Case, OPD Revises Policy for Broken Cameras," *Orlando Sentinel,* May 12, 2015, http://www.orlandosentinel.com/news/breaking-news/os-orlando-police-cameras-policy-20150512-story.html.

14. Google Glass was released to early "Explorers" on April 15, 2013, and I got my pair in April 2014. I wore them almost continuously through February 2015. The end of the Explorer stage of Glass on January 15, 2015, does not mean the device failed. Using data gathered during the Explorer stage, Google announced it was returning to the lab to continue developing the prototype for eventual widespread release.

15. Fitzgerald, Drew, "Now Google Glass Can Turn You into a Live Broadcast," *Wall Street Journal*, June 24, 2014, http://www.wsj.com/articles/now-google-glass-can-turn-you-into-a-live-broadcast-1403653079.

16. Shteyngart, Gary, "O.K., Glass," *The New Yorker*, August 5, 2013, http://www.newyorker.com/magazine/2013/08/05/o-k-glass.

17. Mann's latest model is called EyeTap. See Miller, Paul, "Project Glass and the Epic History of Wearable Computers," *The Verge*, June 26, 2012, http://www.theverge.com/2012/6/26/2986317/google-project-glass-wearable-computers-disappoint-me.

18. The project was started in 1986 under the auspices of Alex "Sandy" Pentland, then a newly minted professor at MIT. See Rhodes, Bradley, "A Brief History of Wearable Computing," MIT Wearable Computing Project, MIT Media Lab, n.d. (accessed September 30, 2016), https://www.media.mit.edu/wearables/lizzy/timeline.html; and Konnikova, Maria, "Meet the Godfather of Wearables," *The Verge*, May 6, 2014, http://www.theverge.com/2014/5/6/5661318/the-wizard-alex-pentland-father-of-the-wearable-computer.

19. Mann, Steve, "'Reflectionism' and 'Diffusionism': New Tactics for Deconstructing the Video Surveillance Superhighway," *Leonardo* 31, no. 2 (1998), pp. 93–102, http://wearcam.org/leonardo/reflectionism.htm; Mann, Steve, Jason Nolan, and Barry Wellman, "Sousveillance: Inventing and Using Wearable Computing Devices for Data Collection in Surveillance Environments," *Surveillance & Society* 1, no. 3 (2003), pp. 331–355, http://www.surveillance-and-society.org/articles1(3)sousveillance.pdf.

20. The word "surveillance" was imported into English during France's Reign of Terror, when surveillance committees busied themselves by monitoring, arresting, and sometimes executing citizens suspected of harboring royalist sympathies. The term is derived from the Latin *super* ("over") and *vigilare* ("watchfulness"). Mann substituted *sous* ("under") for *sur* to describe the tactic of watching authorities from below.

21. Mann, Steve, with Hal Niedzviecki, *Cyborg: Digital Destiny and Human Possibility in the Age of the Wearable Computer* (Toronto: Doubleday Canada, 2001), p. 82.

22. Mann, Steve, "Wearable Computing as a Means for Personal Empowerment," keynote address delivered at the International Conference on Wearable Computing, Fairfax, Virginia, May 12, 1998, http://wearcomp.org/wearcompdef.html.

23. Horvitz, Eric, and Matthew Barry, "Display of Information for Time-Critical Decision Making," *Proceedings of the Eleventh Conference on Uncertainty in Artificial Intelligence*, Montreal, August 18–20, 1995 (San Francisco: Morgan Kauffman, 1995), pp. 296–305, http://research.microsoft.com/users/horvitz/ftp/vista.pdf; Horvitz, Eric, Corinne Ruokangas, Sampath Srinivas, and Matthew Barry, "A Decision-Theoretic Approach to the Display of Information for Time-Critical Decisions: The Vista Project," *Sixth Annual Workshop on Space Operations Applications and Research: Proceedings of a Workshop Sponsored by the National Aeronautics and Space Administration, Washington, D.C., the U.S. Air Force, Washington, D.C., and the University of Houston-Clear Lake, Houston, Texas*, Houston, August 4–6, 1992 (Houston: NASA Johnson Space Center, 1993), pp. 407–441, http://research.microsoft.com/en-us/um/people/horvitz/ftp/soar.pdf.

24. Miller, George A., "The Magical Number Seven Plus or Minus Two: Some Limits on Our Capacity for Processing Information," *Psychological Review* 63, no. 2 (March 1956), pp. 81–97, http://psycnet.apa.org/psycinfo/1957-02914-001.

25. Waugh, Nancy C., and Donald A. Norman, "Primary Memory," *Psychological Review* 72, no. 2 (March 1965), pp. 89–104, http://psycnet.apa.org/journals/rev/72/2/89.

26. As of August 2015, Livejasmin.com is the third most popular "adult" site on the web. This example of "jasmine" was inspired by another search term, "ebony," suggested by Jan Pedersen, distinguished engineer at Microsoft at the time of this writing. A person searching for "ebony" could be looking for information about the wood, the magazine, a town in Texas, a comic-book character, the Stevie Wonder song, or a subset of sex video sites. In fact, a very high percentage of the people searching for "ebony" click on a sex site, whether or not that was what the person was looking for.

27. The purpose of the noise was to blur the resolution of geolocation data available to civilians and foreign governments. US military devices could always get an accuracy of a few meters, simply by filtering out the noise, which was created with an algorithm. See Lendino, Jamie, "The History of Car GPS Navigation," *PC Magazine,* April 16, 2012, http://www .pcmag.com/article2/0,2817,2402755,00.asp.

28. Leveson, Ira, "The Economic Value of GPS: Preliminary Assessment," presentation to the National Space–Based Positioning, Navigation, and Timing Advisory Board Meeting, June 11, 2015, http://www.space.commerce.gov/presentation-on-gps-economic-study.

29. "Humphreys Research Group Develops New Centimeter-Accurate GPS System," Cockrell School of Engineering, University of Texas at Austin, press release, May 5, 2015, https://www.ae.utexas.edu/news/features/834-humphreys-cm-accuracy.

30. Humphreys, Todd, "How to Fool a GPS," TEDxAustin presentation, Austin, TX, February 11, 2012, http://www.ted.com/talks/todd_humphreys_how_to_fool_a_gps.

31. Steven [user testimonial], "Tile Makes It Easy to Find Each Other," Tile App, November 17, 2015, https://www.thetileapp.com/stories/the-family-plan; Mike [user testimonial], "Stolen Office Projector Tracked Down to Pawn Shop," Tile App, n.d. (accessed September 30, 2016), https://www.thetileapp.com/blog/stolen-office-projector-pawn-shop.

32. One such GPS jammer, called the Wave Bubble, was designed by a graduate student at MIT as an experiment. See Fried, Limor, "Wave Bubble: A Design for a Self-Tuning Portable RF Jammer," May 17, 2011, http://www.ladyada.net/make/wavebubble.

33. Strunsky, Steve, "N.J. Man Fined $32K for Illegal GPS Device That Disrupted Newark Airport System," *New Jersey Star-Ledger,* August 8, 2013, http://www.nj.com/news/index .ssf/2013/08/man_fined_32000_for_blocking_newark_airport_tracking_system.html.

34. Humphreys, "How to Fool a GPS."

35. Kopytoff, Verne, "Why Stores Are Finally Turning On to WiFi," *Fortune,* December 14, 2012, http://fortune.com/2012/12/14/why-stores-are-finally-turning-on-to-wifi.

36. Giles, Jim, "Cameras Know You by Your Walk," *New Scientist,* September 22, 2012, https://www.newscientist.com/article/mg21528835-600-cameras-know-you-by-your-walk.

37. Davis, Lauren, "Fashion That Will Hide You from Face-Recognition Technology," *io9,* January 6, 2014, http://io9.gizmodo.com/how-fashion-can-be-used-to-thwart-facial -recognition-te-1495648863.

38. Kelion, Leo, "Face Scanners Added to Chip-and-Pin Terminals," *BBC News,* September 30, 2015, http://www.bbc.co.uk/news/technology-34399896.

39. Jones, Charisse, "MasterCard Tries Out 'Selfie Pay' for Online Purchases," *USA Today,* October 20, 2015, http://www.usatoday.com/story/money/personalfinance/2015/10/20 /mastercard-selfie-pay-online-purchases/72982264.

40. Daugman, John, "Probing the Uniqueness and Randomness of IrisCodes: Results from 200 Billion Iris Pair Comparisons," *Proceedings of the IEEE* 94, no. 11 (2006), pp. 1927–1935, http://ieeexplore.ieee.org/document/4052470.

41. Venugopalan, S., U. Prasad, K. Harun, K. Neblett, D. Toomey, J. Heyman, and M. Savvides, "Long Range Iris Acquisition System for Stationary and Mobile Subjects," *International Joint Conference on Biometrics,* October 11–13, 2011, Washington, DC, http://ieeexplore.ieee.org/document/6117484.

42. Sharma, Amol, "India Launches Project to ID 1.2 Billion People," *Wall Street Journal,* September 29, 2010, http://www.wsj.com/articles/SB10001424052748704652104575493490951809322.

43. Vigilant is the leading company in the sector; see Cushing, Tim, "Private Companies Continue to Amass Millions of License Plate Photos, Hold onto the Data Forever, *Tech-Dirt,* March 16, 2015, https://www.techdirt.com/articles/20150308/14332230253/private-companies-continue-to-amass-millions-license-plate-photos-hold-onto-data-forever.shtml. Illinois-based MVTRAC owns the other big privately held database of license plate spottings in the United States.

44. Cushing, Tim, "DHS Takes Another Stab at License Plate Database, But This Time with More Privacy Protections and Transparency," *TechDirt,* April 7, 2015, https://www.techdirt.com/articles/20150403/10114630537/dhs-takes-another-stab-license-plate-database-this-time-with-more-privacy-protections-transparency.shtml.

45. As of 2014, auto-repo company Advanced Recovery was among the data collectors working with Digital Recognition Network, the "partner" company that provides private license plate recognition data to Vigilant. See Orr, Steve, "License Plate Data Is Big Business," *USA Today,* November 2, 2014, http://www.usatoday.com/story/news/nation/2014/11/02/license-plate-data-is-big-business/18370791.

46. "Documents Show Location Records Being Kept on Tens of Millions of Innocent Americans," ACLU press release, July 17, 2013, https://www.aclu.org/news/aclu-releases-documents-license-plate-scanners-some-300-police-departments-nationwide.

47. Wu, Huadong, Mel Siegel, and Pradeep Khosla, "Vehicle Sound Signature Recognition by Frequency Vector Principal Component Analysis," *IEEE Transactions on Instrumentation and Measurement* 48, no. 5 (October 1999), pp. 1005–1009, http://ieeexplore.ieee.org/iel5/19/17382/00799662.pdf. Even electric and hybrid cars, whose engines are seemingly silent to the naked ear, have sound signatures: under the Pedestrian Safety Enhancement Act of 2010, manufacturers must add "notification sounds" as a signal to drivers and pedestrians.

48. Sottek, T. C., "The Xbox One Will Always Be Listening to You, in Your Home," *The Verge,* May 21, 2013, http://www.theverge.com/2013/5/21/4352596/the-xbox-one-is-always-listening; Kobie, Nicole, "Shh, the TV's Listening: Voice Is the New Privacy Frontline," *Motherboard,* February 9, 2015, http://motherboard.vice.com/read/shh-the-tvs-listening-voice-is-the-new-privacy-frontline.

49. "This Is What a Security Camera Should Be," Google Nest Cam, n.d. (accessed January 6, 2016), https://nest.com/camera/meet-nest-cam.

50. Anonymous interview with author, October 2015.

51. "Tokyo's Train Stations Use Theme Songs to Put a Jingle in Your Squashed Journey," *Time Out Tokyo,* March 25, 2015, http://blogs.timeout.jp/en/2015/03/25/train-melodies.

52. Perez, Sarah, "Social Travel App Jetpac Ditches Facebook, Pivots to Instagram-Based 'City Guides' for At-a-Glance Recommendations," *TechCrunch,* December 5, 2013, http:// techcrunch.com/2013/12/05/social-travel-app-jetpac-ditches-facebook-pivots-to-instagram -based-city-guides-for-at-a-glance-recommendations. Originally, Jetpac crawled photos uploaded to public profiles on Facebook, capturing the images as well the titles, captions, and descriptions. This was perfectly legal because Facebook wanted search engines to be able to index public profiles and generate traffic to the site when people were searching for an individual's name.

53. Glusac, Elaine, "With New App, Photos Become a Travel Guide," *New York Times,* February 4, 2014, http://intransit.blogs.nytimes.com/2014/02/04/with-new-app-photos -become-a-travel-guide.

54. Perez, "Social Travel App Jetpac Ditches Facebook."

55. Hardy, Quentin, "The Peril of Knowledge Everywhere," *New York Times,* May 10, 2014, http://bits.blogs.nytimes.com/2014/05/10/the-peril-of-knowledge-everywhere.

56. The risks of using a photo-processing app to find a gay bar in Tehran would be very high, with little and possibly no upside. If the mullahs wanted to arrest a person for being gay, they would surely be willing to crack any identity. Similar dangers also accrue to text and image postings on private message forums and dating apps.

57. Olsen, Erik, "Scientists Uncover Invisible Motion in Video," *New York Times,* February 27, 2013, http://bits.blogs.nytimes.com/2013/02/27/scientists-uncover-invisible-motion -in-video; Rubinstein, Michael, Eugene Shih, John Guttag, Frédo Durand, and William T. Freeman, "Eulerian Video Magnification for Revealing Subtle Changes in the World," paper presented at the ACM Special Interest Group on Computer Graphics and Interactive Techniques, July 2012, http://people.csail.mit.edu/mrub/papers/vidmag.pdf.

58. Santus, Rex, "This Wristband Works with Your Heartbeat to Pay for Things," *Mashable,* November 5, 2014, http://mashable.com/2014/11/04/wristband-heartbeat-payments /#S8Re1Kn648qR; Tempterton, James, "Halifax Uses Heartbeat Sensor to Secure Online Banking," *Wired UK,* March 13, 2015, http://www.wired.co.uk/article/2015–03/13 /halifax-ecg-login.

59. "A Heart to My Key," *The Economist,* May 9, 2013, http://www.economist.com /blogs/babbage/2013/05/biometrics; Agrafioti, Foteini, Francis Minhthang Bui, and Dimitrios Hatzinakos, "System and Method for Enabling Continuous or Instantaneous Identity Recognition Based on Physiological Biometric Signals," US Patent application no. US20140188770 A1, July 3, 2014, http://www.google.com/patents/US20140188770.

60. Warden, Pete, "Software That Can See Will Change Privacy Forever," *MIT Technology Review,* July 29, 2014, http://www.technologyreview.com/view/529396/software -that-can-see-will-change-privacy-forever.

61. Ekman, Paul, and Wallace V. Friesen, *Facial Action Coding System: A Technique for the Measurement of Facial Movement* (Palo Alto: Consulting Psychologists Press, 1978).

62. See, for example, Fasel, B., and Juergen Luettin, "Automatic Facial Expression Analysis: A Survey," *Pattern Recognition* 36, no. 1 (January 2003), pp. 259–275, http://www .sciencedirect.com/science/article/pii/S0031320302000523; and Bartlett, Marian Stewart, Gwen Littlewort-Ford, Javier Movellan, Ian Fasel, and Mark Frank, "Automated Facial Action Coding System," US Patent no. US8798374 B2, August 26, 2009, https://www.google .com/patents/US8798374.

63. Ekman, Paul, *Emotions Revealed: Recognizing Faces and Feelings to Improve Communication and Emotional Life* (New York: Times Books, 2003), pp. 3–8.

64. Ibid., p. 220.

65. The resolution used—4K—is found in mainstream consumer electronics models. Author interview with Javier R. Movellan, co-founder and lead researcher, Emotient, November 14, 2015.

66. Dwoskin, Elizabeth, and Evelyn M. Rusli, "The Technology That Unmasks Your Hidden Emotions," *Wall Street Journal,* January 28, 2015, http://www.wsj.com/articles /startups-see-your-face-unmask-your-emotions-1422472398. For the video of faked pain expressions used to train the model, see "Are These People in Real Pain or Just Faking It?," *New York Times,* April 28, 2014, http://www.nytimes.com/interactive/2014/04/28/science /faking-pain.html.

67. Truong, Alice, "This Google Glass App Will Detect Your Emotions, Then Relay Them Back to Retailers," *Fast Company,* March 6, 2014, http://www.fastcompany.com/3027342 /fast-feed/this-google-glass-app-will-detect-your-emotions-then-relay-them-back-to-retailers.

68. Kokalitcheva, Kia, "Apple Acquires Startup That Reads Emotions From Facial Expressions," *Fortune,* January 7, 2016, http://fortune.com/2016/01/07/apple-emotient-acquisition.

69. "Does My Ad Evoke the Emotions I Want It To? LG, 'Stage Fright,'" Realeyes, n.d. (accessed September 30, 2016), http://www.realeyesit.com/case-study-lg. LG's finished ad can be seen at https://www.youtube.com/watch?v=Yf636vLep8s.

70. Picard, Rosalind W., "Future Affective Technology for Autism and Emotion Communication," *Philosophical Transactions for the Royal Society of London Series B, Biological Sciences* 364, no. 1535 (December 2009), pp. 3575–3584, https://www.ncbi.nlm.nih.gov /pmc/articles/PMC2781888/.

71. Bosker, Bianca, "Affectiva's Emotion Recognition Tech: When Machines Know What You're Feeling," *Huffington Post,* December 24, 2012, http://www.huffingtonpost .com/2012/12/24/affectiva-emotion-recognition-technology_n_2360136.html.

72. Researchers have found that using mel-frequency cepstral coefficient, a mathematically derived description of sound frequency, is more accurate than simple pitch measures for speech and emotion recognition software. I've chosen to use the term "pitch" for simplicity's sake.

73. For the *Vocal Expressions of Nineteen Emotions across Cultures* corpus, actors were directed to express three levels of intensity for nineteen emotions: affection, amusement, anger, contempt, disgust, distress, fear, guilt, happiness, interest, lust, negative surprise, neutral, positive surprise, pride, relief, sadness, serenity, and shame. See Laukka, Petri, Hillary Anger Elfenbein, Wanda Chui, and Nutankumar S. Thingujam, "Presenting the VENEC Corpus: Development of a Cross-Cultural Corpus of Vocal Emotional Expressions and a Novel Method of Annotating Emotion Appraisals," *Proceedings of the LREC 2010 Workshop on Corpora for Research on Emotion and Affect* (Malta: European Language Resources Association, 2010), pp. 53–57, http://www.diva-portal.org/smash/record .jsf?pid=diva2%3A373848&dswid=760.

74. Neiberg, Daniel, and Joakim Gustafson, "Cues to Perceived Functions of Acted and Spontaneous Feedback Expressions," *Proceedings of the Interdisciplinary Workshop on Feedback Behaviors in Dialog,* September 7–8, 2012, Stevenson, WA, pp. 53–56, http://www .cs.utep.edu/nigel/feedback/proceedings/full-proceedings.pdf.

75. Lutfi, Syaheerah Lebai, Fernando Fernández-Martínez, Juan Manuel Lucas-Cuesta, Lorena López-Lebón, and Juan Manuel Montero, "A Satisfaction-Based Model for Affect Recognition from Conversational Features in Spoken Dialog Systems," *Speech Communication* 55, nos. 7–8 (September 2013), pp. 825–840, http://www.researchgate.net /publication/257012012_A_satisfaction-based_model_for_affect_recognition_from _conversational_features_in_spoken_dialog_systems.

76. Lunden, Ingrid, "LiveOps Raises Another $30M, Acquires UserEvents to Expand Its Cloud Contact Center Platform," *TechCrunch,* January 27, 2014, http://techcrunch .com/2014/01/27/liveops-raises-another-30m-acquires-userevents-to-expand-its-cloud -contact-center-platform-with-routing.

77. Bertolucci, Jeff, "Big Data: Matching Personalities in the Call Center," *Information-Week,* February 17, 2015, http://www.informationweek.com/big-data/big-data-analytics /big-data-matching-personalities-in-the-call-center/d/d-id/1319108.

78. Thrun, Sebastian, "From Self-Driving Cars to Retraining People," Next:Economy O'Reilly Summit: What's the Future of Work?, November 12, 2015, San Francisco, CA, http://conferences.oreilly.co/nextcon/economy-us-2015/public/schedule/detail/44930.

79. Kanevsky, Dimitri, "IBM 5 in 5: Hearing," IBM Research News, December 17, 2012, http://ibmresearchnews.blogspot.co.uk/2012/12/ibm-5-in-5–2012-hearing.html.

80. Valenza, Gaetano, Luca Citi, Antonia Lanatá, Enzo Pasquale Scilingo, and Riccardo Barbieri, "Revealing Real-Time Emotional Responses: A Personalized Assessment Based on Heartbeat Dynamics," *Nature Scientific Reports* 4, no. 4998 (May 21, 2014), http://www .nature.com/articles/srep04998.

81. The Xbox also has a standard camera to analyze physical movements and, presumably, facial expressions are already part of the package or will be. See Wortham, Jenna, "If Our Gadgets Could Measure Our Emotions," *New York Times,* June 1, 2013, http://www .nytimes.com/2013/06/02/technology/if-our-gadgets-could-measure-our-emotions.html.

82. Kellner, Tomas, "Meet the Fearbit: New Sweat Sensors Will Sniff Out Fatigue, Stress, and Even Fear," *GE Reports,* August 12, 2014, http://www.gereports.com/post /93990980310/meet-the-fearbit-new-sweat-sensors-will-sniff-out.

83. Turner, Matthew A., Stephan Bandelow, L. Edwards, P. Patel, Helen J. Martin, Ian D. Wilson, and Charles L. Paul Thomas, "The Effect of Paced Auditory Serial Addition Test (PASAT) Intervention on the Profile of Volatile Organic Compounds in Human Breath: A Pilot Study," *Journal of Breath Research* 7, no. 1 (February 27, 2013), http://iopscience.iop .org/article/10.1088/1752-7155/7/1/017102/meta.

84. Hernandez, Javier, Xavier Benavides, Patti Maes, Daniel McDuff, Judith Amores, and Rosalind M. Picard, "AutoEmotive: Bringing Empathy to the Driving Experience to Manage Stress," paper presented at the ACM Conference on Designing Interactive Systems, June 21–25, 2014, Vancouver, BC, Canada, http://affect.media.mit.edu/pdfs/14. Hernandez_et_al-DIS.pdf; Hernandez, Javier, Judith Amores, Daniel McDuff, and Xavier Benavides, "AutoEmotive," MIT Affective Media Lab presentation at the VW Data Driven Hackathon, January 21, 2014, http://autoemotive.media.mit.edu/#about.

85. For a review of the debates around the psychology of emotions, see Beck, Julie, "Hard Feelings: Science's Struggle to Define Emotions," *Atlantic,* February 24, 2015, http://www.theatlantic.com/features/archive/2015/02/hard-feelings-sciences-struggle -to-define-emotions/385711.

86. Barrett, Lisa Feldman, Batja Mesquita, Kevin N. Ochsner, and James J. Gross, "The Experience of Emotion," *Annual Review of Psychology* 58 (January 2007), pp. 373–403, http://www.ncbi.nlm.nih.gov/pmc/articles/PMC1934613.

87. Ekman, *Emotions Revealed*, p. 57.

88. Charlton, Alistair, "Future Supermarket Will Track Shoppers' Eye Movements," *International Business Times*, May 1, 2013, http://www.ibtimes.co.uk/future-supermarket-adverts-track-eye-gaze-sideways-463288.

89. Kahneman, Daniel, and Jackson Beatty, "Pupil Diameter and Load on Memory," *Science* 154, no. 3756 (December 23, 1966), pp. 1583–1585, http://science.sciencemag.org/content/154/3756/1583.

90. Engbert, Ralf, and Reinhold Kliegl, "Microsaccades Uncover the Orientation of Covert Attention," *Vision Research* 43, no. 9 (April 2003), pp. 1035–1045, http://www.sciencedirect.com/science/article/pii/S0042698903000841.

91. Marks, Paul, "Fitbit for the Mind: Eye-Tracker Watches Your Reading," *New Scientist*, February 12, 2014, https://www.newscientist.com/article/mg22129563-700-fitbit-for-the-mind-eye-tracker-watches-your-reading.

92. Bulling, Andreas, Daniel Roggen, and Gerhard Tröster, "What's in the Eyes for Context-Awareness?," *IEEE Pervasive Computing* 10, no. 2 (April–June 2011), pp. 48–57, https://perceptual.mpi-inf.mpg.de/files/2013/03/bulling11_pcm.pdf.

93. Author interview with Wilkey Wong, director of knowledge services, Tobii Technology, December 16, 2015.

94. Amir Shareghi, Antonija Mitrovic, and Kourosh Neshatian, "Eye Tracking and Studying Examples: How Novices and Advanced Learners Study SQL Examples," *Journal of Computing and Information Technology* 23, no. 2 (2015), pp. 171–190, https://www.researchgate.net/publication/279230237_Eye_Tracking_and_Studying_Examples_How__Novices_and_Advanced_Learners_Study_SQL_Examples.

95. Litchfield, Damien, Linden J. Ball, Tim Donovan, David J. Manning, and Trevor Crawford, "Viewing Another Person's Eye Movements Improves Identification of Pulmonary Nodules in Chest X-Ray Inspection," *Journal of Experimental Psychology Applied* 16, no. 3 (September 2010), pp. 251–262, http://www.ncbi.nlm.nih.gov/pubmed/20853985.

96. Tourassi, Georgia D., Sophie Voisin, Vincent C. Paquit, and Elizabeth Krupinski, "Investigating the Link Between Radiologists' Gaze, Diagnostic Decision, and Image Content," *Journal of the American Medical Informatics Association* 20, no. 6 (November–December 2013), pp. 1067–1075, http://www.ncbi.nlm.nih.gov/pubmed/23788627.

97. Julian, David P., "Systems and Methods for Counteracting a Perceptual Fading of a Movable Indicator," US Patent no. 8,937,591, January 20, 2015, https://patents.google.com/patent/US8937591B2.

98. Vidal, Mélodie, Jayson Turner, Andreas Bulling, and Hans Gellersen, "Wearable Eye Tracking for Mental Health Monitoring," *Computer Communications* 35 (2012), pp. 1306–1311, http://www.sciencedirect.com/science/article/pii/S0140366411003549.

99. Di Stasi, Leandro L., Michael B. McCamy, Andres Catena, Stephen L. Macknik, Jose J. Canas, and Susana Martinez-Conde, "Microsaccade and Drift Dynamics Reflect Mental Fatigue," *European Journal of Neuroscience* 38, no. 3 (August 2013), pp. 2389–2398, http://www.ncbi.nlm.nih.gov/pubmed/23675850.

100. Bixler, Robert, and Sidney D'Mello, "Toward Fully Automated Person-Independent Detection of Mind Wandering," in Dimitrova, Vania, Tsvi Kuflik, and David Chin et al., eds., *User Modeling, Adaptation, and Personalization* (New York: Springer, 2014), pp. 37–48.

101. Killingsworth, Matthew A., and Daniel T. Gilbert, "A Wandering Mind Is an Unhappy Mind," *Science* 330, no. 6006 (November 12, 2010), p. 932, http://www.sciencemag.org/content/330/6006/932. The app is still available for download at https://www.trackyourhappiness.org.

102. Kahl, Martin, "Eyeballing the Driver: Eye-Tracking Technology Goes from Vision to Reality," *Automotive World,* April 16, 2015, http://www.automotiveworld.com/analysis/eyeballing-driver.

103. Killingsworth, and Gilbert, "A Wandering Mind Is an Unhappy Mind," p. 932. 104. Ibid., p. 204.

105. Sociometric Solutions was founded by Sandy Pentland and three of his PhD students at MIT: Ben Waber, Taemie Kim, and Daniel Olguin. I'm especially indebted to Taemie for sharing case studies in my UC–Berkeley class in 2014, and highly recommend Ben's book *People Analytics: How Social Sensing Technology Will Transform Business and What It Tells Us About the Future of Work* (Upper Saddle River, NJ: FT Press, 2013).

106. This study was conducted in two stages over fourteen weeks, with the first stage used for collecting data about existing team dynamics and the second for the A/B test. Each of the teams was composed of twenty employees. Call handle time decreased 23 percent and the staff turnover decreased 28 percent for teams that took breaks together, according to Taemie. For Taemie's presentation on sociometrics at my UC–Berkeley class in November 2014, see https://www.youtube.com/watch?v=zXmukPb6ijs.

107. Westen, Drew, Pavel S. Blagov, Keith Harenski, Clint Kilts, and Stephan Hamann, "Neural Bases of Motivated Reasoning: An fMRI Study of Emotional Constraints on Partisan Political Judgment in the 2004 U.S. Presidential Election," *Journal of Cognitive Neuroscience* 18, no. 11 (November 2006), pp. 1947–1958, http://www.ncbi.nlm.nih.gov/pubmed/17069484.

108. Keuken, Max C., Christa Muller-Axt, and Robert Langner et al., "Brain Networks of Perceptual Decision-Making: An fMRI ALE Meta-Analysis," *Frontiers in Human Neuroscience* 8, no. 445 (June 2014), n.p., http://www.ncbi.nlm.nih.gov/pmc/articles/PMC4063192.

109. Muehlemann, Thomas, Daniel Haensse, and Martin Wolf, "Wireless Miniaturized Near-Infrared Scans," *Optics Express* 16, no. 14 (July 7, 2008), pp. 10323–10330, http://www.ncbi.nlm.nih.gov/pubmed/18607442; Piper, Sophie K., Arne Krueger, Stefan P. Koch, Jan Mehnert, Christina Habermehl, Jens Steinbrink, Hellmuth Obrig, and Christoph H. Schmitz, "A Wearable Multi-Channel fNIRS System for Brain Imaging in Freely Moving Subjects," *NeuroImage* 85, no. 1 (January 15, 2014), pp. 64–71, http://www.sciencedirect.com/science/article/pii/S1053811913007003. The development of NIR technology has been fitful, particularly with comparison to fMRI; see Strangman, Gary, Joseph P. Culver, John H. Thompson, and David A. Boas, "A Quantitative Comparison of Simultaneous BOLD fMRI and NIRS Recordings During Functional Brain Activation," *NeuroImage* 17, no. 2 (October 2002), pp. 719–731, http://www.sciencedirect.com/science/article/pii/S1053811902912279; and Wolf, Martin, Marco Ferrari, and Valentina Quaresima,

"Progress of Near-Infrared Spectroscopy and Topography for Brain and Muscle Clinical Applications," *Journal of Biomedical Optics* 12, no. 6 (November–December 2007), n.p., http://biomedicaloptics.spiedigitallibrary.org/article.aspx?articleid=1351966.

110. Greenberg, Andy, "Want an RFID Chip Implanted into Your Hand? Here's What the DIY Surgery Looks Like," *Forbes,* August 13, 2012, http://www.forbes.com/sites /andygreenberg/2012/08/13/want-an-rfid-chip-implanted-into-your-hand-heres-what -the-diy-surgery-looks-like-video.

111. The MinION, a portable device for analyzing DNA, RNA, proteins, and small molecules in real time, has been built by Oxford Nanopore Technologies, https://www .nanoporetech.com.

112. Brad was chairman of the board of the Electronic Frontier Foundation (EFF) from 2000 until 2010. See Hardy, Quentin, "What's Lost When Everything Is Recorded," *New York Times,* August 17, 2013, http://bits.blogs.nytimes.com/2013/08/17 /whats-lost-when-everything-is-recorded.

113. Zilla van den Born and my fake friend Rebecca, who you met at the start of Chapter 3, aren't the only ones faking online profiles. Legitimate and illegitimate businesses— including government spy agencies—use fake profiles to contact individuals with all sorts of "enticing" offers.

114. Calkins, Kelley, "Dutch Woman Fakes Trip to Southeast Asia, Surfaces Universal Truth," *Huffington Post,* September 12, 2014, http://www.huffingtonpost.com/ravishly /dutch-woman-fakes-trip-to_b_5807572.html.

115. Mims, Christopher, "What Happens When Police Officers Wear Body Cameras," *Wall Street Journal,* August 18, 2014, http://www.wsj.com/articles/what-happens -when-police-officers-wear-body-cameras-1408320244.

116. The head of technology for the City of Los Angeles explained to me that, per the policy at the time, the bodycams were deployed was to have the video sensors "on" at all times, but that the video was saved to the police department's database only when an officer pushed a "record" button on the unit (author interview with Ted Ross, general manager and chief information officer, City of Los Angeles Information Technology Agency, November 3, 2015).

117. El Nasser, Haya, "Los Angeles Police Roll Out the First of 7,000 Body Cameras for Officers," *Al Jazeera America,* August 31, 2015, http://america.aljazeera.com/articles /2015/8/31/los-angeles-police-roll-out-the-first-of-7000-body-cameras-for-officers.html.

118. Meyer, Robinson, "Film the Police: A New App Makes It Easier," *Atlantic,* May 6, 2015, http://www.theatlantic.com/technology/archive/2015/05/film-the-police/392483.

119. Williams, Timothy, "Downside of Police Body Cameras: Your Arrest Hits YouTube," *New York Times,* April 26, 2015, http://www.nytimes.com/2015/04/27/us/downside-of -police-body-cameras-your-arrest-hits-youtube.html.

120. The channel is SPD BodyWornVideo, https://www.youtube.com/channel/UC cdSPRNt1HmzkTL9aSDfKuA.

121. Plaugic, Lizzie, "Seattle's Police Department Has a YouTube Channel for Its Body Camera Footage," *The Verge,* February 28, 2015, http://www.theverge.com /2015/2/28/8125671/seattle-police-body-cameras-youtube-channel; and Chan, Manila, "Seattle PD's YouTube Channel Met with Blowback from Public," *RT America,* February 27, 2015, https://www.youtube.com/watch?v=MJER8aYeMRM.

Chapter 5: Seeing the Controls

1. This quote is often attributed to one of my heroes, Albert Einstein, but there is no evidence that he said it in these words. See Cameron, William Bruce, *Informal Sociology: A Casual Introduction to Sociological Thinking* (New York: Random House, 1963), p. 13.

2. I'm playing here with database jargon, where users can be granted "read" rights, or permissions, to see information in the database, or "write" rights, to edit it.

3. The original German is *Die Grenzen meiner Sprache bedeuten die Grenzen meiner Welt*. See Wittgenstein, Ludwig, *Tractatus Logico-Philosophicus*, trans. by C. K. Ogden (London: Kegan Paul, Trench, Trubner & Co., 1922), p. 76, sec. 5.6, https://www.gutenberg.org /files/5740/5740-pdf.pdf. Wittgenstein wrote the tract during World War I; the original German publication was published in 1921 under the title *Logisch-Philosophische Abhandlung*.

4. Or as Wittgenstein might have put it, "play a new language game."

5. Carrns, Ann, "Why You Have 49 Different FICO Scores," *New York Times*, August 27, 2012, http://bucks.blogs.nytimes.com/2012/08/27/why-you-have-49-different-fico-scores.

6. Mayer, Caroline, "The Truth About Those New Free Credit Scores," *Forbes*, February 5, 2014, http://www.forbes.com/sites/nextavenue/2014/02/05/the-truth-about-those-new -free-credit-scores.

7. Duhigg, Charles, "How Companies Learn Your Secrets," *New York Times Magazine*, February 16, 2012, http://www.nytimes.com/2012/02/19/magazine/shopping-habits.html.

8. Carroll, Evan, "972,000 U.S. Facebook Users Will Die in 2016," The Digital Beyond, January 22, 2016, http://www.thedigitalbeyond.com/2016/01/972000-u-s-facebook -users-will-die-in-2016.

9. Fowler, Geoffrey A., "Life and Death Online: Who Controls a Digital Legacy?," *Wall Street Journal*, January 5, 2013, http://www.wsj.com/news/articles/SB1000142412788732 4677204578188220364231346.

10. Oremus, Will, "Dying on Facebook Just Got a Little Less Awkward," *Slate*, February 12, 2015, http://www.slate.com/blogs/future_tense/2015/02/12/facebook_legacy_contact _who_manages_account_when_you_die.html.

11. Kleinman, Zoe, "Facebook Suspends Photo Tag Tool in Europe," *BBC News*, September 21, 2012, http://www.bbc.co.uk/news/technology-19675172.

12. Several scales are used for hygiene ratings. In California, for instance, a 100-point scale is used, with 100 being the best rating available, while in New York City, grades from A to F are assigned. In the United Kingdom, a 6-point numerical scale is used (0 to 5), and in China, a mash-up of "traffic signal" colors and "smiley" icons is typical (with green smile for "excellent," yellow neutral face for "pass," and red frown for "fail").

13. Mary Mallon, known as "Typhoid Mary," was an asymptomatic carrier of typhoid fever who, unfortunately, worked in the early twentieth century as a cook for several families, many of whom became ill. See Marinelli, Filio, Gregory Tsoucalas, Marianna Karamanou, and George Androutsous, "Mary Mallon (1869–1938) and the History of Typhoid Fever," *Annals of Gastroenterology* 26, no. 2 (spring 2013), pp. 132–134, http://www.ncbi.nlm.nih. gov/pmc/articles/PMC3959940.

14. Researchers at Oxford University and Edinburgh's Medical Research Council Institute of Genetics and Molecular Medicine have developed a smartphone app that can be used to analyze patient photos against a database of rare genetic conditions. See Coghlan, Andy,

"Computer Spots Rare Diseases in Family Photos," *New Scientist,* June 24, 2014, https:// www.newscientist.com/article/dn25776-computer-spots-rare-diseases-in-family-photos.

15. Goodman, Marc, *Future Crimes: Inside the Digital Underground and the Battle for Our Connected World* (New York: Doubleday, 2015), p. 175.

16. Up to 70 million customers were affected. The data were stolen through software installed on credit- and debit-card readers. See Stone, Jeff, "Target Hackers Had Access to All of Chain's U.S. Cash Registers in 2013," *IBT,* September 21, 2015, http://www.ibtimes.com /target-hackers-had-access-all-chains-us-cash-registers-2013-data-breach-report-2106575.

17. About 145 million customers were affected. The data were stolen by hackers who grabbed log-in credentials for a few employees. See "eBay Hack 'One of the Biggest Data Breaches in History,'" *The Week,* May 22, 2014, http://www.theweek.co.uk /technology/58624/ebay-hack-one-of-the-biggest-data-breaches-in-history.

18. About 75 million households and 7 million small businesses were affected. The hackers gained access through a list of the company's software and web applications, which they used to uncover "back doors" to data. See Silver-Greenberg, Jessica, Matthew Goldstein, and Nicole Perlroth, "JPMorgan Chase Hacking Affects 76 Million Households," *New York Times,* October 2, 2014, http://dealbook.nytimes.com/2014/10/02 /jpmorgan-discovers-further-cyber-security-issues.

19. Malware installed via a phishing attack erased all data stored on nearly half the studio's personal computers and more than half of its servers; the Social Security numbers for 47,000 people, as well as salary lists, movie scripts, and finished films, were posted online. See Elkind, Peter, "Sony Pictures: Inside the Hack of the Century," *Fortune,* July 1, 2015, http://fortune.com/sony-hack-part-1.

20. Hackers gained access to a database of 78 million Anthem customers after an employee clicked on "a phishing email that was disguised to look like an internal message." See Scannell, Kara, and Gina Chon, "Cyber Security: Attack of the Health Hackers," *Financial Times,* December 21, 2015, http://www.ft.com/cms/s/2/f3cbda3e-a027-11e5-8613 -08e211ea5317.html.

21. As of April 2016, the Philippines Election Commission database breach was the largest government hack known, affecting 55 million registered voters. See Hern, Alex, "Philippine Electoral Records Breached in 'Largest Ever' Government Hack," *Guardian,* April 11, 2016, https://www.theguardian.com/technology/2016/apr/11/philippine -electoral-records-breached-government-hack.

22. For a great visualization of large data hacks and breaches since 2004, see McCandless, David, "World's Biggest Data Breaches and Hacks," Information Is Beautiful, February 16, 2016, http://www.informationisbeautiful.net/visualizations/worlds-biggest-data-breaches-hacks.

23. Quoted in Elkind, "Sony Pictures: Inside the Hack of the Century."

24. Ibid.

25. Mangalindan, J. P., "Kevin Mandia: Why Selling Mandiant Made Sense," *Fortune,* February 13, 2014, http://fortune.com/2014/02/13/kevin-mandia-why-selling-mandiant -made-sense.

26. As of 2016, encryption is done through either a secure sockets layer (SSL) or a transport layer security (TLS). In August 2015, the Electronic Frontier Foundation and several partners, including Mozilla, Cisco, and the University of Michigan, launched the free "Let's Encrypt" certificate authority system, which they hope will help move more companies from

the HTTP protocol to the HTTPS protocol. EFF and technology experts assert that the HTTP protocol is far more susceptible to account hijacking, identify theft, malware, and unauthorized tracking. See Eckersley, Peter, "Launching in 2015: A Certificate Authority to Encrypt the Entire Web," Electronic Frontier Foundation, November 18, 2014, https://www.eff.org/deeplinks/2014/11/certificate-authority-encrypt-entire-web.

27. For example, in 2004 an AOL engineer stole 90 million screen names and email addresses from the email provider, then sold them for $28,000 to spammers, who sent out 7 billion emails to these addresses. The engineer was sentenced to fifteen months in prison; he also had to pay damages, three times as much as what he made in the deal—but to AOL, for harm to its business! See "Ex-AOL Worker Who Stole E-mail List Sentenced," Associated Press, August 17, 2005, http://www.nbcnews.com/id/8985989/ns/technology_and_science-security/t/ex-aol-worker-who-stole-e-mail-list-sentenced.

28. A whistle-blower revealed the incident and forced improvements in internal data handling. See Singel, Ryan, "Probe Targets Archives' Handling of Data on 70 Million Vets," *Wired*, October 1, 2009, http://www.wired.com/2009/10/probe-targets-archives-handling-of-data-on-70-million-vets.

29. Angwin, Julia, and Steve Stecklow, "'Scrapers' Dig Deep for Data on Web," *Wall Street Journal*, October 12, 2010, http://www.wsj.com/articles/SB10001424052748703358504575544381288117888.

30. Ibid.

31. Ruddermann, Adam, "Economy of Trust: Building Relationships with Security Researchers," Facebook blog, March 17, 2016, https://www.facebook.com/notes/facebook-bug-bounty/economy-of-trust-building-relationships-with-securityresearchers/1249035218444035; Kumar, Mohit, "Ever Wondered How Facebook Decides How Much Bounty Should Be Paid?," *Hacker News*, March 17, 2016, http://thehackernews.com/2016/03/facebook-bug-bounties.html.

32. Silva, Reginaldo, "XXE in OpenID: One Bug to Rule Them All, or How I Found a Remote Code Execution Flaw Affecting Facebook's Servers," personal website, January 16, 2014, http://www.ubercomp.com/posts/2014-01-16_facebook_remote_code_execution; "We Recently Awarded Our Biggest Bug Bounty Payout Ever," Facebook Bug Bounty blog, January 22, 2014, https://www.facebook.com/BugBounty/posts/778897822124446.

33. Farivar, Cyrus, "Professor Fools $80M Superyacht's GPS Receiver on the High Seas," *Ars Technica*, July 30, 2013, http://arstechnica.com/security/2013/07/professor-spoofs-80m-superyachts-gps-receiver-on-the-high-seas.

34. Greenberg, Andy, "Hackers Remotely Kill a Jeep on the Highway—with Me in It," *Wired*, July 21, 2015, http://www.wired.com/2015/07/hackers-remotely-kill-jeep-highway.

35. In 2015, dozens of news outlets covered the story of internet-connected baby monitors being "hacked." Many of these hacks involved families who had continued to use the default password set at the time the monitors were shipped to stores. See Hill, Kashmir, "Hackers Breaking into Baby Cams Are Actually Trying to Help," *Fusion*, April 7, 2015, http://fusion.net/story/115649/hackers-breaking-into-baby-cams-are-actually-trying-to-help. You can see a sample screenshot of the "Big Brother Is Watching You" site through the Internet Archive's Wayback Machine at https://web.archive.org/web/20150107213904/http://spycam.cdn7.com.

According to Qadium, an information consulting company co-founded by my former student Shaun Maguire, it's not merely moms and pops—or hospital personnel—who forget to change the default password on connected cameras and other devices; IT managers at Fortune 500 corporations forget to do so, too. Qadium has found cases of major corporations allowing unsecured access to cameras in secure areas as well as to power supplies for critical equipment.

36. Reel, Monte, and Jordan Robertson, "It's Way Too Easy to Hack the Hospital," *Bloomberg Businessweek,* November 2015, http://www.bloomberg.com/features/2015-hospital-hack.

37. Hackett, Robert, "How Much Do Data Breaches Cost Big Companies? Shockingly Little," *Fortune,* March 27, 2015, http://fortune.com/2015/03/27/how-much-do-data -breaches-actually-cost-big-companies-shockingly-little.

38. Ibid.

39. Dwork, Cynthia, and Aaron Roth, "The Algorithmic Foundations of Differential Privacy," *Foundations and Trends in Theoretical Computer Science* 9, nos. 3–4 (2014), p. 22, https://www.cis.upenn.edu/~aaroth/Papers/privacybook.pdf.

40. Cynthia, like many theoretical computer scientists, does a worst-case analysis. Alternatively, the average loss would characterize the expected cost across users.

41. I was first introduced to the metaphor of a "burn rate" for privacy by Cynthia. For an overview, I suggest her talk "I'm in the Database (But Nobody Knows)," Dean's Lecture, University of California–Berkeley School of Information, February 4, 2015, http://www .ischool.berkeley.edu/events/deanslectures/20150204/audio. A video is available at https:// www.youtube.com/watch?v=RWpG0ag6j9c.

42. Office of Transportation and Air Quality, "Fuel Economy Testing and Labeling," US Environmental Protection Agency, publication no. EPA-420-F-14–015, April 2014, p. 2, https://www3.epa.gov/otaq/carlabel/documents/420f11017a.pdf.

43. Gates, Guilbert, Jack Ewing, Karl Russell, and Derek Watkins, "Explaining Volkswagen's Emissions Scandal," *New York Times,* April 28, 2016, http://www.nytimes.com /interactive/2015/business/international/vw-diesel-emissions-scandal-explained.html.

44. For instance, see Taysom, John Graham, and David Cleeveley, "Method of Anonymising an Interaction Between Devices," patent application, US Patent no. US20110276404A1, November 10, 2011, http://www.google.com/patents/US20110276404.

45. Ginger, Dan, "John Taysom: 18 IPOs and Counting," *EntrepreneurCountry Global,* January 22, 2015, http://www.entrepreneurcountryglobal.com/united-kingdom/ecosystem -economics/item/john-taysom-18-ipos-and-counting.

46. I have focused on Facebook Log-In rather than Google Sign-In here since the data shared with Facebook are more often shared explicitly rather than implicitly.

47. Reichheld, Frederick F., "One Number You Need to Grow," *Harvard Business Review* (December 2003), https://hbr.org/2003/12/the-one-number-you-need-to-grow.

48. Ibid.

49. For criticisms of the Net Promoter Score, see, for instance, Keiningham, Timothy L., Bruce Cooil, Tor Wallin Andreassen, and Lerzan Aksoy, "A Longitudinal Examination of Net Promoter and Firm Revenue Growth," *Journal of Marketing* 71, no. 3 (July 2007), pp. 39–51, http://journals.ama.org/doi/abs/10.1509/jmkg.71.3.39.

50. Unlike a car dashboard, the refinery dashboard would not display real-time reading. Rarely do we need to make a split-second decision about a refinery as we do while driving. Further, the data safety audit would be conducted semi-regularly. Although it would be possible to calculate the privacy efficiency and return-on-data metrics far more frequently, and

potentially in real time, constantly updating the metrics would make it far more difficult for users to compare refineries.

51. I would propose a visual display similar to the one used to communicate the energy-efficiency rating of appliances in the European Union, where the entire scale is shown from the top performance (in green) to the worst (in red), and the machine's rating is indicated with a marker on the scale, with raw numbers provided at the bottom for the various components of the rating. (To see example labels for everything from air conditioners to vacuum cleaners, visit http://www.newenergylabel.com/index.php/uk/home.)

Chapter 6: Taking the Control(s)

1. This quote comes from Kant's essay "Answering the Question: What Is Enlightenment?," published in the September 1784 issue of *Berlin Monthly*. See Kant, Immanuel, *Kant: On History*, trans. by Lewis White Beck (Indianapolis: Bobbs-Merrill, 1963), p. 7. The original German text: Kant, Immanuel, "Beantwortung der Frage: Was ist Aufklärung?," *Berlinische Monatsschrift* (September 1784), http://gutenberg.spiegel.de/buch/-3505/1.

2. This statistic is for spam detected by the information technology security firm Trend Micro; see "Global Spam Map," Trend Micro, March 16, 2016, http://www.trendmicro.com/us/security-intelligence/current-threat-activity/global-spam-map.

3. Finkel, Irving, and Jonathan Taylor, *Cuneiform* (London: British Museum Press, 2015), p. 11.

4. Not all of the tablets discovered by archaeologists deal with accounting matters. See Kilmer, Anne, with Richard L. Crocker and Robert R. Brown, *Sounds from Silence: Recent Discoveries in Ancient Near Eastern Music* (Berkeley, CA: Bit Enki, 1976).

5. Graeber, David, *Debt: The First 5,000 Years* (Brooklyn, NY: Melville House, 2011), p. 39.

6. Warden, Pete, "Data Ownership and the Future of Data," presentation to class on the Social Data Revolution, School of Information, University of California–Berkeley, November 18, 2014, https://www.youtube.com/watch?v=N_C00zQpcqw&feature=youtube; Crawford, Harriet, *Sumer and the Sumerians* (Cambridge: Cambridge University Press, 2004), p. 89.

7. Warden, "Data Ownership and the Future of Data."

8. Schechner, Sam, "Google Honors 'Right to Forget' Tantric Workshop," *Wall Street Journal*, July 18, 2014, http://www.wsj.com/articles/google-honors-right-to-forget-tantric-workshop-1405717183.

9. Ibid.

10. The 2016 Panama Papers leak involved about 5 million emails and 5 million files. The largest leak before that was in 2010, when 250,000 classified cables to and from the US State Department were published by WikiLeaks. See Greenberg, Andy, "How Reporters Pulled Off the Panama Papers, the Biggest Leak in Whistleblower History," *Wired*, April 4, 2016, https://www.wired.com/2016/04/reporters-pulled-off-panama-papers-biggest-leak-whistleblower-history.

11. Founded by Good World Solutions, LaborLink allows workers to anonymously report on workplace conditions from any mobile phone, with aggregated data shared with clients ranging from corporate HQs to NGO watchdogs. Individuals phone a number and receive a call back to answer a key-response survey, to ensure that no voices are recorded (and

identifiable). More than half a million employees in sixteen countries have participated in the project. For more information, visit http://goodworldsolutions.org/#labor-link.

12. The Frequency Monitoring Network (FNET, also known as GridEye)—at the University of Tennessee at Knoxville, the Virginia Institute of Technology, and Oak Ridge National Laboratory—monitors power system frequencies and disturbances around the world. The variations are taken by frequency disturbance recorders (FDRs) that plug into an outlet and communicate electricity and geolocation data. You can watch a map of frequencies in North America at http://fnetpublic.utk.edu/gradientmap.html.

13. I first learned about this technique from Linda Walter, co-founder of Future Challenges (Berlin), during the panel "The Promise of Video: Documenters, Technology, and Accountability," 2016 RightsCon Silicon Valley, Mission Bay Conference Center, San Francisco, CA, March 30, 2016, https://rightscon.sched.org/event/6Isn/the-promise-of-video -documenters-technology-accountability.

14. Interestingly, the "true" identity of the person who invented Bitcoin remains unknown, despite the efforts of many investigative reporters, and probably even more government agents around the world. The person is known only by the pseudonym Satoshi Nakamato. See Nakamoto, Satoshi, "A Peer-to-Peer Electronic Cash System," Bitcoin.org, October 31, 2008, http://www.bitcoin.org/bitcoin.pdf.

15. In fact, a person can embed a note about anything in the blockchain—it doesn't have to be related to his Bitcoin transaction or to the currency in general.

16. Buterin, Vitalik, "On Public and Private Blockchains," Ethereum Blog, August 7, 2015, https://blog.ethereum.org/2015/08/07/on-public-and-private-blockchains.

17. Krause, Andreas, and Eric Horvitz, "A Utility-Theoretic Approach to Privacy in Online Services," *Journal of Artificial Intelligence Research* 39 (September–December 2010), pp. 633–662, http://research.microsoft.com/en-us/um/people/horvitz/pvoijair_jair.pdf.

18. Bertrand, Marianne, and Sendhil Mullainathan, "Are Emily and Greg More Employable Than Lakisha and Jamal? A Field Experiment on Labor Market Discrimination," National Bureau of Economic Research working paper no. 9873, July 2003, http:// www.nber.org/papers/w9873; "No Names, No Bias?," *The Economist,* October 31, 2015, http://www.economist.com/news/business/21677214-anonymising-job-applications -eliminate-discrimination-not-easy-no-names-no-bias.

19. I have chosen a vibrator as my example product here because of an experience my colleagues and I had at Amazon. In the week leading up to Mother's Day, Amazon did what it did every Mother's Day: it suggested gift ideas for your mom when you landed on the home page. To start, the recommendation algorithms served random selections from relevant categories, and then increasingly showed the items that garnered the most clicks. As the day progressed, one product quickly rose and stayed in the pole position: a vibrator. The vibrator made it to the top because a category in which it was listed, "Women's Health Care," was used to seed the promotion. Then people clicked on the ad because they were surprised to see a vibrator suggested as a Mother's Day gift.

20. Kemp, Joe, and Daniel Beekman, "'Pressure Cooker' and 'Backpack' Internet Search Prompts Visit from Feds: Long Island Woman Claims," *New York Daily News,* August 1, 2013, http://www.nydailynews.com/news/national/long-island-woman-claims-online-search -pressure-cooker-helped-prompt-visit-feds-article-1.1415101.

21. Warner, Stanley L., "Randomized Response: A Survey Technique for Eliminating Evasive Answer Bias," *Journal of the American Statistical Association* 60, no. 309 (March 1965), pp. 63–69, http://www.popline.org/node/516223.

22. I first considered the power of applying sliders or knobs to data in the 1990s, after using a demonstration project, called "HomeFinder," developed by University of Maryland professor of computer science Ben Shneiderman. The software allowed users to search for housing in the Washington, DC, metropolitan area that fit their criteria. A person looking to rent a place with five bedrooms for no more than five hundred dollars a month might discover that there were no matching properties available (represented as "points of light" on a map). But she could then slide the cost per month up or the number of bedrooms down, until the query highlighted matching results. See Shneiderman, Ben, "Information Visualization: Dynamic Queries, Starfield Displays, and LifeLines," in Ben Shneiderman, ed., *Sparks of Innovation in Human-Computer Interaction* (Norwood, NJ: Ablex Publishers, 1993), http://www.cs.umd.edu/hcil/members/bshneiderman/ivwp.html.

23. This principle may be most famously encapsulated in Steve Krug's mantra of web design: "Don't make me think." See Krug, Steve, *Don't Make Me Think, Revisited: A Common Sense Approach to Web and Mobile Usability,* 3rd ed. (San Francisco: New Riders, 2014).

24. Mayer-Schönberger, Viktor, and Kenneth Cukier, *Big Data: A Revolution That Will Transform How We Live, Work, and Think* (New York: Houghton Mifflin Harcourt, 2004).

25. Amazon also has email addresses associated with each purchase. In the past, Amazon surfaced products that were especially popular among people who shared email addresses with the same domain name. The program ended when some well-known companies complained that their employees' aggregated purchases might reveal strategic decisions. As a purely hypothetical example, if there were a sudden surge of books on blockchain technology bought by people using an @gs.com address, or shipped to 200 West Street, New York, NY 10282, people would intuit that Goldman Sachs was getting into blockchain before the company made a formal announcement.

26. Vara, Vauhini, "How an Airline Fare Loophole Could Hurt Passengers," *The New Yorker,* January 5, 2015, http://www.newyorker.com/business/currency/united-skiplagged-problem -hidden-city-ticketing; and Jansen, Bart, "Judge Throws Out United Airlines Case Against Skiplagged," *USA Today,* May 4, 2015, http://www.usatoday.com/story/todayinthesky/2015 /05/04/united-skiplagged-lawsuit-federal/26864961.

27. Tversky, Amos, and Daniel Kahneman, "Judgment Under Uncertainty: Heuristics and Biases," *Science* 185, no. 4157 (September 27, 1974), pp. 1124–1131, http://science .sciencemag.org/content/185/4157/1124. For an introduction to the field, I highly recommend many of the chapters (including Danny and Amos's "The Simulation Heuristic" and Baruch Fischhoff's "Debiasing") contributed to the wonderful collection Kahneman, Daniel, Paul Slovic, and Amos Tversky, eds., *Judgment Under Uncertainty: Heuristics and Biases* (Cambridge: Cambridge University Press, 1982).

28. Anders, George, "LinkedIn Offers College Choices by the Numbers," *MIT Technology Review,* January 22, 2014, https://www.technologyreview.com/business-report /data-and-decision-making.

29. Several refineries offer users the option of receiving a raw dump of their data. Google's Takeout, Facebook's information download, and Amazon's order history download are but three examples.

30. Cook, James, "Uber's Internal Charts Show How Its Driver-Rating System Actually Works," *Business Insider,* February 11, 2015, http://www.businessinsider.com/leaked -charts-show-how-ubers-driver-rating-system-works-2015-2.

31. Many of these details are based on conversations with hundreds of drivers on four continents as well as with developers at several ride-sharing platforms. See also Herrera, Doug, "Fired from Uber: Why Drivers Get Deactivated, and How to Get Reactivated," Ride Sharing Driver blog, April 21, 2016, http://www.ridesharingdriver.com /fired-uber-drivers-get-deactivated-and-reactivated.

32. The specific numbers depend on the city. Lyft's acceptance rate is calculated to include rides accepted but never completed: Acceptance Rate = (Rides Completed + Rides Marked as "No-Show") / (Total Ride Requests).

33. Some markets also required drivers to be available to pick up riders in specific "hot zones" during the window of time when guaranteed hourly earnings were offered. See Huet, Ellen, "Uber's Clever, Hidden Move: How Its Latest Fare Cuts Can Actually Lock In Its Drivers," *Forbes,* January 9, 2015, http://www.forbes.com/sites/ellenhuet/2015/01/09/ubers -clever-hidden-move-how-fare-cuts-actually-lock-in-its-drivers; and "Guarantees Terms and Conditions," Uber Newsroom, April 16, 2016, https://newsroom.uber.com/sf/guarantees -terms-and-conditions.

34. Wenger, Albert, "Labor Day: Right to an API Key (Algorithmic Organizing)," Continuations blog, September 1, 2014, http://continuations.com/post/96355016855/labor -day-right-to-an-api-key-algorithmic.

35. For a lengthier discussion of on-demand workers' rights, see Grossman, Nick, and Elizabeth Woyke, *Serving Workers in the Gig Economy: Emerging Resources for the On-Demand Workforce* (Boston: O'Reilly Media, 2016), http://www.oreilly.com/iot/free/serving-workers -gig-economy.csp.

36. I am indebted to Klaus May at Bosch for sharing information on the history of ABS. For a detailed history of ABS, Klaus suggests Johnson, Ann, *Hitting the Brakes: Engineering Design and the Production of Knowledge* (Durham, NC: Duke University Press, 2009).

37. Jones, Ann, "From Dynamometers to Stimulations: Transforming Brake Testing Technology into Antilock Braking Systems," in Joerges, Bernward, and Terry Shinn, eds., *Instrumentation Between Science, State and Industry* (Dordrecht: Kluwer Academic, 2001), pp. 213–214.

38. ABS has been required on all new cars sold in the European Union since 2004 and in the United States since 2011. It has also been required on new trucks and buses in the European Union since 2015. The systems are not required everywhere, however; as of 2010, only two out of every three new cars in China, and one out of seven new cars in Brazil, ships from the factory with ABS installed. See May, Klaus, email to author, March 23, 2016; and "Der Weg des ABS vom Flugzeug ins Auto," *Auto Motor und Sport,* March 19, 2010, http://www.auto-motor-und-sport.de/news/abs-die-geschichte-des-anti-blockier -systems-1790991.html.

39. Toyota and Lexus were scheduled to ship the first car models with AEB systems as a standard feature in 2017. See Chew, Jonathan, "Toyota Will Put Automatic Braking in Almost All Cars by 2017," *Fortune,* March 22, 2016, http://fortune.com/2016/03/22/toyota -auto-braking-models.

40. Durbin, Dee-Ann, "Study Finds Automatic Braking Cuts Rear-End Crash Risk," *Phys.org,* January 28, 2016, http://phys.org/news/2016-01-automatic-rear-end.html.

Chapter 7: Rights into Realities

1. Kay was chief scientist of Atari when in 1982, during an educational technology conference, he noted this principle from his years at the legendary Xerox PARC, where he spearheaded the work to develop graphical user interfaces for computers. Quoted in Wise, Deborah, "Experts Speculate on Future Electronic Learning Environment," *InfoWorld* 4, no. 16 (April 26, 1982), p. 6.

2. "'Baacode' Traces Clothes' Origins," *Vancouver Sun,* September 23, 2008.

3. The uses of the Baacode outlined here are based on my conversations over several years with Jeremy Moon, Icebreaker's founder, executive chairman, and creative director, and its CEO, Rob Fyfe. Unfortunately, the Baacode was phased out in the first half of 2016. Rob told me that the decision was made because only 1 percent of customers were looking up their garments and the company's manufacturing now requires mixing wool from different sheep farms in a single garment (email from Rob Fyfe, July 12, 2016).

4. Martin, Claire, "Is That Real Tuna in Your Sushi? Now, a Way to Track That Fish," *New York Times,* August 13, 2016, http://www.nytimes.com/2016/08/14/technology/is-that-real-tuna-in-your-sushi-now-a-way-to-track-that-fish.html.

5. Author interview with Christoph Franz, chairman, Roche Holding AG, August 8, 2016. See also Kremen, Rachel, "Catching Fake Meds in a Snapshot," *MIT Technology Review,* September 8, 2009, https://www.technologyreview.com/s/415218/catching-fake-meds-in-a-snapshot.

6. Ossola, Alexandra, "Authentic Drugs Tagged with Plant DNA Could Help Snare Fake Meds," *Scientific American,* January 12, 2016, http://www.scientificamerican.com/article/authentic-drugs-tagged-with-plant-dna-could-help-snare-fake-meds.

7. As one example, customers who register their purchase, including contact information, with the luggage manufacturer Briggs & Riley (http://www.briggs-riley.com) are enrolled in a lifetime warranty program and a lost-luggage reporting facility.

8. For more information about Trash Track, see http://senseable.mit.edu/trashtrack.

9. Saeb, Sohrab, Mi Zhang, Christopher J. Karr, Stephen M. Schueller, Marya E. Corden, Konrad P. Kording, and David C. Mohr, "Mobile Phone Sensor Correlates of Depressive Symptom Severity in Daily-Life Behavior: An Exploratory Study," *Journal of Medical Internet Research* 17, no. 7 (July 2015), p. e175, http://www.jmir.org/2015/7/e175.

10. The first company in this space, the fare-prediction analytics company Farecast, was acquired by Microsoft in 2008. Microsoft and its Bing search engine stopped offering the prediction service in 2014. See Cook, John, "Farewell, Farecast: Microsoft Kills Airfare Price Predictor, to the Dismay of Its Creator," *GeekWire,* April 8, 2014, http://www.geekwire.com/2014/farewell-farecast-microsoft-kills-airfare-price-predictor-dismay-creator.

11. Ewen, Nick, "Airline Elite Status Match and Challenge Options for 2015," The Points Guy blog, July 15, 2015, http://thepointsguy.com/2015/07/airline-elite-status-match.

12. This shift in mindset was led by Doc Searls and his colleagues, first in a 1999 internet posting; then in the book *The Cluetrain Manifesto: The End of Business as Usual,* published in 2000; and more recently with so-called Vendor Relationship Management, or VRM, which Doc discusses in his book *The Intention Economy: When Customers Take Charge* (Cambridge, MA: Harvard Business Review Press, 2012).

13. Reisinger, Don, "Why Facebook Profiles Are Replacing Credit Scores," *Fortune,* December 1, 2015, http://fortune.com/2015/12/01/tech-loans-credit-affirm-zest.

14. Rao, Leena, "PayPal Co-Founder Raises $275 Million to Reinvent Credit," *Fortune,* May 6, 2015, http://fortune.com/2015/05/06/affirm-raises-275-million; Levchin, Max, "Fireside Chat with Max Levchin: All Things Data, Fintech, and How to Solve Hard, Valuable, Fun Problems," EECS Department Colloquium Series, Department of Electrical Engineering and Computer Sciences, University of California–Berkeley, October 29, 2014, http://events.berkeley.edu/index.php/calendar/sn/eecs.html?event_ID=82684.

15. Hardy, Quentin, "Using Algorithms to Determine Character," *New York Times,* July 26, 2015, http://bits.blogs.nytimes.com/2015/07/26/using-algorithms-to-determine-character.

16. Lippert, John, "ZestFinance Issues Small, High-Rate Loans, Uses Big Data to Weed Out Deadbeats," *Washington Post,* October 11, 2014, https://www.washingtonpost.com/business/zestfinance-issues-small-high-rate-loans-uses-big-data-to-weed-out-deadbeats/2014/10/10/e34986b6-4d71-11e4-aa5e-7153e466a02d_story.html.

17. Author interview with Darwin Tu, founder and CEO of 51credit.com, June 17, 2016.

18. Ibid.

19. The US Securities and Exchange Commission is investigating the veracity of the $14 billion figure. See Clover, Charles, "SEC Probe on Alibaba Focuses on Singles Day Sales," *Financial Times,* May 26, 2016, http://www.ft.com/cms/s/0/5d4f4ff6-232f-11e6-9d4d-c11776a5124d.html.

20. Lunt, Christopher, "Authorization and Authentication Based on an Individual's Social Network," US Patent no. 9,100,400, August 4, 2015, http://www.google.com/patents/US9100400.

21. Kim, Ryan, "SigFig Offers to Tune Up Your Investment Portfolio," *GigaOm,* May 1, 2012, https://gigaom.com/2012/05/01/sigfig-offers-to-tune-up-your-investment-portfolio.

22. Woodruff, Mandi, "You Won't Know Your Broker's Screwing You Over Till It's Too Late," *Business Insider,* May 17, 2012, http://www.businessinsider.com/nothings-stopping-brokers-from-turning-clients-into-their-own-personal-cash-cows-2012-5?IR=T.

23. These figures for retail customers investing directly through SigFig were reported on the company's home page, http://www.sigfig.com, as of June 14, 2016; see also Delman, Gregg, "SigFig Lauches 'SigFig Guidance' to Help the 90% of Investors Losing Money Due to Common Mistakes," SigFig press release, *BusinessWire,* March 18, 2015, http://www.businesswire.com/news/home/20150318005206/en/SigFig-Launches-%E2%80%98SigFig-Guidance%E2%80%99–90-Investors-Losing.

24. In the spring of 2016, SigFig received an infusion of $40 million in venture capital and announced partnerships with Cambridge Savings Bank of Massachusetts and UBS. See Moyer, Liz, "New Financial Investment Rules May Aid Robo Advisers," *New York Times,* April 7, 2016, http://www.nytimes.com/2016/04/08/business/dealbook/new-financial-investment-rules-may-aid-robo-advisers.html; and Verhage, Julie, "Robo-Advisor Sig-Fig Raises $40 Million from Investors Including UBS, Eaton Vance," *Bloomberg Technology,* May 24, 2016, http://www.bloomberg.com/news/articles/2016-05-24/robo-advisor-sigfig-raises-40-million-from-investors-including-ubs-eaton-vance.

25. Author interview with Darwin Tu, founder and CEO, 51credit.com, June 17, 2016.

26. J. P. Rangaswami went on to work for BT Global Services and Salesforce.com but, as of January 2016, has returned to Deutsche Bank as chief data officer. See Zelenka, Anne, "A CIO Revolutionizes the Rules of Email," *GigaOm,* May 1, 2007, https://gigaom.com/2007/05/01/a-cio-revolutionizes-the-rules-of-email.

27. He created a second, confidential email account for managers to use when they needed to contact him about personnel issues. Author interview with J. P. Rangaswami, chief data officer, Deutsche Bank, June 24, 2016.

28. Author interview with J. P. Rangaswami, chief data officer, Deutsche Bank, June 24, 2016.

29. Jacobs, Samuel P., "How Email Killer Slack Will Change the Future of Work," *Time,* October 29, 2015, http://time.com/4092354/how-e-mail-killer-slack-will-change -the-future-of-work.

30. I am an investor in Percolata and serve as an adviser.

31. Chapman, Lizette, "Percolata Emerges from Stealth with $5M for New Sensors for Retail Stores," *Wall Street Journal,* January 12, 2015, http://blogs.wsj.com/venturecapital /2015/01/12/percolata-emerges-from-stealth-with-5m-for-new-sensors-for-retail-stores.

32. The three unique identifiers of a mobile phone are IMEI (International Mobile Equipment Identity), which establishes your connection to a base station so that you can make a call; wifi; and Bluetooth.

33. These figures are as reported by Percolata in June 2016 at http://www.percolata.com.

34. Email to author from Gam Dias, founder and CEO of MoData, June 19, 2016.

35. Gapper, John, "Bridgewater Is Troubled over 'Radical Transparency,'" *Financial Times,* February 10, 2016, http://www.ft.com/cms/s/0/789399f0-cf62-11e5-831d-09f7778e7377. html; Feloni, Richard, "Ray Dalio Explains Why 25% of Bridgewater Employees Don't Last More Than 18 Months at the Hedge Fund Giant," *Business Insider,* March 23, 2016, http:// uk.businessinsider.com/biggest-challenges-new-bridgewater-employees-face-2016-3.

36. Feloni, Richard, "Ray Dalio, Head of the World's Largest Hedge Fund, Explains His Succession Plan for Bridgewater and How Its 'Radically Transparent' Culture Is Misunderstood," *Business Insider,* March 21, 2016, http://uk.businessinsider.com/bridgewater-ray -dalio-succession-radically-transparent-culture-2016-3.

37. Horowitz, Sara, "Freelancing in America 2015 Report," Freelancers Union, October 1, 2015, https://blog.freelancersunion.org/2015/10/01/freelancing-america-2015.

38. Dewey, John, *Democracy and Education: An Introduction to the Philosophy of Education* (New York: Macmillan, 1916), p. 46. The full text of Dewey's book is available at https:// www.gutenberg.org/files/852/852-h/852-h.htm.

39. This diagnosis of what ails our classrooms has been vigorously put forward by Sir Ken Robinson in his books and lectures. See Robinson, Ken, "Do Schools Kill Creativity?" TED Talk, Monterey, CA, February 2006, https://www.ted.com/talks/ken_robinson _says_schools_kill_creativity.

40. Mazur, Eric, "From Questions to Concepts: Interactive Teaching in Physics," presentation at the Derek Bok Center for Teaching and Learning, Harvard University, Cambridge, MA, 2008, quoted in Light, Gregory, and Marina Macari, *Making Scientists: Six Principles for Effective College Teaching* (Cambridge, MA: Harvard University Press, 2013), p. 58.

41. Paul, Annie Murphy, "Why Floundering Is Good," *Time,* April 25, 2012, http://ideas. time.com/2012/04/25/why-floundering-is-good; Kapur, Manu, and Katerine Bielaczyc, "Designing for Production Failure," *Journal of the Learning Sciences* 21, no. 1 (January 2012), pp. 45–83, http://www.tandfonline.com/doi/abs/10.1080/10508406.2011.591717.

42. Curtis, Jennifer, "Increased Engagement Through the Power of Group Learning," Pearson Learning Catalytics, n.d. (accessed September 30, 2016), https://www.pearson highered.com/products-and-services/course-content-and-digital-resources/learning -applications/learning-catalytics/user-stories/jennifer-curtis.html.

43. Author interview with Ben Nelson, founder and chief executive officer, Minerva Project, September 10, 2014.

44. Kamenetz, Anya, "Study in Your PJs? What a High School 'Work from Home Day' Looks Like," *NPR,* February 23, 2016, http://www.npr.org/sections/ed/2016/02 /23/466460375/study-in-your-pjs-what-a-high-school-work-from-home-day-looks-like.

45. Singer, Natasha, "ClassDojo Adopts Deletion Policy for Student Data," *New York Times,* November 18, 2014, http://bits.blogs.nytimes.com/2014/11/18/classdojo-adopts -deletion-policy-for-student-data.

46. Shoda, Yuichi, Walter Mischel, and Philip K. Peake, "Predicting Adolescent Cognitive and Self-Regulatory Competencies from Preschool Delay of Gratification: Identifying Diagnostic Conditions," *Developmental Psychology* 26, no. 6 (November 1990), pp. 978–986, http://psycnet.apa.org/?&fa=main.doiLanding&doi=10.1037/0012–1649.26.6.978.

47. Mischel, Walter, and Ebbe B. Ebbesen, "Attention in Delay of Gratification," *Journal of Personality and Social Psychology* 16, no. 2 (October 1970), pp. 329–337, http://psycnet .apa.org/journals/psp/16/2/329.

48. Shoda, Mischel, and Peake, "Predicting Adolescent Cognitive and Self-Regulatory Competencies from Preschool Delay of Gratification."

49. Topol, Eric, *The Patient Will See You Now: The Future of Medicine Is in Your Hands* (New York: Basic Books, 2015), p. 276.

50. Quoted in Markel, Howard, "'I Have Seen My Death': How the World Discovered the X-Ray," *PBS NewsHour:* "The Rundown," December 20, 2012, http://www.pbs.org/newshour /rundown/i-have-seen-my-death-how-the-world-discovered-the-x-ray.

51. International Human Genome Sequencing Consortium, "Finishing the Euchromatic Sequence of the Human Genome," *Nature* 431, no. 21 (October 21, 2004), pp. 931–945, http://www.nature.com/nature/journal/v431/n7011/abs/nature03001.html.

52. Mettler, Fred A., Jr., Michael Davis, Charles A. Kelsey, Robert Rosenberg, and Arvis Williams, "Analytical Modeling of Worldwide Medical Radiation Use," *Health Physics* 52, no. 2 (February 1987), p. 133, http://www.ncbi.nlm.nih.gov/pubmed/2434447; Global Industry Analysts, "Computed Tomography (CT) Scanners: A Global Strategic Business Report," January 2016, http://www.strategyr.com/Computed_Tomography_Scanners _CT_Scan_Market_Report.asp; European Magnetic Resonance Forum, "Magnetic Resonance: A Peer-Reviewed, Critical Introduction," 9th ed., March 2016, http://www.magnetic -resonance.org/ch/21–01.html; Hadfield, James, and Nick Loman, "Next Generation Genomics: World Map of High-Throughput Sequencers, http://omicsmaps.com/#.

53. Hill, Kashmir, "In the Future, Your Insurance Company Will Know When You're Having Sex," *Fusion,* April 14, 2015, http://fusion.net/story/119745/in-the-future-your-insurance -company-will-know-when-youre-having-sex.

54. Topol, *The Patient Will See You Now,* pp. 159–179.

55. Esch, Tobias, Roanne Mejilla, Melissa Anselmo, Beatrice Podtschaske, Tom Delbanco, and Jan Walker, "Engaging Patients Through OpenNotes: An Evaluation Using

Mixed Methods," *BMJ Open,* January 29, 2016, http://bmjopen.bmj.com/content/6/1/e 010034.full.

56. The passage of the Patient Protection and Affordable Care Act of 2010 made it illegal in the United States to deny healthcare coverage to an individual based on a previously diagnosed condition. However, given that health care accounts for about 17 percent of US GDP ($3 trillion), it is no surprise that the law is constantly challenged. I believe it will take at least a generation before people stop fearing that they will not be able to get health insurance based on a preexisting condition.

57. The Health Insurance Portability and Accountability Act of 1996, or HIPAA, was the first effort in the United States to create a standard code for communicating and protecting healthcare data. HIPAA privacy rules require that patients have access to their medical records, have the ability to amend those records, and authorize any sharing of their records with others. For more information about HIPAA rules, see http://www.hhs.gov/hipaa /for-individuals/medical-records/index.html.

58. Esch, Mejilla, Anselmo, Podtschaske, Delbanco, and Walker, "Engaging Patients Through OpenNotes."

59. Crotty, Bradley H., Melissa Anselmo, Deserae N. Clarke, Linda M. Famiglio, Lydia Flier, Jamie A. Green, Suzanne Leveille, Roanne Mejilla, Rebecca A. Stametz, Michelle Thompson, Jan Walker, and Sigall K. Bell, "Opening Residents' Notes to Patients: A Qualitative Study of Resident and Faculty Physician Attitudes on Open Notes Implementation in Graduate Medical Education," *Academic Medicine* 91, no. 3 (March 2016), pp. 418–426, http://www.ncbi.nlm.nih.gov/pubmed/26579794. See also the OpenNotes website http:// www.opennotes.org/who-is-sharing-notes.

60. Quoted in Sun, Lena H., "Boston Hospital Pilot Gives Patients Electronic Access to Their Therapists' Notes," *Washington Post,* May 18, 2014, https://www.washingtonpost. com/national/health-science/boston-hospital-pilot-gives-patients-electronic-access-to-their -therapists-notes/2014/05/18/2d891bac-cfe5-11e3-a6b1-45c4dffb85a6_story.html.

61. Meyers, Austin, Nick Johnston, Vivek Rathod, Anoop Korattikara, Alex Gorban, Nathan Silberman, Sergio Guadarrama, George Papandreou, Jonathan Huang, and Kevin P. Murphy, "Im2Calories: Towards an Automated Mobile Vision Food Diary," IEEE International Conference on Computer Vision, Santiago, Chile, December 7–13, 2015, pp. 1233–1241, http://www.cv-foundation.org/openaccess/content_iccv_2015/html/Meyers _Im2Calories_Towards_an_ICCV_2015_paper.html.

62. "What Small Retailers Can Learn from Discovery's Vitality Incentive Program," *Loyalty Box,* March 13, 2015, http://www.theloyaltybox.com/blog/loyalty-ideas/what-small -retailers-can-learn-from-discoverys-vitality-incentive-program; Nossel, Craig, "Incentives That Create Healthy Behavior," seminar, C3 Collaborating for Health, London, July 21, 2011, http://www.c3health.org/wp-content/uploads/2011/08/Craig-Nossel-seminar-FINAL -20110817.pdf.

63. Sturm, Roland, Ruopeng An, Darren Segal, and Deepa Patel, "A Cash-Back Rebate Program for Healthy Food Purchased in South Africa: Results from Scanner Data," *American Journal of Preventive Medicine* 44, no. 6 (June 2013), pp. 567–572, http://www.ncbi .nlm.nih.gov/pmc/articles/PMC3659342.

64. Hernandez, Daniela, "The Social Network for People Who Want to Upload Their DNA to the Internet," *Fusion,* February 11, 2015, http://fusion.net/story/40034 /the-social-network-for-people-who-want-to-upload-their-dna-to-the-internet.

65. Christakis, Nicholas, and James Fowler, *Connected: The Surprising Power of Our Social Networks and How They Shape Our Lives* (New York: Little, Brown, 2009).

66. Lazer, David, and Ryan Kennedy, "What We Can Learn from the Epic Failure of Google Flu Trends," *Wired,* October 1, 2015, http://www.wired.com/2015/10/can -learn-epic-failure-google-flu-trends.

67. Christakis and Fowler, *Connected: The Surprising Power of Our Social Networks and How They Shape Our Lives,* pp. 108–111.

68. "About the Precision Medicine Initiative Cohort Program," US National Institutes of Health, n.d. (accessed September 30, 2016), https://www.nih.gov/precision -medicine-initiative-cohort-program; Office of Press Secretary, "The Fact Sheet: President Obama's Precision Medicine Initiative," White House press release, January 30, 2015, https://www.whitehouse.gov/the-press-office/2015/01/30/fact-sheet-president -obama-s-precision-medicine-initiative; Office of Press Secretary, "The Fact Sheet: Obama Administration Announces Key Actions to Accelerate Precision Medicine Initiative," White House press release, February 25, 2016, https://www.whitehouse.gov /the-press-office/2016/02/25/fact-sheet-obama-administration-announces-key-actions -accelerate. The European Union has also made substantial investments in the field under the Innovative Medicines Initiative. An initial ten-year phase of the project, which ran from 2008 to 2013, had a budget of €2 billion; the second phase, which began in 2014, has a budget of €3.3 billion. See Hamill, Ken, "Worldwide Efforts to Accelerate Precision Medicine," *SciEx,* April 18, 2016, http://sciex.com/community/blogs/blogs /worldwide-efforts-to-accelerate-precision-medicine.

69. Roth, Alvin, *Who Gets What—and Why: The Hidden World of Matchmaking and Market Design* (New York: Houghton Mifflin Harcourt, 2015), pp. 35–38.

70. Maddaus, Gene, "Kicked Out of San Francisco, MonkeyParking App Plans a Fresh Start in Santa Monica," *LA Weekly,* September 18, 2014, http://www.laweekly.com/news /kicked-out-of-san-francisco-monkeyparking-app-plans-a-fresh-start-in-santa-monica -5080436.

71. Eskenazi, Joe, "MonkeyParking Is Back and Ready to Disrupt Your Driveway," *San Francisco Magazine,* March 25, 2015, http://www.sfgate.com/business/article/Monkey Parking-is-back-and-ready-to-disrupt-your-6158479.php.

Epilogue

1. Jowett, Benjamin, trans., *The Republic of Plato: An Ideal Commonwealth* (New York: Colonial Press, 1901), p. 209, https://catalog.hathitrust.org/Record/001193269. To introduce the "Allegory of the Cave" dialogue between Socrates and Glaucon in Book VII, Jowett chose the title "On Shadows and Realities in Education."

INDEX

Andreas Weigend is one of the world's foremost experts on the future of big data, social-mobile technologies, and consumer behavior, the combination of which he calls the social data revolution. The founder and director of the Social Data Lab, he was previously the chief scientist of Amazon. He consults to a wide range of companies in the areas of retail, travel, finance, transportation, and telecommunications with clients including Alibaba, Hyatt, Lufthansa, and MasterCard. He has a PhD in physics from Stanford University and teaches at Stanford, the University of California–Berkeley, and Fudan University in Shanghai, China. He lives in San Francisco, California, and Shanghai, but can always be found at www.weigend.com/where.

Photograph by Social Data Lab